The **Ashes** • *Aunty Jack* • Big Pineapple • Sir Do • Burke and Wills • **Chesty Bond** • *Cop Shop* • *Countdown* • Dad and Dave

Davis Cup • *Don's Party* • **Driza-bone** • Eight Hour Day • Esky • **Eureka Flag**

• Federation • *Four Corners* • **Gallipoli** • Goanna Oil • Granny Smith Apple • Hill's Hoist •

Harold **Holt** • *Home and Away* • Humphrey B. Bear • **INXS** • **Jackeroo**

• Elizabeth **Jolley** • Barry Jones • Ned **Kelly** • Nicole **Kidman** • Kings Cross • Lamington •

Lasseter's Reef • Henry **Lawson** • Leyland Brothers • Dennis **Lillee** • Jeannie Little • Eddie **Mabo**

• **Mad Max** • Elle MacPherson • Manly Ferry • Ray Martin • Men at Work •

Mietta • Kylie Minogue • Olivia Newton-John • Sidney **Nolan** • *Number 96* • Penfolds Grange

• Phar Lap • *Picnic at Hanging Rock* • Pie Floater • *Play School* • Puffing Billy • *Punch* •

Qantas • *rage* • Rats of Tobruk • Reconciliation • Fred Schepisi • The **Seekers** • Sentimental Bloke

• silverchair • Skipping Girl • Dick **Smith** • Snugglepot and Cuddlepie • Speedo • *Strictly*

Ballroom • *The Sullivans* • **TAB** • Tatts • Sigrid Thornton • **Thongs** • Truganini • Uluru •

Vegemite • Victa • *Waltzing Matilda* • Steve **Waugh** • Weeties • Gough **Whitlam**

• The **Wiggles** • R.M. **Williams** • Working Dog • Cliff Young • Carla Zampatti

Hullo Mate! I thought you were only
a Billy Tea Advertisement.

TRUE BLUE

Viking
Penguin Books Australia Ltd
250 Camberwell Road, Camberwell, Victoria 3214, Australia
Penguin Books Ltd
80 Strand, London WC2R ORL, England
Penguin Putnam Inc.
375 Hudson Street, New York, New York 10014, USA
Penguin Books Canada Limited
10 Alcorn Avenue, Toronto, Ontario, Canada M4V 3B2
Penguin Books (N.Z.) Ltd
Cnr Rosedale and Airborne Roads, Albany, Auckland, New Zealand
Penguin Books (South Africa) (Pty) Ltd
5 Watkins Street, Denver Ext 4, 2094, South Africa
Penguin Books India (P) Ltd, 11, Community Centre, Panchsheel Park
New Delhi 110 017, India

Printed in China by Toppan Printing

National Library of Australia
Cataloguing-in-Publication data

Hutchinson, Garrie, 1949– .
    True blue: the A to Z of Australian ads, art and icons.

    ISBN 0 670 90317 5.

    1. Advertising - Australia - History. 2. Commercial art -
    Australia - History. I. Title.

741.670994

Disclaimer: The publisher cannot accept responsibility for any errors
or omissions.

TRUE BLUE

GARRIE HUTCHINSON

VIKING

It's True Blue...

It's True Blue if it's a mosaic, a visual A-to-Z, a personal anthology of the pictures, the icons, the images that make up who we are. It's True Blue if it's an alphabetical story of Australian words, people and places, from Ablett to Zampatti, if it's nostalgic and contemporary. It's True Blue if it's dinky-di and fair dinkum. It's True Blue if it's a book or a painting, a poet or a cartoonist, an advertisement or a logo which is part of the fabric of Australian culture.

This is an unashamedly biased and personal collection of the images and icons that make up my Australian culture. Readers might find that while my heart is in my mouth over the selection, my tongue is also firmly in my cheek, and quite possibly adjacent to the foot in my mouth. If the boot was on the other foot I am sure you would come up with an equally selective selection.

Garrie Hutchinson

Sydney Sorry Day, 2000, a True Blue image

Ken Done's image of Sydney, Australia

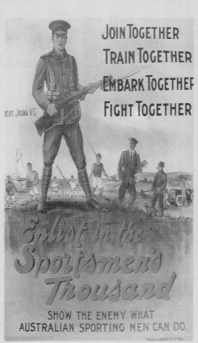

A call to arms

Hello Possums, says Dame Edna

Forward! by H.G. Nelson

My very good friends, make no mistake: Australia is the greatest nation in the world. It has the best of everything. It always has. The world has not caught up with this simple fact. *True Blue* makes this fact as plain as the hooter on your bonce.

For too long Australians have been bumping about in the dark wondering just how bloody good we are. *True Blue* flicks the switch and shines the bright light on our own brilliance. Flicking through these fabulous pages it is as though the nation is camped in the room of mirrors having a good hard look at itself. Once we step through the beckoning door to the world at large

all we do is scream with joyful glee, 'You bloody beauty!' This book is that good. It is a kick up the date with the size twelves Clark ripple-sole desert boots.

As you know, 2001 was a magical year. It was our greatest year ever. The celebrations that marked the Centenary of Federation will live with us forever. This special twelve months allowed the nation to pause and have a long lingering look over the dusty dirt road with barbed wire fence we have travelled along for the past two centuries. Now we can see clearly where we have come from and with *True Blue* wedged firmly in tucker bag we can get a sniff of where we are

headed. This great nation can, at last, set the coordinates with confidence for the solid patch of blue up through the haze ahead.

I love this book. It would be un-Australian not to love it. Who wouldn't want to set aside a couple of hours a day to snuggle under the doona or plonk the bot onto the Fowlerware in the smallest room, licking your lips in anticipation at having a good hard squizz at Garrie's A–Z handiwork?

So do the Australian thing – settle back with a large one handy and simply savour our brilliance.

Hats off Garrie! Pants off Australia!

Australia is a Big Country, and we feel we deserve a full array of big things. Other countries may have other kinds of symbols, but here we like the gentle self-mockery of celebrating minor aspects of national life on a monumental scale. Perhaps this means that sheep, pineapples, bananas, cricket captains, premiers, guitars, prawns, cows, avocados and, in Leunig's accurate eye, lamingtons, are important in our culture, and if you don't get it you've fallen for a Big Joke. But even jokes are useful to

The Big Thing that started it all

Big Things

the tourist industry. It seems that the Big Banana in Coffs Harbour was the first big item on the agenda, though the phrase, one of the highest praise, has been around forever. Millions travel to Coffs just to see it, but perhaps not as many as are attracted to Nambour to gaze in wonder at the Big Pineapple. Tamworth is home to the Country Music festival. Its Big Man is Slim Dusty, and its big attraction is the mighty Big Guitar. It's not too far from the Big Merino at Goulburn. Competition among towns over Big Things is as fierce as it is over the Tidy Town award. Cricket fans will recall that Warwick Armstrong was known as the Big Ship and that the controversial early 1930s NSW premier, Jack Lang, was the Big Fella.

The Big Ship's things at the MCG Museum

The Big Merino, pride of Goulburn

The 'Big Fella'

JACK LANG **AND THE AUSTRALIAN LABOR PARTY 1891–1949**

BEDE NAIRN

The Big Fella's biography, by Bede Nairn

8

The Big Pineapple, Australia's favourite big thing

The Big Lobster hails from Kingston S.E., the Big Banana from Coffs Harbour

Michael Leunig's Australia Day card – The Big Lamington, something we can all live in

Kylie Minogue (left), Gladys Moncrieff (above)   Louise Lovely, film star of the 1920s

Divine Divas

Dame Nellie Melba was the original Australian Diva, and since her glorious career (1890s–1920s) all antipodean Divas have had to choose whether to make names for themselves overseas or to remain to shine as stars Down Under, like the Southern Cross. Kylie Minogue among the modern Divas can illuminate two hemispheres, while essentially living in the north and keeping a flat in Richmond. Dame Edna is a welcome visitor to Australia, but could be said never to have left. Film Diva Louise Lovely, who had the AFI awards named for her in 2000, was a star of the local screen. Singers Nellie Stewart, and 'Our Glad' Gladys Moncrieff also stayed with us. Dame Joan Sutherland, for whom opera fans queued in the 60s, has expatriated her wonderful voice to Switzerland.

Nellie Stewart, musical star of the 1880s   Dame Joan Sutherland

Dame Nellie Melba, the greatest of them all, in a sketch by Florence Rodway

Breaker Morant, executed

Squizzy Taylor's last stand

Ben Hall, bushranger

Rogues & Ratbags

Founded as an inconvenient place to send felons, Australia took little time in developing its own brand of roguery. Perhaps it was because of a feeling that we were upside down at the bottom of the world, or in a melancholy consideration of the bizarre mammal population, but the Australian ratbag has a set of qualities that perhaps make him (it is the male of the species under consideration here): he has more front than Myers; he believes his own bull****; he believes himself loved by all, but at the same time is completely misunderstood; he has grand plans and sometimes carries them out; and all ratbags have a Fatal Flaw which is a love of money. All have become larrikin folk heroes, some after serving time or even after execution.

Alan Bond paid a world record US$49 million for Van Gogh's *Irises* in 1987

Ned Kelly, folk hero and early film subject

Christopher Skase, wheeler-dealer on the run

John Wren by Will Dyson

The lifesaver's prominent skull cap

Cricket's baggy green cap

A stack of Akubras

Hats off Australia

Hats on the 1960s TV show *Homicide*

Hats at the races, 1940s

From the pioneer's cabbage tree hat, made from natural local materials, to the globally engineered backwards-facing peaked cap of Lleyton Hewitt, hats and caps have shaded the heads of Australians for over two centuries, and form part of the Australian iconography. Hats are an important protective device in sport, but have also made a fashion statement under other heads. The Digger's slouch hat is the most honoured. Cricket's baggy green cap is the most aspirational. The Akubra, staple of the rabbit-fur industry, has heroic supporters in Greg Norman and Slim Dusty, while the pork pie is confined to *Homicide* fans and racing stewards. And women's millinery has, since the 1960s, been more or less confined to the Melbourne Cup.

Fashionable hat in 1938

Slouch hats in New Guinea, 1942

Melbourne Cup hats, 1962

Manning Clark and Ned Kelly, historical hats

Rita Pauncefort and Dorothy Foister were hatted radio stars of the 1940s, Ada & Elsie

Uluru, the big red rock

The Blues' Big Red, Lance Whitnall

Garry Lyon of the Melbourne 'Redlegs'

The Big Reds

Phar Lap was a Big Red

Australia is the big red country, which has at its centre a big red rock, Uluru, and in its heart a champion racehorse, Phar Lap.

We have a taste for big reds as well, not your squeamish continental wines, but a big full-flavoured red, of which the most expensive is Penfolds Grange. Of course those Coonawarra reds are grown on that 'terra rossa' soil. Our painters have been fond of the colour red, and not least among them was Sir Hans Heysen, who loved the big red rivergums. Redgums also gave their name to a radical-tinged folk band in the 1970s. This might not have happened in the 1950s and early 1960s when we were suspicious of Reds, under the bed or sweeping down from the north.

But we've always been attracted to red heads.

A big river redgum in a dry creek near Broken Hill

Redheads once were made here   Penfolds Grange, the big red wine

IT'S YOUR CHOICE: WHERE DO YOU DRAW THE LINE AGAINST COMMUNIST AGGRESSION?

The big red menace of 1966, a Liberal Party ad

17

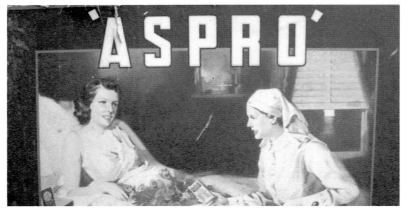
Nurse says, 'Aspro is the world's master medicine'

Many brands once Australian owned and developed have seen changes in ownership, Chesty Bond and Aeroplane Jelly among them. Others, such as R.M. Williams and Mambo have resisted, finding the local niche and export to be satisfactory markets. Ownership is less important than local jobs. Some brands, such as Qantas and Vegemite, are forever Australian. Whatever the ownership, the brands define what it is to be Australian.

Made in Australia?

Chesty Bond in fine fettle

Mambo's loud logo

An old Nugget boot tanning outfit

Qantas' bright livery, Wunala Dreaming

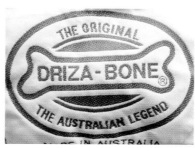

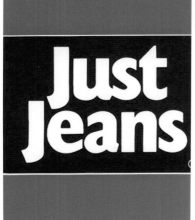

The beautiful Blue Mountains

The Shearers' Strike of the 1890s, a mighty Big Blue

Something Blue

Swaggie with his bluey

The Australian sky is blue, the flag (for the moment) is blue, and some of our greatest comedians have been decidedly blue: Mo, George Wallace, Graham Kennedy. We like a good blue, at least to watch at the cricket or the footy. Our great nation-building events have been pretty big blues – Eureka, the Shearers' Strike, World War I and II. Bluey and Curley made us laugh during the Second. At the time of the Depression (that gave many Australians the blues) blokes had to hump a bluey around the Blue Mountains and tune into *Blue Hills* on the wireless if they landed a job a decade or so later. Their kids are watching *Blue Heelers*, and those dags in D-Gen send up Bluey calling him Bargearse. NSW's colours are the Two Blues, and Carlton is the old, dark Navy Blues.

The chief Blue Heeler, John Wood, on stage

Alex Gurney's classic strip

Blue Hills, the ABC's long-running radio serial

Norman Lindsay's Bunyip Bluegum at the races

Carlton, the mighty Blues

The Eureka Stockade, the 1854 blue that launched an independent Australia, by J.B. Henderson

Ausflag design, 3rd People's Choice 1998

19th place, 1998 competition

Franck Gentil's design was preferred by the Ausflag judges in the 1998 competition

Flying the Flags

5th place, People's Choice, 1998 competition

Judge's Top 10, 1998 competition

8th place, 1998 competition, Ausflag design

The present Australian flag was adopted after a magazine competition in 1901 which drew 32 823 entries. Entry restrictions meant that the winner was destined to incorporate the British ensign and a badge symbolising Australia. In the end Annie Dorrington of Perth, Ivor Evans of Melbourne, Leslie Hawkins of Sydney, Egbert Nuttall of Melbourne and William Stevens of Auckland offered almost identical designs and shared the £200 prize money. Prime Minister Edmund Barton made the announcement on 3 September, 1901, to some consternation. Some thought the design was ugly, others thought it insufficiently patriotic. Originally a red background was nominated for civil use, the blue was for government. Since 1902, when King Edward VII gave the flag royal approval, the design has remained much the same except in the matter of the number of points on the stars. However, it was not adopted as Australia's official national flag until the passing of the Flag Act in 1953. The Aboriginal flag was designed by Harold Thomas in 1971; in it the black represents the Aboriginal people, the red the earth and the Aborigines' spiritual relationship with the land, and the yellow the sun. It was proclaimed a 'Flag of Australia' under the Flag Act in 1995. Since the establishment of the Ausflag organisation by Harold Scruby in 1981, thousands of designs have been submitted in various competitions. Some are preferred by the public and others by designers. The winners of the 1998 Australian Flag Professional Competition were announced on Australia Day 2000.

Judges' 3rd prize 1998, by Peter Lambert

Australia's first official flag, 1901

Australia's current national flag

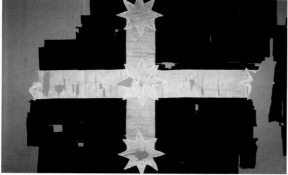

The Eureka Flag 1854 has no official status, hijacked by extreme groups

The Aboriginal flag designed by Harold Thomas in 1971

Kangaroo in top ten of the 1998 competition

2nd, People's Choice, Neville Cowland, Judith North

Winner of 1993 competition, by Mark Tucker

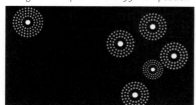

One of the top ten in the 2000 competition

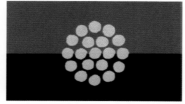

Symbol of Australia as a meeting place of all cultures

Second place in 1993, by Roderick Simpson

George Maragaritis' design, 2nd, 2000

6th place, 1998 competition, People's Choice

Third place in 1993, by Tony Burton

Boxing Kangaroo, 1983

23

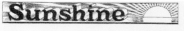

David Unaipon, Aboriginal inventor, featured on another Australian invention; an ad for the Sunshine harvester; Sir Howard Florey, discoverer of penicillin

Bright Ideas

Australians have always been a practical bunch. From the beginnings of settlement here 60 000 or more years ago, there have been people who look at the materials available, and the problem – such as how to knock down a fat magpie goose – and find a way. Hence the boomerang. Later the stump-jump plough, the Sunshine harvester and the Granny Smith apple were other applications that had a good deal to do with the need to eat. Technology has been an Australian passion as well, and has resulted in useful backyard items such as the rotary clothes hoist, or the Triton workbench. The ute was invented in order to carry things around for the backyard, or the shed. And great Australians such as Graeme Clark and Howard Florey have achieved wonders in medicine.

The first ute proved utilitarian and useful

French view of the boomerang's origins

The stump-jump plough

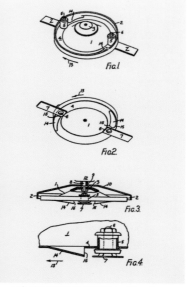

Left, the rotary clothesline with a view;
above, the rotary lawn mower patent
sketch; right, a Granny Smith

Edwin Flack won our first 1500m gold in 1896

Roger Bannister passes John Landy, 1954

1500 Metre Sports

Australia's first gold medallist was Edwin Flack who, at the first modern Olympic Games in Athens in 1896, won gold in the 800 metres, and naturally enough in the 1500 metres. Since then, on the track and in the pool, Australians have had a peculiar affinity with the mile and its metric equivalent.

On the track, champion performances have been seen from many athletes – not least of these was John Landy stopping to help young Ron Clarke in the 1956 qualifying event. Herb Elliott, Percy Cerutty–trained, was never beaten over the distance, and won gold in 1960 in Rome.

In the pool the tradition began with the amazing Frank Beaurepaire, who won bronze in 1908 in London, and in 1920 in Antwerp. Harold Hardwick won bronze in Stockholm in 1912, Andrew 'Boy' Charlton silver in Amsterdam in 1928, and John Marshall a silver in London in 1948. Our first gold medallist was Murray Rose in Melbourne, 1956, followed by John Konrads at Rome, 1960, Bob Windle, Tokyo, 1964, Greg Brough, bronze at Mexico, 1968, Graham Windeatt, silver at Munich, 1972. Steve Holland's gallant bronze at Montreal, 1976, brought about a sea change in Australian attitudes to Olympic sport, causing the establishment of the Australian Institute of Sport. Kieren Perkins' double gold, Grant Hackett's triumph over Perkins in Sydney were the result.

Herb Elliott wins gold, Rome, 1960

Frank Beaurepaire, bronze in 1908 and 1920

Boy Charlton, silver in 1928

Murray Rose, gold at Melbourne, 1956

Kieren Perkins, gold at Barcelona

Steve Holland's 1976 bronze led the way

Grant Hackett, gold at Sydney

Australia's monuments tell us something about the diverse spirit of the nation, and the nature of its two biggest cities. Melbourne's monument is the MCG where Australia's identity has been forged. It was where Australian football was invented, where the first cricket Test was played, and where Australia's first Olympics was held. For better or worse, Melbourne is the sporting heart of Australia, and the MCG, with the Great Southern Stand, is the image of the people's ground.

For a city largely devoid of good architecture, Sydney has managed to erect two of the world's greatest monuments, the Sydney Harbour Bridge and the Opera House, both set around the beautiful harbour. The harbour provided the theatrical setting for both of them, the environment in which they are used to celebrate the city. The New Year's fireworks that explode on the bridge have come to represent the essence of the city – transient fun and celebration. The image of the Opera House and the Bridge is of fireworks, New Year's Eve 1999, the supposed turning of the millennium year. The great stroke was to light up the word 'eternity', which Arthur Stace (1884–1967) had chalked in copperplate on the pavements of Sydney over half a million times.

And while dreaming of eternity, Uluru is the monument that represents the natural, and for some the spiritual, heart of Australia. It can hardly be coincidental that it is also at the physical centre of the continent.

Monuments of Oz

The Great Southern Stand at the MCG, the lights, a full house – that's the heart of Melbourne

Fireworks, a party, the Bridge, the Opera House – that's the image of Sydney

Locally owned and managed in partnership, the central icon of Australia – that's the soul of Australia

Matthew Flinders surveys his legacy

Burke and Wills, heroic failures

Sir John Monash, Australian leader

Aussie Legends

In the Australian language, calling someone a legend can mean precisely the opposite, the word sometimes being harvested with the tall poppies. On the other hand, there are some Australians whose deeds have made them more than heroes, or heroines. Australian legends and heroes, unlike those in classical history, are real people who have performed great deeds, and are not mythical personalities. The recently deceased Don Bradman was a cricketing legend, his statistics prove that he was twice as good as any other player in the history of the game. When he played he was an Australian hero, our champion representing us against the world. In the past 50 years he became something more, a legend embodying a chunk of what it means to be an Australian. Cathy Freeman became a legend in a similar way, not by winning world championships and Olympic gold medals – that is the currency of heroes – but in the Sydney Olympic Opening Ceremony where she became the embodiment of reconciliation. General Sir John Monash is a military legend rather than a brave hero because in World War I he became the post-Gallipoli leader of the new nation. In World War II Weary Dunlop, a doctor and leader on the infamous Burma–Thailand Death Railway, was first a hero, but turned into a legend because through self-sacrifice he became an exemplar of survival – and reconciliation. Burke and Wills are legends of exploration who died in pursuit of a dream, an Australian tale of bad luck. And Matthew Flinders, a legend of the sea, circumnavigated the continent and named our country.

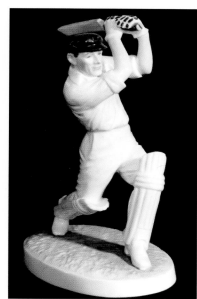

Don Bradman, cricket immortal

Weary Dunlop, still serving at the Shrine

Cathy Freeman ignites the flame for Australia at the Sydney Olympics

A

The ANZAC Book written on Gallipoli, edited by C.E.W. Bean

Ablett takes a 'speccie'

ABC personalities Caroline Jones and Bill Peach parade at the 1969 Waratah Festival

ABC

The activities of the national broadcaster (b. 1932) are a continuing topic of vigorous discussion among and between its audience, management, government and media commentators. Issues such as the alleged bias of current affairs programs, privatisation and/or advertising by stealth, the adequacy of funding, a decline in standards and questions about the audience which is too small, middle class and loyal, or too widespread and diverse to rate – all this besets 'Aunty'. Nevertheless, the ABC is crucial in giving Australia a sense of cultural continuity, and at its best, a feeling of national identity.

Ablett, Gary

The AFL footballer known as 'God' because of the miraculous individual

A long way to the top if you want to rock'n'roll

things he could do, Gary Ablett was, at the same time, a player with the 'devil' in him: unpredictable, moody, and not necessarily a team player. He played 6 games with Hawthorn, then 242 games for 1021 goals with Geelong. His greatest moment on field was the 1989 Grand Final which he nearly won off his own boot; his lowest off-field moment was in 2000 when a young woman died in his company in a hotel room while they were on a binge. Ablett was an extraordinary, mortal footballer.

AC/DC

Formed by Malcolm Young in 1973 after his previous band dissolved; he quickly brought in his younger brother Angus Young. Their sister Margaret named the band after the letters on the back of mum's vacuum cleaner. Margaret also suggested that Angus, who was only fifteen at the time, wear his school uniform on stage. The original line-up had Phil Rudd on drums, Mark Evans on bass and Dave Evans on lead vocals – Bon Scott, the band's chauffeur, became their lead singer when Evans refused to go on stage in Melbourne. Their massive power chord sound became one of the 70s most influential sounds. *Highway to Hell* in 1979 was their first million-selling album. When Scott died in 1980 he was replaced by Brian Johnson.

One of George Adams' legacies

Patsy Adam-Smith, very popular historian

The Inflammable Adams

A

Adams, Arthur H.

Novelist and playwright Arthur H. Adams (1872–1936) came to Australia from New Zealand in 1898 with the libretto to a comic opera by noted early composer Alfred Hill. This secured him a job with impresario J.C. Williamson at £4 a week. The show *Tapu* was later produced. Adams went on to become editor of the *Bulletin*'s Red Page, *Lone Hand* and the *Sydney Sun*. His best-remembered novels are *Galahad Jones* (1910) and *The Australians* (1920) and his play *Mrs Pretty and the Premier* (1915). Another writer who wrote at least one of everything.

Adams, George

Publican and founder of the Tattersalls empire, George Adams (1839–1904) was born in England and came to Australia in 1855. His first pub was the Steam Packet Inn at Kiama in 1875. He frequented O'Brien's Hotel, home of the Tattersalls Club, in Pitt Street Sydney, and in 1878 George struck it rich when three mates bought him the hotel – because 'George Adams liked O'Brien's, and they liked George Adams'. Adams paid them back in six years, and was on his way to becoming a rich man. He ran sweepstakes on Australian race meetings from the pub, and in 1881 ran the first public Tattersalls sweep on the Sydney Cup. He was legislated out of NSW and then Queensland, moving his lottery business to Tasmania in 1895, where Tatts stayed for 58 years. 'A ticket in Tatts' became many Australians' dream of escaping the rat-race.

Adam-Smith, Patsy

Best known for her book *The Anzacs* (1978), Patsy Adam-Smith (1926–2001) was a popular historian in the best sense of the word. *Anzacs* was a major influence in restirring interest and emotion in Anzac and Gallipoli. She had a lifelong interest in railways and her railwayman Dad, and her auto-biography *Hear the Train Blow* (1964) is a classic. Other Australians she dealt with include shearers, women at war, mutton birds, merchant sailors and all manner of outback heroes.

Adams, Phillip

Phillip Adams' (b. 1939) career has included stints in advertising, television and journalism, but it is his contribution to the Australian film industry which truly stands out. A foundation member of the Australia

We liked the jelly when it was home owned

Down goes the *Admella*, in the illustration submitted to a South Australian competition

John Pascoe Fawkner's copy of the first edition of the *Age*

Council and foundation chairman of the Film, Radio and Television Board, he was also at the heart of the establishment of the Australian Film Development Fund and the Experimental Film Fund. He has won eight Australian Film Festival Awards and two gold medals in international competition. He produced the seminal Australian films *The Adventures of Barry McKenzie* (1972), *Don's Party* (1976), *The Getting of Wisdom* (1977) and *We of the Never Never* (1982).

Admella

The wreck of the 395-ton steam-assisted sailing ship *Admella*, on Carpenter Rocks near the border of South Australia and Victoria in 1859, is one of the most heart-wrenching sea disaster stories of Australia. The ship broke up, stranding 40 people on the forward section and 50 on the stern in huge seas. While fruitless attempts to save them were made, people were alive on the ship for over a week, dropping off one by one until just 22 were rescued. Three of the four horses on their way to the Australasian Sweepstakes in Melbourne also survived.

Aeroplane Jelly

Aeroplane Jelly possesses one of TV's most recognisable advertising jingles, penned by Les Woods:

I like Aeroplane Jelly,
It's Aeroplane Jelly for me,
I like it for dinner, I like it for tea,
A little each day is a good recipe.

The Aeroplane Jelly Company was founded by Bert Appleroth in Sydney in 1928. Aeroplane Jelly was also one of the products 'reinvented' by Dick Smith in his 'fight back' campaign following the news that it had passed into foreign hands. His version was called Helicopter Jelly.

Age, The

Melbourne's quality broadsheet founded in 1854 by John and Henry Cooke, the *Age* was from its inception a liberal daily of world standard. It was quickly taken over by David and Ebenezer Syme, in whose family it remained until control was sold to the Sydney Fairfaxes in 1987. Less crusading in the 1990s than the 1890s but capable of annoying governments, especially during the Kennett years. It has remained the newspaper of choice for Melburnians who love classified ads, real estate, cars, food and the arts.

35

A

Young 'Sharky' waves Greg Norman's Akubra

Peter Allen and then wife Liza Minnelli

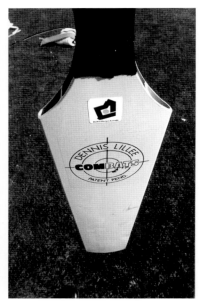

Dennis Lillee's promotional opportunity

Akubra

After arriving in Australia in the 1870s, Benjamin Dunkerley developed a mechanical method of removing the hair tip from rabbit fur so that the underfur could be used in felt hat making, and the technique allowed him to start a hatmaking business in Sydney. However, it was Stephen Keir who began branding the hats 'Akubra' after Dunkerley's death in 1918, and he also won large contracts to supply 'slouch' hats for the army in both world wars. Now in its fourth generation of family ownership, the Akubra has become an enduring national symbol.

Allen, Peter

Born Peter Woolnough (1944), he began playing piano when he was four years old. When he was fourteen

he met guitarist Chris Bell, formed 'The Allen Brothers' and made their debut on TV's *Teen Time*. The pair toured extensively, recorded their debut single *First Kiss* in 1960 and recorded for Pye, EMI and Festival Records in 1961. His shortlived marriage to Liza Minnelli began in 1967 and ended in 1970, the same year he and Bell parted ways. He recorded two solo albums, *Peter Allen* (1971) and *Tenterfield Saddler* (1972), before recording his first album with a major label, *Continental American* (1973), and becoming a leading light in the cabaret revival scene in New York. His biggest success, however, was the album *I Go To Rio* (1977), which saw him give concerts at the Sydney Opera House and the Paris Olympia. He won a Best Song Oscar for co-writing the theme to the film

Arthur. His final album was *Make Every Moment Count* (1990) before dying in 1992. His life has since been immortalised in the hit musical *The Boy from Oz*.

Aluminium Cricket Bat

Fiery fast bowler Dennis Lillee was also a bit of a larrikin, involving himself in a number of 'incidents'. One was his promoting a cricket bat made from aluminium rather than the traditional willow in a Test match against England in 1979, in Perth. Lillee faced four balls with the bat before England captain Mike Gatting complained. Play resumed with a wooden bat. Lillee made 18 and was told by the Australian Cricket Board that his behaviour was 'reprehensible'. Lillee participated in the poet's ideal dismissal in the

Irresistible Alvin Purple makes a conquest

Matilda's tribute to the America's Cup win

Gordon Andrews with one of his banknotes

second innings of this match: Lillee c. Willey b. Dilley 19.

Alvin Purple

The first in a series of blunderingly risque comedies directed by Tim Burstall, starring Graeme Blundell as Alvin, an ugly little guy irresistible to women. The first *Alvin Purple* hit screens in 1973 and the sequel *Alvin Rides Again* arrived a year later. There was also a shortlived ABC TV series which appeared in 1973 but which was taken off air by the then-chairman, the appropriately named Sir Henry Bland. Blundell was a founder director at the Pram Factory, and through the 1980s and 90s directed theatre, television commercials in Sydney and Melbourne, and acted in films as varied as *Don's Party* and *Star Wars*.

He became an entertaining biographer of Brett Whiteley (with Margot Hilton), and Graham Kennedy.

America's Cup

Winning the America's Cup from the New York Yacht Club in 1983, after 132 years and four failed Australian attempts, is inextricably linked with a peculiar period in Australian history, when 'entrepreneurism' took over our national life. The not-yet-disgraced Alan Bond financed the winning bid by *Australia II*, and Bob Hawke told everyone who had stayed up all night to watch the slow-moving event that they could take the day off – and any employer who didn't like it was a 'bum'. The rich man's sport par excellence, America's Cup challengers have been *Gretel* (1962), *Dame Pattie* (1967), *Southern Cross* (1974), and

Australia (1980). *Kookaburra III* lost the 'auld mug' in 1987, year of the stock market crash, and the nadir was reached when the *oneAustralia* sank off San Diego in 1995.

Andrews, Gordon

Gordon Andrews (1914–2001) was the elder statesman of modern Australian design, best known for the original set of decimal bank notes, released in 1966, plus the later $50 and $100 notes. Andrews also designed innovative furniture, the interior of the House of Representatives chamber in the new Parliament House, and masks.

Andrews, John

Born in Sydney (1933), John Andrews set up his own business in Toronto in 1962 before expanding (and

37

Anzac Cove, named by the Turkish government in honour of the Anzacs

returning) to Sydney ten years later. More concerned with the functionality of his buildings and in solving specific site-related issues than in establishing a personal style, his early work is distinctive for its opposition to the romantic architecture of his Australian contemporaries. An understanding of social, climatic and functionality issues distinguishes Andrews' work.

Angus & Robertson

In January 1886, booksellers David Angus and George Robertson joined forces to create a partnership which would go on to become Angus & Robertson Limited in 1907. Pioneers of Australian publishing as well as bookselling, they would publish 'Banjo' Paterson's *The Man from Snowy River* and Henry Lawson's *In the Days When the World Was Wide*. It would continue to operate as a publisher and bookseller for over sixty years before it became the first Australian bookseller to offer bookshop franchises in 1976. In 1978 the publishing and bookselling arms of the company separated, and a merger between the bookselling arm and Bookworld made the new company the tenth-largest retail bookselling business in the world.

Ansett

Founded by Reginald Myles Ansett in 1936 with a single-engine, six-seater Fokker Universal, the first flight was from the Victorian regional town of Hamilton to Melbourne. Originally a purely domestic airline, in 1993 it expanded its services to include international flights.

Anzac

Strictly speaking, ANZAC is the acronym for Australian and New Zealand Army Corps, and was adopted in 1915. Anzac is also that part of the Gallipoli Peninsula taken by Anzac in 1915 – the small cove where they landed and the area above it which they fought for. The Turkish government named it Anzac Cove in 1985. Anzac soon became synonymous with Australian soldiers, whose blood sacrifice at Gallipoli, in the Middle East and in France gave meaning to the newly federated Australia. The first Anzac Day in 1916, commemorating the landing on 25 April 1915, was held by diggers at a service in London attended by royalty, and subsequently in Australia. A bad patch in the 1950s where the commemorative aspect of Anzac was

Sir Reginald Ansett by John Spooner

Jules François Archibald and co-founder of the *Bulletin*, John Haynes

lost in drunken reunions of still young and misunderstood World War II veterans (as depicted in Alan Seymour's scarifying play of intergenerational conflict *The One Day of the Year*, 1961) was followed by the divisive participation of Australia in conscription and the Vietnam War, 1965–72. Anzac Day was rediscovered in the 1980s and 1990s, spurred on by the 75th Anniversary events 'Australia Remembers' in 1990, and the diminishing number of 'original Anzacs'. It is now our national day, the birthday of Australia's secular religion.

Archer

Racehorse, winner of the first two Melbourne Cups, 1861–62. Legend has it that Archer walked from NSW to Melbourne for the first Cup, but recent research has revealed that the horse most probably came by boat – but no one wants to believe that.

Archibald, J.F.

Journalist and editor, Jules François Archibald (1856–1919) was born John Feltham but changed his name when young. His career began on the *Warrnambool Examiner* as an apprentice printer and he was briefly a clerk in the Victorian Education Department before going back to journalism in Sydney in 1878. In 1880 Archibald and John Haynes began publishing the *Bulletin*. Archibald was the literary editor and accepted contributions from the soon-to-be-great, including Henry Lawson and 'Banjo' Paterson. In 1882 he and Haynes were jailed for not paying the costs of a libel action, which amount

was raised through a public appeal. While in jail the *Bulletin* was published by W.H. Traill who had written the libellous article, and Archibald found himself working for him. Archibald was editor from 1886–1902, when forced to retire because of ill health. He sold his interest in 1914. Archibald was a great editor, and created the most popular, irreverent and Australian magazine of his time – its motto 'Australia for the white man'. He endowed the Archibald Prize, and the Archibald Fountain in Hyde Park, Sydney, commemorating the association of France and Australia in World War I.

Archibald Prize

Always controversial, the Archibald Prize is Australia's premier portraiture award and probably Australia's most

39

The Argonauts pose around the microphone

Argus 1956 Olympic souvenir

recognised award for the visual arts.
Begun in 1921 as the result of a
bequest from Jules François
Archibald, it created a stir in 1944
when William Dobell won with a
painting of Joshua Smith which many
critics described as so distorted that
it no longer constituted a portrait.
The issue was decided in court where
Justice Roper found that the painting,
although 'characterised by some
startling exaggeration and distortion
… bears, nevertheless, a strong
degree of likeness to its subject.'
Other notable winners have included
Brett Whiteley (1976, 1978), Judy
Cassab (1960, 1967) and Clifton Pugh
(1965, 1971, 1972). In 1988 a People's
Choice section was included in the
award. Adam Cullen won in 2000
with a portrait of *SeaChange* heart
throb David Wenham.

Argonauts, The

An ABC radio club built around an
afternoon program that ran in
Melbourne in 1933–34, and nationally
from 1941–72. The idea was that
children around Australia could join
the studio presenters in becoming
Argonauts, rowers on Jason's ship the
Argo in search of the Golden Fleece.
They would have names such as Illyria
42 (Robert Dessaix). Jeffrey Smart
presented talks on painting, Ruth Park
wrote the *Muddle Headed Wombat*
(first voice Leonard Teale) for the
Children's Hour, of which the
Argonauts Club was part. Kids sent
their stuff in and received awards,
Barry Humphries' first work was made
for the Argonauts Club. It flourished
in middle-class Australia from the
1940s to the 1960s, before TV. Song:
Fifty mighty Argonauts,

Bending to the oars,
Today we go adventuring
To yet uncharted shores. Row! Row!
Merry oarsmen, Row!
A more innocent Australia and a jolly
good night to you and you and you
and you and YOU!

Argus, The

The great rival of the *Age* newspaper,
the *Argus* appeared daily in
Melbourne between 1846 and 1957.
On 15 November 1952 the *Argus* was
the first daily newspaper in the world
to publish colour photographs.

Arrighi, Luciana

Luciana Arrighi's design career began
in Australia with the Australian
Elizabethan Theatre Trust, before
moving to England for further study.
She designed Ken Russell's three

Luciana Arrighi in costume   An Arkley in uncharacteristic mono   Neil Armfield and Patrick White

startling TV specials, *Isadora*, *Rousseau* and *Rossetti*, and in 1969 designed *Women in Love*. She returned to Australia for Patrick White and Jim Sharman's *The Night the Prowler*, and Gillian Armstrong's *My Brilliant Career*. She won Academy Awards for production design of Merchant Ivory's *Howard's End* in 1993 and for *The Remains of the Day* in 1994.

Arkley, Howard
Best known for his colourful airbrush paintings of Australian suburbia, Howard Arkley (1951–99) was born and raised in the suburbs and never really left. His luminous, hypnotic canvases portrayed brick-veneer houses reframed in pastel hues or primary colours. His tragic death from a heroin overdose in 1999 came only a few weeks after a successful showing

at the Venice Biennale, where he represented Australia, a sell-out exhibition in Los Angeles and invitations to show in Paris and London. Arkley's prices skyrocketed after his death, and his widow argued strongly that royalties should be paid by auction houses using images for their own profit.

Armfield, Neil
Neil Armfield (b. 1955) is one of Australia's top theatre directors. He graduated from Sydney University in 1977, and became co-artistic director of Nimrod Street Theatre Company in 1979. He has directed innumerable productions for every major Australian company since then, and has a particular relationship with actor Geoffrey Rush, and the work of Patrick White. Armfield directed Rush

in *The Marriage of Figaro* for the Olympic Arts Festival and for the English National Opera in 2000. His 'core commitment' is to Sydney's Company B Belvoir, for which he directed Tim Winton's *Cloudstreet*.

Armstrong, Mark
Perhaps his most famous creation was the 2000 Sydney Olympic Games torch. The design contained elements of the boomerang, the Opera House and the Sydney Harbour Bridge.

Armstrong, Warwick
Warwick 'Big Ship' Armstrong (1879–1947) was not only a huge figure in Australian cricket, but a huge man full stop. A brilliant, powerful batsman and useful leg-spinner, he was also a thorn in the side of cricket officials everywhere. A fixture in the

Warwick Armstrong, The Big Ship

William Arnott, the biscuit king

Art In Australia cover, 1941

Australian side, he declined the 1912 tour of England after objecting to how the Board of Control had decreed the side would be managed. Amazingly, he was not only back in the side on their return, but promoted to captain – after which he promptly guided his team to eight consecutive victories. During his first-class career he played 269 matches, scored over 16 000 runs and took 800 wickets. He also played in fifty Tests across a remarkable twenty years.

Arnott's Biscuits

Today Arnott's employs thousands of people and provides biscuits for over forty countries around the world, but it began in a goldfield's pie shop. Founded by William Arnot (he would add another 't' to his name) in 1847 at Bathurst, NSW, he moved to a bakery

in 1857 with some success before three floods over seven years destroyed the business, leaving him heavily in debt. He moved to Newcastle, and opened a new store with money borrowed from friends. It was an instant success and within a year he was able to purchase the building he was renting. In 1877 he opened his first biscuit factory which found success after success, weathering two world wars to become the eighth largest biscuit manufacturer in the world with factories throughout Australia and Asia. In 1997 it was bought by the U.S. Campbell's Soup Company.

Art in Australia

Founded in Sydney by Sydney Ure Smith with others in 1916 to present the works of Australia's artists in

colour and published, usually quarterly, until 1942, it boasted a staff by 1917 that included Lloyd Rees, Roland Wakelin and Percy Leason; the first four-colour publication in Australia, the leading journal on art, music and literature in its day with contributions from Norman, Lionel and Jack Lindsay, Kenneth Slessor, Katharine Susannah Prichard and Mary Gilmore. Margaret Preston designed a number of covers.

Ashbolt, Allan

Allan Ashbolt (b. 1921) was co-founder in 1946 of the Mercury Theatre in Sydney with Peter Finch. From 1951 to 1957 he was drama critic and book reviewer for the *Sydney Morning Herald* and worked as special projects producer and producer of talks at the ABC from 1954 to 1977.

The Ashes, cricket's greatest trophy

Folding the tent at Ashtons Circus, 1950s

Ashes, The

In 1882 following England's defeat by the Australians, the *Sporting Times* published a mock obituary to cricket. The entry ran: 'In Affectionate Remembrance of English Cricket Which Died At The Oval on 29th August 1882, Deeply lamented by a large circle of sorrowing friends and acquaintances R.I.P.' Legend states that in 1882–83, when the Hon. Ivo Bligh (later Lord Darnley) toured Australia, an urn filled with ashes was given to the English team. Supposedly presented by a group of Melbourne women and filled with the burnt remains of a bail used in the Third Test, in 1982 new evidence seemed to suggest that the Ashes were those of a ball and were presented to Bligh by Sir William Clarke in a ceremony before the Test series. Ever since, the little urn has come to represent one of the world's premier sporting rivalries, and its owner is decided by a five Test match series held between Australia and England every two years, the location alternating between the countries.

Ashtons Circus

For almost 150 years, the Ashtons Circus has been a fixture in Australia. James Henry Ashton assembled his first 'bush circus' in 1852 and followed squatters and miners to the outback. The first troupe included acrobats, trapeze artists and a band and its travels through rural Australia forged links which would endure to the present day. In fact, Ashtons performance in Sydney in 1905 was its first there for 40 years. Another Ashton tradition is genuine family ownership. James passed the torch to his two sons, James and Fred, and James ran the circus from 1882 until his death in 1918. His family moved to vaudeville while Fred and his family took over. By 1937, now managed by Fred's son Joe, the circus employed 70 people under its two ring tent. Still run today by the Ashtons, its family focus is especially evident when four generations of the one family perform in the ring simultaneously.

Ashton, Julian & Art School

Julian Ashton (1851–1942) came to Melbourne in 1878 from Surrey to work as an illustrator on David Syme's *Illustrated Australian News*. He moved to Sydney in 1883 and established a very prestigious art school which produced artists such as William Dobell and Sydney Ure Smith.

Storey Hall sports a modern growth

Aunty Jack will 'rip yer bloody arms off'

A

Ashton Raggatt McDougall

Multi award-winning Melbourne architectural firm well known for the organic luminous green redevelopment of RMIT University's Storey Hall in Swanston Street Melbourne and who designed the National Museum of Australia which opened on Acton Peninsula in 2001.

Aunty Jack

TV sketch show directed by Maurice Murphy on the ABC 1972–73, starring Grahame Bond as the cross-dressing motorbike-riding boxing Aunty Jack, with the growly voice threatening to 'rip yer bloody arms off'. Garry McDonald was Kid Eager, Sandy MacGregor was Flange Desire, Rory O'Donohue was Thin Arthur and John Derum was the Narrator. 'Farewell Aunty Jack' reached Number 1 and stayed in the Australian music charts for 22 weeks in 1974.

Aussie: The Cheerful Monthly

Originally launched under the title *Aussie: The Australian Soldier's Magazine* and printed in the field by the AIF, the magazine ran monthly (although it occasionally missed an issue) from 1918 to 1920. In that year it changed its name to *Aussie: The Cheerful Monthly* and continued publication until 1931. Contained fiction, poetry, illustrations, an 'Aussie dictionary' and articles on Australian writers from its long-serving editor Phillip Lawrence Harris.

'Austra-laise', The

Originally winning a prize of a guinea in a song competition run by the *Bulletin* in 1908, C.J. Dennis' the 'Austra-laise' was nicknamed the 'Blanky Austra-laise' by one judge because of the many blank spaces in the text replacing the word 'bloody'. In 1913 an expanded version was published in Dennis' book *Backblock Ballads and Other Verses* and in 1915 it was reprinted in a leaflet for Australian soldiers as a marching song, with the advice that it should be sung to the tune 'Onward Christian Soldiers'. In 1951 it was used as a recruiting song for the Korean War and in 1968 selected as the marching song of the Seventh Battalion, Royal Australian Regiment.

Austral Wheelrace

First held at the MCG between 1887 and 1914, this is the premier professional sprint cycling race in Australia, and was won in its 102nd

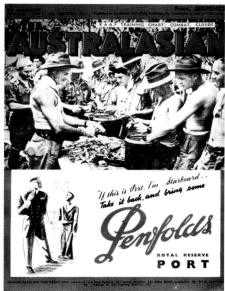

The *Australasian* in wartime

Matthew Flinders' map first identified the continent as Australia

running by Gary Neiwand in 2000 at the Northcote velodrome. Some races since 1887 were lost to war, but 1910 was a highlight when one of the new-fangled flying machines (made by M. Bleriot) took off from the centre of the MCG, but crashed into the bowling green soon after. Stephen Pate is the only cyclist to have won the Austral from scratch, in 1991–92.

Australasian, The
Formed by the 1864 merger of three Melbourne weeklies and then later including *Bell's Life in Victoria* and the *Australian Sketcher with Pen and Paper*, the *Australasian* was the weekend companion to the *Argus* and included contributions from such notable writers as Marcus Clarke and Ada Cambridge. It was Australia's best general-interest weekly for

eighty years. It changed its name to the *Australasian Post* in 1947.
See: Argus

Australia
The Latin word *australis* means 'southern' and it was natural that when searching purposefully for – or finding accidentally – the great land rumoured to exist in the southern hemisphere to balance the great northern landmass, the word 'australis' would be used. Thus sixteenth-century map makers such as Mercator called the great south land, '*continens australis*'. De Quiros discovered Vanuatu in 1606 and thought it connected to the land Australia del Espiritu Santo. In translations of his book he referred to Terra Australis. A Dutch geographer Gerritz rendered de Quiros' land as

Australia Incognita in 1612. Captain Cook thought in 1770 he had discovered not Terra Australis but the east coast of what the Dutch had called New Holland. Cook called it New Wales, and later New South Wales. None of these early usages of Australis took hold. The redoubtable Matthew Flinders wrote in his report *Voyage to Terra Australis*, having circumnavigated the place (1814), 'Had I permitted myself any innovation upon the original term Terra Australis, it would have been to convert it into Australia.' In the charts published of his voyage, the land is referred to as General Chart of Terra Australis or Australia. Governor Macquarie used the word Australia in correspondence and it seems from this official usage it was used by ordinary New South Welshers to refer to their new land.

45

Australia II sets a spinnaker

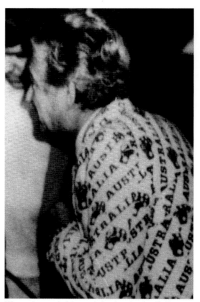

The prime minister celebrates Australia too

Melbourne and Geelong in action, 1880

They also began referring to themselves as Australians, thus avoiding Currency Lad, New South Welshman or Welshwoman. W.C. Wentworth used the word in the 1820s, and it seemed it was in general use as a name for the continent and people by then. Officially the colonies were still colonies, and the Colonial Office seems not to have used the word Australia in the 19th century. The map makers at the Admiralty, however, were not so constrained. Thus when it came time to federate a new nation from the six colonies in the 1890s there seemed little doubt or even discussion about what the Great South Land should be called.

Australia II
Skippered by John Bertrand, *Australia II* wrested the America's Cup from the USA on 27 September 1983 by defeating the defender *Liberty*. The cup had been held by America for 132 years and was the premier prize of 12-metre sailing. The syndicate which financed the boat was headed by Alan Bond, who launched himself into the spotlight with the victory. However it was the legendary 'winged keel', designed by Ben Lexcen, which held the answer to *Australia II*'s remarkable victory.
See: America's Cup; Bond, Alan

Australian Football
Australian football rejoices in a rationalised if not entirely rational history. Aficionados and football scholars debate arcane points of . sporting history most often in Melbourne till the cows come home and beyond. Was it really invented by the introspective all-rounder Thomas Wentworth Wills? Or was it brought to Melbourne by Irish gold-diggers? Or worse, by the 49th Regiment? Or better, was it picked up by Wills as a lad when playing with the local Aborigines, and derived from their game marrngrook? Little is known or will ever be known, so speculation will remain fruitful. The facts, such as they are, include these: Wills did grow up and learn Aboriginal languages on his father Horatio's spread near Ararat in Victoria, there was an Aboriginal game played with a stuffed possum skin involving running and catching, he did attend Rugby School in the 1850s and he did umpire the notional 'first' game between players representing two Melbourne schools on 8 August 1858 after writing the 'foundation letter' to a Melbourne

The Carlton team poses in 1881, before the establishment of the VFL

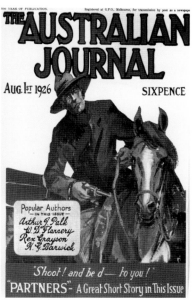

Popular fiction in the 1920s

sporting weekly, *Bell's Life*. Codification of all games, soccer and Gaelic football among them, postdates the first games of Australian football which already possessed its own distinctive take on what is permissible – no kicking each other, running and catching the ball. The game as it was played in the 1860s and 1870s would not have looked much like the game played later in the 19th century, let alone the modern version. There was less running, less marking and fewer tactics. Other codes of football perhaps have a greater affinity of appearance with their 19th-century beginnings, but it is one of the glories of the Australian game that it has changed and developed into today's fast and spectacular test of oval-ball skills. But those old players and those clubs were the direct antecedents of

the game that did develop. The clubs Melbourne and Geelong were formed in 1859, Carlton in 1864. The first rules were promulgated in 1859 and were revised in 1866. The first regular competition, the Victorian Football Association, was organised in 1877. Australian football does have something in common with modern Gaelic football, and games are played under hybrid rules. There is a touch of American football, rugby union and rugby league, and even something from the round-ball games too, from a tactical point of view. It also has a tremendous appeal to Aboriginal footballers, an affinity that has been especially evident in the last twenty years. Many students feel the sport has turned full circle, in one of the more elegant expressions of the reconciliation process.

Australian Journal

For almost one hundred years the *Australian Journal* (1865–1962) held the interest of Australians and, particularly during the editorship of Marcus Clarke (1870–71), supported Australian writing. A weekly publication for its first four years and a monthly thereafter, it serialised not only Marcus Clarke's *His Natural Life* (1870–72) but also Charles de Boos' *Fifty Years Ago* (1869–70) and the shorter fiction of writers such as Charles Harpur and Ada Cambridge.

Australian Legend, The

Russel Ward's influential 1958 book, *The Australian Legend*, helped legitimise Australia's view of itself, before the changes wrought by post-war immigration had taken full effect. Ward claimed that the

Bruce Spence at the Pram Factory

John Romeril's *A Floating World*, designed by Peter Corrigan

national characteristics were mateship, independence, egalitarianism, adaptability, anti-authoritarianism and secularism. Feminism, racism or reconciliation were not on the agenda, though Ward's argument was about what Australians believed rather than what we actually did.

Australian Performing Group

Melbourne's responsibility for the renaissance of the Australian theatre in the late 1960s stemmed from the people involved with the Australian Performing Group (APG), first at La Mama 1968–69, and then at the Pram Factory 1970–81. Graeme Blundell and David Kendall directed Jack Hibberd's micro plays at the University of Melbourne in 1968, and this group was part of the first acting

workshop at La Mama later that year. During 1969 the La Mama Company did extensive work on texts by Hibberd, John Romeril, Barry Oakley, Bertolt Brecht and Alex Buzo. In 1970 the company became the APG, dedicated to developing 'collective work and organisation' at the Pram Factory in Drummond Street, Carlton. First production was *Marvellous Melbourne*, developed by the group from an old melodrama and scripts by Hibberd and Romeril. The popular show brought the 'rough' Australian actors' theatre to the fore. It involved theatre done in the round and in the raw. Later shows owed more to the writers and sometimes to the directors, but APG work was always grounded in what the actor could do. David Williamson's *Don's Party* (1970), Jack Hibberd's *A Stretch of the*

Imagination (1970), John Romeril's *A Floating World* (1974) and the group-developed *The Hills Family Show* (1976) were among the highlights. There was always tension in the APG between the ideologues of different sorts: writers, actors, administrators, collectivists, individualists, directors, designers ... the APG became a kind of home and a structure for anyone who wanted to 'do' something in the theatre, and the headquarters for anyone who had emotion invested in a 'new' Australian theatre, as opposed to the 'old' over-subsidised, proscenium arch version. Along the way the APG spun off all kinds of people – Williamson to Sydney, Hibberd to classical status, Blundell to Sydney via the Playbox, Gillies to satirical stardom and others right out of the theatre. But it is a measure of

Don's Party, 1970

Examples of Robin Boyd's Australian Ugliness – featurism in Australian cities

the success of a decade's work that while the group and the building have gone, just about all the people involved in the APG in its heyday are still ploughing Australian cultural fields of one sort or another.

Australian Ugliness, The

Robin Boyd's splendid diatribe against the ugliness, environmental vandalism and 'featurism' of Australian suburbia, *The Australian Ugliness* was first published in 1960. The attitudes in the book have a lot in common with what Barry Humphries came to celebrate and mock. Boyd defined featurism this way: 'Featurism is not simply a decorative technique, it starts in concepts and extends upwards through the parts to the numerous trimmings.' As Dame Edna once so nicely put it:

The best Highett homes
have hundreds of gnomes
All scattered about on the grass
There's wrought iron too,
in a pale duck-blue
And acres of sand-blasted glass

Boyd's distaste was a reaction to the unplanned suburban sprawl not only in Australia, but overseas. But as he lived here, he wrote about what he saw around him, in Australia. He would see it still today, especially in the mock Victorian and classical Italianate palazzos of outer suburban Melbourne in the year MM. The title *The Australian Ugliness*, unlike Horne's *The Lucky Country*, was unironic.

Australian War Memorial

The Australian War Memorial was the idea of C.E.W. Bean, journalist and Australia's Official War Historian.

Bean landed at Gallipoli on the first Anzac Day, and took it as his task to conserve the memory of the sacrifice of those men in the creation of the 'consciousness of Australian nationhood'. One way was his extraordinary Official History of Australia's participation in World War I, another was the appointment of Official War Artists (such as Arthur Streeton and George Lambert) and yet another was in the creation of the Australian Historical Records Section in 1917. This group collected relics of World War I with the enthusiastic participation of thousands of diggers. While postwar inertia in building Canberra, the writing of the history and changing governments slowed the building of the War Memorial building, a great exhibition of the collected material

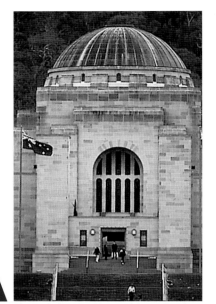

The Australian War Memorial, Anzac Parade

Celebrate Wattle Day on August 1

The Weekly at the Cup, by WEP

A

was held in Melbourne lasting from 1923 to 1925 and in Sydney from 1925 to 1935, and was a success. John Treloar of the Historic Records Section was appointed the first director of the AWM in 1920, and oversaw the eventual construction of the building in all its symbolic resonance. He retired in 1952. An architectural competition in 1927 failed to produce a satisfactory single design for the building, but Sydney architects Emil Sodersteen and John Crust were encouraged to submit a joint design, incorporating Sodersteen's vision for the building and Crust's concept of cloisters to house the Roll of Honour. The joint design forms the basis of the building we see today, completed in 1941. By the time the Roll of Honour was completed in 1959 it had become a list of Australia's dead in all wars,

arranged by units. The Hall of Memory was also completed in 1959 and in 1993 the Tomb of the Unknown Soldier was placed in the Hall of Memory. A program of gallery refurbishment was undertaken during the 1980s starting with the Gallipoli Gallery, which opened in 1984. This was followed by the opening of galleries commemorating the more recent conflicts such as Korea and Vietnam. The redeveloped galleries, Research Centre and Sculpture Garden were officially opened by the prime minister in March 1999.

Australian Wattle Day League

Wattle Day, officially September 1, celebrating the green and gold of the national colours of the national floral emblem, was proclaimed in 1992. The

Golden Wattle *Acacia pycnantha* was made the national floral emblem in 1988. These great achievements came about after over a hundred years of struggle by the Australian Wattle Day League and its predecessors.

Australian Women's Weekly
The brainchild of George W. Warneke, the *Australian Women's Weekly* launched in Sydney on 8 June 1933 and extended its circulation to Victoria and Queensland a few months later, and then to the rest of Australia by 1936. Warneke edited the magazine until 1939 before passing the reins to a series of women editors, including Alice Jackson, Esme Fenton, Dorothy Drain, Ita Buttrose and Dawn Swain. More a reflection of its time than an influence on it, the magazine has held an enviable

Michael and Lindy Chamberlain in 1980

Meryl Streep came to play Lindy Chamberlain

The headline tells the story

circulation throughout its life. A supporter of women as wives and mothers in its early years, the magazine also championed the replacement of women with men in the workforce following World War II, and in the 1990s it switched its focus to celebrity gossip and lifestyle concerns, losing none of its popularity along the way. Urban legend holds that the magazine retained its weekly title despite its monthly frequency because of the 'objectionable' overtones of a magazine called 'Australian Women's Monthly'.

Azaria

The Azaria Chamberlain disappearance combined many of Australian culture's usually hidden obsessions – lost children, wild dingos, bad mothers, legal and police incompetence, and the mysterious big red rock, Uluru. The nine-and-a-half week old Azaria disappeared on 17 August 1980, with her parents, Michael and Lindy Chamberlain, claiming that she had been taken from their tent by a dingo. An inquest in February 1981 found that a dingo had taken the child and that the parents had no involvement in the child's death, but suggested that another person may have been involved in disposing of the baby's body. In February 1982, a second inquest resulted in the Chamberlains being committed for trial for the murder of their daughter. Lindy Chamberlain was found guilty and her husband was found to have acted as an accessory. Lindy, pregnant during the trial, was sentenced to a mandatory life term and gave birth to another daughter in prison. After a matinee jacket was discovered at Uluru in 1986, undermining earlier forensic evidence, Lindy was released. The Chamberlains later had their convictions quashed and were compensated for wrongful conviction. On 13 December 1995, a third inquest into the death of Azaria Chamberlain returned an open verdict. After three inquests, numerous appeals and even a Royal Commission, all that is known for sure is that Meryl Streep playing Lindy Chamberlain in the Fred Schepisi film famously cried, 'A dingo's got my baby' and that this was echoed around the pop culture world. John Bryson's disturbing book *Evil Angels* upon which the film was based and named is the definitive account and analysis of the events prior to Lindy being pardoned.

51

B

Bronzed Aussies performing on the beach in the 1950s

Bert Bailey says 'What this country needs is a darn good laugh', and still does

Alex Stitt cover for Sidney Baker's classic

Babe

One of the highest-grossing Australian films ever made, *Babe* tells the story of a pig in rural NSW which thinks it's a sheepdog. Starring Magda Szubanski and James Cromwell (as well as a host of digitally retouched barnyard animals) it certainly brought home the bacon for the profile of the Australian film industry and talent, grossing more than 500 million dollars worldwide. Written and produced by George Miller, *Babe* was also the feature film debut of director Chris Noonan. The so-called 'darker' sequel, *Babe: Pig in the City* (1998) was written, produced and this time also directed by George Miller, and although it could not repeat the success of the first film, still held its own.
See: Szubanski, Magda

Baggy Green Cap

The baggy green cap of Australia's Test cricketers has come to symbolise more than just membership of the Australian team. Reinstituted by captain Steve Waugh as the headwear of choice in the first fielding session of each Test, the cap has a proud heritage and its laconic appearance is seen by many to reflect the attitude of the country as well as its sportsmen. It has also been the subject of some controversy in the late 1990s, with stolen caps appearing for sale on the internet.

Bailey, Bert

Best known for his portrayal as Dad of *Dad and Dave* fame, Bert Bailey (1868–1939) is also famous for his collaborations with Edmund Duggan. In 1907 they co-authored the bush melodrama *The Squatter's Daughter* before together adapting the stories of Steele Rudd into the phenomenally successful *On Our Selection*. The production was performed from 1912 to 1929. Bailey also starred in the film adaptation in 1932.

Baker, Sidney

Sidney James Baker (1912–76) was first interested in the peculiarly Australian version of the English language when questioned about it in England in the late 1930s. This benign inquiry spurred a series of books and studies on the nature of Australian speech and usage which include *A Popular Dictionary of Australian Slang* (1941), *Australian Pronunciation* (1947) and his most famous work, *The Australian Language* (1945).

Snowy Baker, the complete athlete

A panel of Jim Bancks' *Us Fellers*

Bancks was a great Minties artist

Baker, Snowy

Nicknamed 'Snowy' at an early age because of his hair, Reginald Leslie (1884–1953) found success virtually everywhere he looked. As an athlete he was a swimmer, runner, rugby player, cricketer, rower, horserider and boxer – Reg could do it all. He was also a successful journalist, frequently contributing to the *Sydney Evening News* (1908–10) and even publishing a book, *General Physical Culture* (1910). Between 1918 and 1920 he took these varied skills to the big screen and then America, where he became distracted by business ventures, again finding considerable success.

Baldessin, George

Part of a group of Australian artists in the 1970s who were trying to resist the Americanisation of Australian art,

George Baldessin's (1939–78) work centres around the human figure and natural forms. Perhaps his most recognised work is the *Pear (version No.2)*, a series of sculptures outside the main entrance to the National Gallery of Australia in Canberra. The pears are made from special steel chosen by the artist because it rusts in a predictable way to give a patina of rust at a pre-determined depth – thereby creating a brown 'skin' on the pears.

Bananas in Pyjamas

A hugely successful spin-off from Australia's longest running children's television show *Play School*, Bananas in Pyjamas have spawned their own videos, toys and live shows. Unsurprisingly, they are two giant bananas, dressed in pyjamas.

Bancks, Jim

The highest-paid black-and-white artist of his era, James Bancks (1889–1952) was a full-time artist at the *Bulletin* from 1914 before creating the new full-colour comic strip *Us Fellers* for the *Sydney Sun*. The focus of this strip quickly became the red-headed troublemaker Ginger Meggs, a character who is still a part of popular folklore today.

Bandstand

A copy of American *Bandstand*, with Buddy Holly-like bespectacled host Brian Henderson as the equivalent of the world's teenager Dick Clark, *Bandstand* was sedate (some said sedated compared to the ABC's rockier show Johnny O'Keefe's *Six O'Clock Rock*) but lasted from 1958 to 1972. Its stars were the likes of the

Brian Henderson's *Bandstand* during filming

A portrait of Sir Joseph Banks

Bannerman meets The Don in 1929, and right, after the game, perhaps a cool bottle of Ballarat Bitter

Delltones, Col Joye and the Joy Boys, Dig Richards and the young Frank Ifield (*I Remember You-hoo*) and the very young Bee Gees. Henderson is now Nine newsreading's elder statesman. Johnny O'Keefe, who lived on a wilder side, is in rock heaven.

Banks, Sir Joseph

Banks (1743–1820) was the naturalist with Captain Cook when they landed on the east coast of Australia in 1770. He was initially unimpressed with the unique range of flora and fauna encountered at Botany Bay, noting that 'barren it may justly be called', but after returning with his vast collection of specimens, Australia seemed a much richer place. He was influential in having Botany Bay selected as a site for a convict settlement, and corresponded enthusiastically with early governors of NSW. Bankstown is named for him, and the splendidly Australian genus *Banksia* as well.

Bannerman, Charles

Australia's first sporting hero, Charles Bannerman (1851–1930), faced the first ball bowled in Test cricket, bowled by England's (Albert) Shaw at 1.05 pm on 15 March 1877 at the MCG. He scored a single off the second ball and thereby set in motion the whole history and tradition of international cricket. Bannerman went on to score 165 (290 minutes, 18 fours) and retired hurt when a ball split the index finger of his right hand. This first century made in Test cricket was watched by some 4500 people during the afternoon of the first day. Australia went on to win the first game played between teams of equal numbers by 45 runs. Bannerman was known as the Pocket Hercules; he played just three Tests, unable to cope with the public adulation. His younger brother Alexander 'Alick' Bannerman (1854–1924) played 28 Tests, and toured England six times.

Barassi, Ron

More than any other player, Ron Barassi epitomised the transition from the old Victorian Football League suburban competition which reached its highest point in the 1950s, to the Australia-wide Australian Football juggernaut. Barassi was an orphan taken under the wing of Melbourne supercoach Norm Smith after Ron Barassi Senior, also a Melbourne player, was killed at Tobruk. Young Barassi was an

Ron Barassi by John Spooner

Edmund Barton, second from left, front row, Australia's first Prime Minister, 1903

B

inspirational champion in Norm
Smith's great teams of Demons in the
1950s. Barassi's departure for class
enemy Carlton in 1965, where he
became captain–coach, was seen as
the thin end of the wedge of money
football and professionalism, and so
it turned out to be. Barassi coached
Carlton to two premierships, in 1968
and, most memorably, in 1970, before
'retiring'. He then went to North
Melbourne in 1973, and coached that
club to its first flag in 1975, and again
in 1977. He was unsuccessful as coach
of Melbourne 1981–85 but was long
an advocate of the expansion of
Australian football into Sydney, and
took up the challenge to make the
Swans respectable in 1993. Since
retiring from that coaching position
in 1995, Barassi has become the elder
statesman.

Bardot

Formed as part of a Channel 7 'real
life'-style band search, Bardot
managed a number one single with a
combination of saturation advertising
and careful demographic targeting.
Australia's attempt at the Spice Girls
and the series itself an imitation of
an identical New Zealand show, we
can only hope their moment in the
sun is shortlived.

Barton, Sir Edmund

The first Prime Minister of Australia,
Sir Edmund Barton (1849–1920), was
a leader of the Federation Movement
from 1896, headed the committee
that drafted the Commonwealth
Constitution Bill and led the
delegation which presented it to the
British parliament in 1900.
Rediscovered by the Centenary.

Barnet, Nahum

Melbourne architect Nahum Barnet
designed a number of prominent and
loved Melbourne buildings, even
though most Melburnians don't
know who designed them. Most
prominent is perhaps the Francis
Ormond Building of RMIT in La Trobe
Street, a Gothic building designed by
Barnet and Terry & Oakden in the late
1880s. Or perhaps it is Her Majesty's
Theatre in Exhibition Street. Barnet
designed the first part, then named
the Alexandra Theatre, in 1886. Less
prominent is another Gothic-style
hall and shop building at 119–125
Little Bourke Street, now the Anglican
Chinese Mission of the Epiphany.
Least prominent is the original GTV-9
building in Richmond, designed in
1908 for Hugo Wertheim (Jeff
Kennett's great-grandfather), the

Nahum Barnet, Terry & Oakden's building at RMIT University, Melbourne

Melbourne's first skyscraper, ICI House

Australian piano builder. Prime Minister Alfred Deakin laid the foundation stone, and Wertheim's was soon producing 24 000 pianos a year. Barnet also designed the Melbourne Synagogue in a refined classical style, which opened in 1930.

Base, Graeme
Acclaimed children's author and illustrator Graeme Base (b. 1958) began his career as a designer in advertising before turning his attention to children's books. His titles include *Animalia* (1987) – a beautifully illustrated book of alphabet plates, whose pages are crammed with myriad objects and creatures beginning with the appropriate letter of the alphabet – and *The Eleventh Hour: A Curious Mystery* (1988).

Bates, Daisy
Born Daisy May O'Dwyer Hunt (1863–1951), Daisy Bates worked as a journalist in London before being sent to Australia by the *Times* to investigate reports of ill-treatment of the Aboriginal population. So began a total of 35 years living amongst Aborigines, studying their customs, language and legends. Dressed always in Edwardian clothes, she assisted with the hunting and helped tend each group she stayed with, gaining the nickname 'Kabbarli' or grandmother. Her book *The Passing of the Aborigines* was published in 1938.

Bates, Smart, McCutcheon
Bates Smart has the longest direct lineage of any local architectural firm. It was formed in 1926 by Edward Bates (1865–1931), Charles Smart

(d. 1950) and Osborn McCutcheon (b. 1899), successors (after a number of changes in the composition and name of the firm) to Reed, Henderson and Smart, the firm originally set up by Melbourne's most prominent 19th-century architect, Joseph Reed. After Reed, the buildings of note include the AMP Society building (1928) in Collins Street, described as being in the Commercial Palazzo style, the MLC Assurance building, Sydney (1935), the MLC building in Perth (1955) and then the triumph of Australia's first glass curtain wall skyscraper, ICI House, Melbourne (1958). Other modernist buildings include the Australian Chancery in Washington, DC (1969). Bates Smart was one of the architects involved in the Las Vegas kitsch of Crown Casino on Southbank, and with LAB, as

57

Life's a beach in Australia

Bean at work on his great history

A heavily decorated Frank Beaurepaire

LAB+Bates Smart, the architects for the shattered geometry and new materials involved in building the most modern project in Melbourne, Federation Square (2001).

Beach, The

Life's a Beach was the title of Rennie Ellis' best-selling book of beach pictures, and for many coastal Australians it is true. Robert Drewe's seductive short stories *The Bodysurfers* are imbued with the sexy impact of living near the beach – in Sydney anyway. The beach is not life on the edge, but life on the margin of a stressful urban culture. The beach is hot and sweaty, oily and sensual. A cold shower is available close by. The beach is lazy. It is sleep. Sand in fat beach novels. Endless summer. Secret ogling. Beach cricket, cricket on the radio. Sunset walks. Icons like lifesavers, sharks and surfing are associated with the beach, but they are part of a more energetic culture – the surf culture.

Bean, C.E.W.

Acclaimed Australian war historian Charles Edwin Woodrow Bean (1878–1968) sailed with First Australian Imperial Force to Egypt during World War I and then to Gallipoli where he was wounded but refused to be evacuated. He stayed with the AIF in France for the remainder of the war. He was the author of six of the twelve volumes of the *Official History of Australia in the War of 1914–1918*. In the volumes he conceived the Anzac myth, and explained the Australian character through the sacrifice of the diggers at Gallipoli. Bean was the writer who invented the Australian tradition, and the idea of Australian nationalism which proved itself at Gallipoli.
See: Australian War Memorial

Beaurepaire, Frank

To recover from rheumatic fever, Frank Beaurepaire (1891–1956) turned to swimming. It was a decision that would change his life and help mould Australia's attitudes towards swimming and sport. Remarkably, although he held 15 world records he never won an Olympic gold medal. He won a silver and bronze in 1908 before his career was interrupted by the war, then returned to win a silver in the 1920 Games and a silver and bronze in 1924. On 4 February 1922, Beaurepaire and Jack Chalmers pulled a young man out of the surf in

A rare photo of Clarice Beckett

Randolph Bedford's travel book, and his portrait, by David Low

Sydney after a shark attack. Although the man later died, the two shared in a £5000 reward, and Beaurepaire put his slice into the founding of Beaurepaires tyre service where he proved himself an able businessman. He later became lord mayor of Melbourne and was instrumental in bringing the Olympics to Melbourne as chief promoter of the bid. However, his sudden death on 29 May 1956 stopped him from seeing his beloved Games arrive in his home town.

Beaver, Bruce

An elder statesmen among Australian poets (b. 1928) with books beginning with *Letters to Live Poets* (1969):

I set the seal on a book of letters
never to be posted, ever
to the live poets of my knowing,
not all writers, yet all conscious

of the gift of the living word
It was followed by *Lauds and Plaints* and *Odes and Days*. He is a writer, the poet Kevin Hart noted in reviewing *Poets and Others* (1999), as 'attentive to the sweep and singularity of daily experience, a poet whose eloquence is never far from praise, and a man for whom art is not an addition to life but an index of life itself'.

Beckett, Clarice

Clarice Beckett (1887–1935) is one of the legion of Australian women artists of the 1920s and 1930s who, unlike Nora Heysen, did not live long enough to be fully appreciated in their own lifetime. Some 1200 of her moody, evocative, soft suburban landscapes and studies were found in a barn in 1971, and exhibited to wide acclaim. Impressionist, painterly, they look

back to the Roberts and Streeton's 9x5 cigar box show, but also forward to Howard Arkley. The *Age* critic hailed the rediscovery of a 'remarkable Modernist' when the paintings were shown again in 1971. She suffered the small-town provincialism that was Melbourne's bohemia in her lifetime. Now the paintings seem to be the essence of Melbourne between the wars, as Grace Cossington-Smith's were to Sydney.

Bedford, Randolph

Randolph Bedford (1868–1941) led a varied life. From writer to politician to miner he found both success and failure. He wrote four novels and numerous articles for the *Bulletin* and the *Age*. A militant nationalist, in 1896 he launched the *Clarion* and through it promoted republicanism and 'White

Two Bee Gees in 1964

The cast of *Bellbird* – the ABC's popular soap of the late 1960s

B

Australia'. He lost elections as both a Liberal and Labor candidate before winning a by-election in Warrego in 1923, a seat he held until 1941.

Bee Gees
Australia's answer to The Beatles, the Bee Gees are Barry Gibb (b. 1947) and the twin brothers Maurice and Robin Gibb (b. 1949). A minor hit in the 60s with two other band members, it wasn't until the 70s and the smash hit single *Stayin' Alive* from the film *Saturday Night Fever* (1977) that they really hit the big time. Their falsetto harmonies were synced to John Travolta's hips and it remains the highest-selling soundtrack of all time, clocking up 25 million copies and counting. The Gibb brothers have penned over a thousand songs and continue to contribute music to other

bands and singers such as Tina Arena. Curious fact: The death warrant for Joan of Arc was signed in the priory where Robin Gibb now lives.

Beer, Maggie
South Australia's Stephanie, a restaurateur and food entrepreneur who began by farming pheasants with husband Colin Beer in the Barossa Valley in 1973. They opened the Pheasant Farm Restaurant which closed in 1993, as the Beers concentrated on producing gourmet foods beginning with a pâté. Maggie Beer's Export Kitchen opened in 1997 in Tanunda, and produces a range of preservative-free foods.

Begonia Festival
Featuring Ballarat's world-famous tuberous begonias, the Begonia

Festival is Australia's best example of the Victorian 'gardenesque' landscape style.

Bellbird
Launched in 1967, *Bellbird* would become one of Australia's most enduring soaps. Its unique format saw it aired for fifteen minutes an episode, four nights a week on the ABC. Although it never rated particularly well, its following in country areas was second to none and when real estate nasty Charlie Cousens had to be written out (via a fall from a wheat silo no less) the ABC's *TV Times* magazine was flooded with mail – more than they had received concerning any other TV death in their 21 years of publication. The final episode went to air in 1979. Never quite replaced by Aunty.

Bellbird's Warwick Randall and Maggie Millar

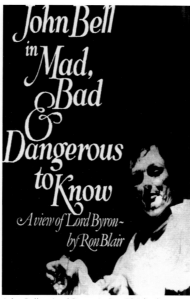

John Bell as Lord Byron, in Ron Blair's play

Joseph Tishler, aka Bellerive

Bellerive

Not only a world-class sporting arena, Bellerive is also the pen name of Joseph Tishler (1871–1957), renowned doggerel writer for the *Bulletin*. Lacking rhythm, rhyme and often meaning, his often unintentionally funny poems were generally printed in response to correspondents' columns over a period of forty years. You can read them in *The Book of Bellerive* (1961), an achievement which gained Tishler the title 'Australia's worst poet' from Douglas Stewart.

Bell, Graeme

A tribute to the preservative qualities of jazz, piano player Graeme Bell (b. 1914) was, in the heyday of his touring 'Dixieland' jazz bands, Australia's most influential jazz musician. He formed his first band

with brother Roger in 1935, and turned professional after World War II. Bell played and helped organise the first Australian Jazz Festival at Melbourne's Eureka Youth League Hall in 1946. Jazz was left-wing music, and the band played at the World Festival of Youth in Prague in 1947 and toured Europe again in 1950, before disbanding in 1953. Bell moved to Sydney in 1957, leaving an association with the fringe Melbourne bohemian community at Montsalvat. He kept playing till the 1980s and in 1997 was inducted into the ARIA Hall of Fame.

Bell, John

The career of actor and director John Bell (b. 1940) has been filled with Shakespeare. He worked briefly with the Royal Shakespeare Company in England before returning to Australia

to set up the Nimrod Theatre in 1970. There he directed indigenous Australian plays such as *The Removalists* and *The Club* by John Williamson as well as *Romeo and Juliet* and *Candide*. In 1990 he set up the Bell Shakespeare Company which aimed to bring Shakespeare to a wider Australian audience.

Bell Shakespeare Company

Australia's only national touring Shakespeare theatre company was established in 1990. Its aim: to produce quality productions which, to quote founder and Artistic Director John Bell '[work] despite the passage of time, the ravages of education, and the shortcomings of productions which so regularly trivialise, vulgarise and distort them, or simply succeed in boring audiences to death.'

61

A contemporary portrait of Bennelong

Richie Benaud (r) with England's Ted Dexter

Edward Dyson's *Benno*

B

Bells Beach

One of the greatest surfing locations in the world, Bells Beach has an enviable reputation. Located at Australia's surf capital Torquay, Victoria, it hosts the longest-established event on the professional surfing circuit – the Rip Curl Pro, held every Easter.

Bell's Life

Bell's Life, running separate editions in Sydney (1845–?71), Melbourne (1857–68) and Adelaide (1861–62) was modelled on *Bell's Life* in London and *Sporting Chronicle* (1822–86). Focusing on sport and politics with a smattering of literary material, its most distinctive feature was verse predictions of horse races. Tom Wills called for the invention of Australian football in a letter to *Bell's* in 1858.

Benaud, Richie

The voice of Australian cricket, Richie Benaud could also apparently hit a ball in his day, although most Australians remember him only for his silver-haired and golden-larynxed, faintly lisping introduction to the next televised Test match.

Bennelong

One of two Aborigines captured by Arthur Phillip in 1789 in an attempt to demonstrate the benefits of European 'civilised' life, Bennelong later escaped and witnessed the spearing of Phillip at Manly. He sailed to England in 1792 with an ailing Phillip and was presented to King George III, but returned due to sickness in 1795 after which he was shunned by both Aboriginal and white communities. He died in a tribal fight in 1813. The point at Sydney Cove where he lived still bears his name, and now, the Sydney Opera House.

Benno

A character in Edward Dyson's larrikin novel, *Benno and Some of the Push* (1911). An early example of the Australian 'o' diminutive. Memorable 'o's include commo, reffo, Jacko, Buzo – who named all his characters in his 60s play *Front Room Boys* thus.

Beresford, Bruce

Bruce Beresford (b. 1940) was instrumental in resuscitating the Australian film industry. A first feature, *The Adventures of Barry McKenzie* (1972) preceded two AFI awards for best director with *Don's Party* (1976) and *Breaker Morant*

Bruce Beresford deep in thought

The Big Issue exposing the pseudo-poor

A wartime ad for Bex, and right, Big Day Out logo

(1979). He received international attention for Academy Award-winner *Driving Miss Daisy* (1989).

Bernborough
The most exciting galloper since Phar Lap, in the 1940s Bernborough attracted the biggest crowds Australian racing had ever seen. The greatest ability of the 'Toowoomba Tornado' was to carry tremendous weights and still win races.

Between Wars
Michael Thornhill's 1974 pic, written by Frank Moorhouse, about a doctor with problems stemming from World War I (dealing with shell shock, psychiatry, fascists and strange goings-on in country NSW) previewed Moorhouse's interests in his novels *Grand Days* and *Dark Palace*.

Bex
Barry Humphries made famous the the great Aussie remedy 'a cup of tea, a Bex and a good lie down'.

Beynon, Richard
Richard Beynon (b. 1925) began life as an actor, and travelled to England in 1947 to further his career, but on return to Australia in 1956 he entered his play *The Shifting Heart* in the Playwright's Advisory Board competition. He won first prize and the play, along with Lawler's *Summer of the Seventeenth Doll*, marked a renaissance in the Australian stage.

Bicentenary
The Sydney Bicentenary was a flawed 'celebration of a nation' in 1988. Too Sydney-centred, it never really caught the attention of the European

Australians – even in the nationalistic Hawke era. Australia's day, it was felt, was not the foundation of Sydney day – perhaps Anzac Day or 1 January, to celebrate Federation.

Big Day Out Festival
Australia's premier youth music festival, spawned by Triple J.

Big Issue, The
An imported idea but a good one still, the *Big Issue* magazine was launched in England in in 1991 and in Australia in June 1996. Now boasting a circulation of 13 000, it is sold by homeless and unemployed people with half of the purchase price going to the vendor. A general interest magazine, its dedication to the less fortunate is an admirable and worthwhile cause.

63

Billy Tea, a kangaroo and a swag: Australian!

Ric Birch on Opening Ceremony night

Graeme Clark accepts a bionic award

B

Big M

Dairy industry campaign that flourished in 1980s – successfully selling flavoured milk as young and sexy – had disappeared by the end of the 1990s when those young people grew old.

Bilby

A small native marsupial with rabbit-like ears, it has recently been immortalised in chocolate as an attempt to steal a little thunder away from the Easter bunny. Money from sales of the Bush Billie Bilbies through Coles is put toward saving the real-life bilbies.

Billy

Billy tea, cooked in a billy, a tin can, is drunk by the campfire in the bush and brewed by taking the handle of the can while it's boiling and swinging it around in huge, round-arm arcs. The addition of a gum leaf for flavour is optional. A modern version is now manufactured by Lyons Tetley (Australia Pty Ltd), although it lacks the gum leaf.

Bilson, Tony

Chef who started his career in Carlton's then hippy-bohemian hotel the Albion, before joining a succession of Sydney eateries, Tony's Bon Gout most notably, then Berowra Waters before reaching for the big time with the failed Ampersand.

Bionic Ear

An Australian invention of global importance, the bionic ear has restored the ability to hear to many people who could not be helped by conventional hearing aids. Developed over ten years by a team at the University of Melbourne led by Professor Graeme Clark. In 1983, Cochlear was formed to manufacture and market the device and it now exports to over 30 countries.

Birch, Ric

Australia's Olympian Busby Berkeley rose to fame with Matilda the blow-up Kanga at the Brisbane Commonwealth Games 1982, before going to bigger things at LA and Atlanta. Triumphed over previous bad reviews (kangas on bikes at Atlanta previewing Sydney) with an awe-inspiring celebration at Sydney Opening Ceremony. It might have had corrugated iron tap dancing but it also had Cathy Freeman and the Aboriginal dreaming stories.

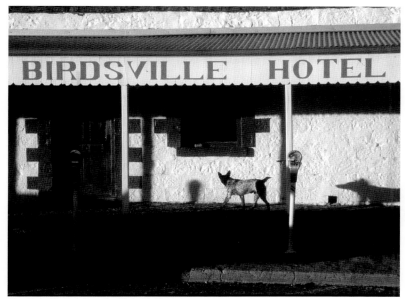

The Birdsville Hotel, on the Birdsville Track

Sir Joh and friend

Birdsville Track

One of the earliest stock routes in the country, the Birdsville Track traces 500 km between Marree in SA and Birdsville in Queensland, now a much-travelled 4WD route.

Bjelke-Peterson, Flo & Joh

Joh was the politically canny but apparently bumbling peanut-farming premier of Queensland from 1968 to 1987, who presided over the midnight state of the white shoe brigade. Flo was a Queensland Senator, but was more famous for her promotion of the concept of the pumpkin scone.

Black Box Flight Recorder

The prototype for the black box flight recorder was developed in 1954 by Australian Dr David Warren of Aeronautical Research Laboratories. A compact, sturdy, fire- and crash-proof recorder, the black box is designed to automatically record cockpit voice communications and register the main flight parameters for easy dissection if the plane should crash. However the idea was rejected by both the RAAF and the Australian Department of Civil Aviation and Warren was forced to seek out American and British companies to market and sell the design. It is now standard equipment on all commercial aircraft and many military craft throughout the world.

Black Days

Black Tuesday was the 1929 Stock Market crash, Black Wednesday (Victorian) was when Premier Graeme Berry sacked the public service, Wednesday 8 January 1878; Black Thursday was a day of bad bushfires on 6 February 1851, near Melbourne; Black Friday was the very bad bushfire day, 13 January 1939; Black Sunday was at Bondi on 6 Feb 1938 when 300 were saved by lifesavers after being sucked out by a rip, with five dead. There seem to be no Black Mondays except for those back at work, or Saturdays, when your team loses.

Blackburn, James

An ex-convict architect and engineer transported to Van Dieman's Land in 1833, pardoned 1841, James Blackburn (1803–54) first worked in Hobart, designing churches and penal buildings, but moved to Melbourne in 1849. His greatest and most lasting contribution was the design of Melbourne's first water supply, the Yan Yean reservoir. He died of typhoid.

John Blackman with hair (some)

Not the Black Stump, but Black Flag in Western Australia, which was beyond it

Blacket, Edmund

Edmund Blacket (1817–83) was the leading church architect of his day in Sydney, with Christ Church St Laurence (1843) and St Stephen's in Newtown. He also designed the first buildings of the University of Sydney, and Mort's Wool Stores.

Blackman, Charles

Charles Blackman (b. 1928), a painter of slightly sinister schoolgirls, cats, scenery, flowers and scenes from *Alice in Wonderland*, has been a popular and accessible artist all his long life. He was Australia's highest-selling living artist in 1999 with sales of $2.66 million. The sinister streak is best illustrated by the 1950s Schoolgirls paintings where images filled with a sense of foreboding and vulnerability were inspired by the story of a 12-year-old Melbourne girl who was raped and murdered in 1921. Blackman was so disturbed that girls could be in such danger from society that he channelled his torment into canvases filled with shadows, anonymous figures and a deep sense of foreboding.

Blackman, John

The throaty voice in the booth for Australia's longest-running variety show *Hey, Hey It's Saturday*, John Blackman provided the voice for (among other things) that delightful head on a stick 'Dicky Knee'. Now working as a radio host on Melbourne AM station 3AK.

Black Stump

When you're beyond the black stump you've officially left civilisation behind. A mystical object, few people ever see it, but they know when they're past it. Most commonly used in the phrase 'this (or the other) side of the black stump'.

Blainey, Geoff

In 1984 the distinguished historian Geoffrey Blainey made some remarks about the pace of Asian immigration being 'far ahead of public opinion'. His view that the old discredited White Australia policy had now become a 'surrender Australia' policy turned into a fevered cause celebre, with books and counter books being written, and carrels of historians disassociating themselves from Blainey's analysis. The Pauline Hanson One Nation phenomenon of the 1990s surely supported his analysis – the trouble was that millions didn't.

Geoffrey Blainey – an independent mind

Thomas Blamey inspects the troops in New Guinea

Associated with the argument over Asian immigration was another one about reconciliation and the 'black armband' view of history. Once again Blainey was not on the side of the politically correct. A great coiner of phrases – another of his books was called *The Tyranny of Distance* – the black armband was soon taken up by conservative commentators as describing the negative view of Australia held by commentators supportive of Mabo, Wik, reconciliation, Sorry. Blainey later said he did not mean the phrase to be anti-Aboriginal. He meant it to be understood in the Australian football context where a black armband is worn in respect of a former player who has died. But the fact was that the phrase came to be an anti-Aboriginal phrase, and even Blainey

used it that way, referring to the High Court as a 'black armband tribunal'. The good aspect of this is that the debate about Australian and Aboriginal history is out in the open. Blainey's own view by the end of the century seems to be that white and Aboriginal cultures were in 1788 profoundly irreconcilable, and that misunderstandings would arise. He also believes that over the past 213 years the good in Australian culture has outweighed the bad. Blainey is that rare being in Australia, an opinionated, independent scholar historian with the gift of the gab, and love him or hate him, we have to listen to what he says. His books include *A Short History of the World*, *The Rush That Never Ended*, *The Causes of War* and *The Triumph of the Nomads*.

Blamey, Sir Thomas

Blamey (1884–1951) is the only Australian soldier to attain the rank of Field Marshal. A professional soldier, he was a staff officer at Gallipoli and in France under Sir John Monash in World War I. Between the wars he was a controversial Chief Commissioner of Police in Victoria in 1925–36, resigning under a cloud over allegations about his love of the night life. These views, as believed by ordinary soldiers, coloured their appreciation of him as Australian Commander in Chief after commanding the AIF in North Africa and Greece. This appointment, and further soldiers' beliefs, gave rise to the bitter poem *An Inscription for Dog River* by Kenneth Slessor, then a war correspondent. 'Having bestowed on him all we had to give/in battles few

Cate Blanchett, a bright star in moody light

Blinky Bill embarking on an advertising career

The cover of a *Blue Heelers* novelisation

B

can recollect … Even our descendants' right to live/Having given him everything, in fact,/except respect.' Blamey's subordinate role once Douglas Macarthur was appointed supreme Allied commander, and his decisions to use Australian troops in what many saw as senseless waste of life in operations in 1945, led to a diminution in reputation among the men involved. None of this seemed to affect the high esteem in which Blamey was held by government.

Blanchett, Cate

An 'accidental' actress, Cate Blanchett (b. 1969) took a year out from an economics course at university to travel through Europe, and on her return won small roles at La Mama. She quit economics and attended the National Institute of Dramatic Art

(NIDA). Roles with the Sydney and Melbourne Theatre companies followed before she landed the lead role in *Oscar and Lucinda* (1997). The next step was world stardom as she won a Golden Globe and a BAFTA for her performance as the lead in *Elizabeth* (1998) and was nominated for an Oscar.

Bledisloe Cup

Donated for the 1931 Australian rugby union tour of New Zealand, the cup's annual series has come to represent one of the pre-eminent rivalries in world sport. Won by the New Zealanders in 1931, Australia took it first in 1934, and since then the two countries' positions as the premier sides in world rugby union have ensured fanatical interest in the result of the tournament.

Blinky Bill

Lovable and sellable, Blinky Bill is a mascot, a cartoon character, an interactive CD-ROM and a licensing agreement all rolled into one. Created by Dorothy Wall, the koala in clothes debuted in the picture book *Blinky Bill the Quaint Little Australian* (1933) and starred in several sequels. Revived for another round in the 70s, Blinky Bill is to this day a perennial children's favourite.

Blue Heelers

Somewhere between British cop sensation *The Bill* and *Neighbours* is Australia's number one rating drama series. First aired in February 1994, it tells the tale of the mythical town of Mt Thomas and the men and women who police its streets. It also spawned Australia's sweetheart Lisa McCune

Lucky Grills as Bluey, aka Bargearse

EXCITED CROWD CHAIRS WOODFULL AFTER AUSTRALIA'S TEST WIN

Bodyline – Australia won the Melbourne Test

as Maggie Doyle. Although the source of its overwhelming success is something of a mystery, consider this quote from the producers: 'In the city, police work is too often just a clinical matter of life and death. In our overburdened society, victims become as nameless as their assailants. The result is an equally anonymous style of policing. But in the country, real community-based policing connects directly with the rural lifestyle.' Good honest country people + police drama + colourful characters + strong moral stance = success.

Bluey
A bluey is a swag. *Bluey* was a TV show starring Lucky Grills in 1976–77. The D-Generation redubbed Bluey as Bargearse in 1993.

Bodyline
One of the defining events in Australian sport, the Bodyline series of 1932–33 was intended to stop a resurgent Australian cricket team – and especially Don Bradman. The technique, devised by English captain Douglas Jardine, was not technically illegal but was both dangerous and unsportsmanlike. It involved stacking the legside field and then bowling a persistent series of short balls at the batsman's leg side. This gave the batsman a choice between taking a risky swing or letting the ball hit him. Players were hit in the chest and head, and Bill Oldfield received a fractured skull in the third Test. Australian captain at the time, Bill Woodfull, remarked after the third Test (described by *Wisden* as the most unpleasant ever played) 'There are

two sides out there. One is trying to play cricket, the other is not.' England won the Ashes that series but Bodyline was soon outlawed.

Bolte, Sir Henry
Henry Bolte (1908–90) Victorian Liberal premier 1955–72 who swam to power on the anti-Communist tide of the mid 1950s and stayed there for as long as he wanted on a mixture of country charm, naivete, ruthlessness and support from the anti-Labor Catholic DLP. He was a resolute social conservative, opposing all the causes of the 60s – he was anti-abortion, pro-censorship and pro-hanging.

Bond, Alan
A spectacularly short-lived entrepreneur, Alan Bond (b. 1938) made headlines when his syndicate's

Neville Bonner on campaign trail

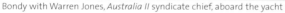

Bondy with Warren Jones, *Australia II* syndicate chief, aboard the yacht

Bondi tram in heavy traffic

B

yacht won the America's Cup in 1983. His empire at its peak had interests in oil, land, gold, newspapers and television. His personal wealth was estimated at $400 million in the 1980s, but the stockmarket crash of 1987 took Bond with it. He was bankrupt in 1992. The receivers took over and Bond was imprisoned for criminal dishonesty. As an interesting side-note, Bond has always been involved in art. His purchase of Van Gogh's *Irises* for $54 million was the beginning of the end for Bond, and while in prison he began painting curious portraits of football players.

Bondi

Roughly a kilometre long and enclosed by headlands, Bondi in east Sydney is one of the best-known beaches in the world. The site of almost continual

uproar, the most recent trouble arose over the building of a temporary Olympic beach volleyball stadium on the foreshore. Luckily, after the Games the stadium disappeared and Bondi was returned to the unusually tanned and relaxed flesh of Sydney.

Bondi Tram

Electric tram services to Bondi Beach began on 19 October 1902, and the last one 'shot through' on Sunday, 18 February 1960. An R-class corridor tram, it left Bondi at 3.30 am with a full load of passengers, and bounced and ricketed to the Dowling Street depot. Along the way it lost almost all of its fixtures to souvenir hunters, including handrails, upholstered seat cushions, the lifting jack, and even a headlight. Apparently a warehouse of ghost trams still exists.

Bonner, Neville

Neville Bonner (1922–99) was the first Aboriginal person to sit in Federal Parliament, as a Senator for Queensland, from 1971 to 1983. Life did not begin so easily however, and when he was only seven Bonner was already having to help his family earn a living by clearing bush. After the 1967 referendum gave Aborigines the vote, Bonner joined the Liberal Party and entered politics. 'You've got to get into the system, work through the system and make the changes. If you say a law is a bad law, you don't break it, you try to change the law.' Throughout his twelve years in politics he was a strong campaigner for civil rights and equality in Australia. Unhappily he was abandoned by the Liberal Party when he wanted to continue in Parliament.

Big-hitting George Bonnor

Young Boonie with hair but no helmet

Allan Border after another victory

Bonnor, George
A big-hitting 19th-century batsman known as the Colonial Hercules, George Bonnor (1855–1912) played 17 Tests for Australia. He made 128, including 113 in a session in the fourth Test, 1884–85. He once threw a cricket ball 119 yards.

Boomerang
A curved, flat wooden missile used by Aborigines for hunting and warfare. Contrary to popular belief, there are actually two types. The returning boomerang was designed to hover over a flock of birds the way a hawk would, scaring them into a dive which would bring them into nets which had been strung between two trees. The non-returning boomerang was used primarily as a weapon and for sale to overseas tourists.

Boonie
A nuggety little Tasmanian, David Boon (b. 1960) broke into the Australian team in 1984 and was a mainstay until his retirement in 1996. An aggressive opener, he scored over 7000 runs in 106 Test matches, a feat matched only by the drinking record he reportedly holds for the flight from Australia to England.

Border, Allan
Australian cricket captain Allan Border (b. 1955) became world cricket's most prolific runscorer in 1994, passing 11 000 runs and picking up other records along the way, including most Tests played, most catches and fifties in Tests and most Tests as captain. He is also the only batsman to hit 150 runs in both innings of a Test.

Bourke, Back o'
A place in the Never Never, somewhere near the Black Stump. Australia must have more descriptions for 'back of beyond' than any other place. Bottom of the Harbour is an urban equivalent, named for where asset-stripped companies ended up in a series of tax frauds perpetrated in the 1980s.

Bowyang
The word comes from the English dialect word 'bowy-yanks' which were leather leggings worn by agricultural labourers. The Australian version found a home on the goldfields, describing a piece of string or a leather strap tied around the trouser leg below the knee. The aim was to stop dirt or dust getting in and to stop the trouser leg from dragging.

Ben Bowyang writes a letter, by Percy Leason

The Boyd Clan, Arthur left, Merric second from right

B

Bowyang, Ben

Ben Bowyang is a character invented by C.J. Dennis. His misspelt letters to the Melbourne *Herald* purported to be from 'Bill Bowyang' to his son in the city. It later became a comic strip, and the term 'bowyang' came to refer to simple country folk everywhere.

Box, The

A TV series set in a television station, *The Box* was Melbourne's answer to the adult soapiness of *No. 96*, living and loving on Ten, 1974–77.

Boxing Kangaroo

The green and gold (red-gloved) Boxing Kangaroo flag was made famous during Alan Bond's successful campaign to win the America's Cup in 1983. Since then it has become a kind of unofficial Australian sporting

flag – but was officially endorsed for waving at the Sydney Olympics. And kangaroos do box, don't they?

Boyd, Arthur

A reclusive but fiercely visionary painter, Arthur Boyd (1920–99) was not so flamboyant and public as contemporary painters such as Sid Nolan, but was their equal as a painter's painter. He loved to paint, he loved the integrity of the work. Brought up as an artist, he worked in camouflage and cartography during World War II, and fell in with the crowd around the Contemporary Art Society. Boyd's Wimmera landscapes are from the wartime period, and the powerful 1946–47 painting of Melbourne called *Mining Town (Casting the money-lenders from the temple)* derives from his agonies over

the war and its aftermath. He designed a now-lost large sculpture outside cousin Robin Boyd's Olympic Pool in 1956. He moved to London in 1959 and painted the deeply felt Australian paintings around the Nebuchadnezzar image – a substantial success. In the 1970s, he rediscovered the Australian landscape and later bought the property Bundanon, on the Shoalhaven River in southern New South Wales, which in 1993 the Boyd family donated to the Australian people for use as an artists' retreat and gallery. On his death in 1999, Paul Keating said 'It has fallen to people like Arthur to define what it is to be Australian on canvas and to let us understand that we're not Europeans anymore, that we're not anything other than Australians. This is the debt we really owe him.'

Arthur Boyd at Bundanon, by Michel Lawrence

Ben Boyd's Tower

Boyd, Ben

NSW developer and adventurer, Ben Boyd (1803–51) prefigures some of the entrepreneurs of later generations. He arrived in Australia from Scotland in 1842, opened the Sydney branch of the Bank of Australia with £200 000 of capital in 1843 and rapidly became a major landholder. He tried to use labourers from Vanuatu in 1847, but the 'children of nature' had to be repatriated as unsuitable. He built two towns at Twofold Bay on the NSW South Coast, Boydtown and East Boyd, as bases for whaling and export, but ambition and legal costs led to financial ruin in 1849. He had kept his schooner and set out for the Californian goldfields, where he failed to strike it rich and returned to the Pacific, and in June 1851 landed on Guadalcanal in the Solomons. He failed to return from a hunting excursion – and despite rumours of having simply 'disappeared' it is believed he was killed by the locals. Perhaps not – maybe he was a kind of Lord Jim.

Boyd, Martin

Originally a student of theology, and then architecture, Martin a'Beckett Boyd (1893–1972) came from Switzerland to Australia in 1893. During World War I he served with an English regiment and later the Royal Flying Corps, fighting in France during the period 1915–18. After the war he moved to England to again pursue a religious vocation, this time in a Franciscan order of the Church of England, before finally finding his feet as a fiction writer. His first major work *The Montforts* (which sought to catalogue the life of his mother's family in Australia from the goldrush to the war) won the very first Australian Literature Society's Gold medal. He is perhaps best known for his Langton tetralogy which includes *Cardboard Crown* (1952), *Outbreak of Love* (1957) and *When Blackbirds Sing* (1962). He also wrote two works of non-fiction and a pair of evocative autobiographies. In 1948 he returned to Australia, where he settled in his grandfather's house in Berwick until 1951, when ill health caused him to return to Europe.

Boyd, Robin

Robin Boyd (1919–71) was a modernist architect and writer whose books *The Australian Ugliness* (1960) and *Australia's Home* (1952) made a deep impression on Australia of the 1950s

Robin Boyd and Neil Clerehan

Russell Boyd pre-*Crocodile Dundee*

Braddon's *Naked Island* (1952)

– critical of 'Austerican' suburbia yet showing that there was an indigenous domestic history. He worked with Roy Grounds and Frederick Romberg designing many commercial and domestic buildings, including project homes, motels and a fish restaurant (the Fishbowl). His affectionate but critical nationalism, and modernism is still missed.

Boyd, Russell

Cinematographer Russell Boyd (b. 1944) made the jump from advertising to cinema with the Australian film industry, starting at the top with Peter Weir's *Picnic at Hanging Rock* (1975), then *Gallipoli* (1981), *Crocodile Dundee* (1985) and then in the 1990s in the United States with such films as *Forever Young* and *Liar, Liar*.

Brack, John

John Brack (1920–99), painter and teacher, is unfairly perhaps best remembered for his rather Orwellian painting *Collins St 5pm*, a comment on the mass-produced urban Melburnian, but his work ranged further and wider, from the figurative foreground to a bringing out of the landscape background in the 1970s and 1980s.

Braddon, Russell

Russell Braddon (1921–95) was born in Sydney. He was imprisoned in Changi for four years during World War II, and his controversial book, *The Naked Island* (1952), describing his and his mates' awful experiences as prisoners of war of the Japanese, sold more than a million copies. He wrote biographies, novels, histories and TV

scripts. He lived in Britain from 1949 until 1993, and died in NSW in 1995. His other books included *Nancy Wake* (1956), *Joan Sutherland* (1962), *Roy Thomson of Fleet Street* (1965), *Suez* (1973) and *Predator* (1980).

Bradfield, John

Civil engineer John Bradfield (1867–1943) was responsible for the breakthrough idea of a single arch cantilever bridge connecting Sydney to the north shore. It was approved by a parliamentary committee in 1913, and the final design and building plan was approved by Bradfield, before completion in 1932. He also devised the ambitious but slightly hare-brained scheme to dam Queensland's eastern rivers, and pipe the water west to irrigate the inland.

John Bradfield on site

Bradman cigarette card, 1938

Bradman enters his arena, SCG

Bradman, Sir Donald

Towards the end of the twentieth century, as Don Bradman (1908–2001) approached his personal centenary, he grew from a mere cricketing great to something more. He became, like the centenarian Gallipoli veterans, a kind of Living National Treasure, a Living Legend, a connection to an old Australia, a heroic age when heroes were created. It was as if some veteran of the Trojan War were still alive: Achilles perhaps. Bradman was a kind of Australian hero in the 1930s, someone who fitted the bill in those days when national confidence had been shaken by the war, Depression and social change. Bradman was, with Phar Lap and Walter Lindrum, so good that they (the English) went to war against him. Phar Lap 'they' killed, of course, and Lindrum had the rules

changed to 'fix' him. Bradman had the special privilege of 'representing' this new nation, on the cricket field as the Diggers did on the battlefield. When he proved so incredibly efficient at scoring runs on the 1930 tour (974 runs in just seven Test innings) the Old Enemy devised the hateful and unsporting tactic of Bodyline for the 1932–33 England tour of Australia. That was war, and while Australia might have lost the series and the battle, Bradman still averaged 56, and we won the war when 'scone theory' was not used again, and Bradman and others plundered the ponderous Poms. Songs and movies were made about him in the 1930s, and he became something more than a sportsman, more than a mere celebrity. Bradman's batting was relentless

rather than stylish, so it wasn't perfect. Which is why as he approached his last innings in his last Test on the Invincible tour of England in 1948, needing four runs for a perfect Test average of 100, he had the god-given tear in his eye which saw him bowled for a duck. He averaged 'only' 99.94, still far beyond the reach of any other batsman in the history of the game. With that slight human imperfection, he became an immortal. Which is why as he approached that human century, a great wave of affection and protection rose up. The Don might permit a street named after him in Adelaide, but when the local shops start calling themselves the Bradman this or that, well that wasn't cricket. When a publisher tried to sell some business letters the whole country

75

SIR DONALD BRADMAN'S
Scores in First-class Cricket

Bradman's complete first-class scores list

Bradman's song by Lumsdaine and Bradman

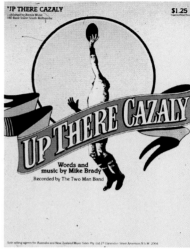

Brady's *Up There Cazaly*

B
He Writes for the
TELEGRAPH

was outraged: it was an invasion of a holy privacy. A special act of parliament was passed unanimously, promoted by the white picket fence, self-confessed 'cricket tragic' Prime Minister John Howard, to protect The Don's copyright. In another country this might seem bizarre, but Australia as a national concept has been created around a small number of ideas, and sport, particularly cricket, is one of them. And inasmuch as there can be a representative icon of sport, something approaching a god-like perfection, it was Don Bradman. He, or the idea of him, was unselfconsciously worshipped despite the niggling feeling that over his long life other human imperfections had shown through – he threatened to withdraw from a 1930s Test tour over money. But the

greatest batsman world cricket has ever known towered above both his contemporaries and those who came after. On average, he scored a century in every third innings, he scored the most double centuries ever and was the only man to have scored two triple centuries. Interest did not wane after his retirement from cricket in 1949. Bradman was the measure of perfection in any sport, his statistical feats double those of any other batsman, and beyond the ken of the merely great. His death in February 2001 was the occasion for an international outbreak of mourning. For the first time he made it to the 90s but did not go on to a century.

Brady, Mike
Smoky-voiced composer of the football anthem *Up There Cazaly*

(1979), Brady was a member of the 60s band MPD Ltd, who had a hit in 1966 with Paul Anka's tune *Little Boy Sad*. He became a well-known advertising music writer in the 1970s, composing such commercial jingles such as a favourite: SPC Baked Beans and Spaghetti 'for hungry little human beans.'

Brent of Bin Bin
Six novels of Australian country life, beginning with *Up the Country* (1928), were published by 'Brent of Bin Bin'. Before the war there was much speculation about the real identity of the author. In the 1950s it was definitively established to be a pseudonym of Miles Franklin, whose motives for using it are not entirely clear, but may relate to the mixed reception of *My Brilliant Career*.

Lily Brett contemplates her next book

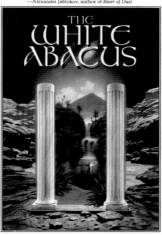

Damien Broderick's *White Abacus*

Bryan Brown in *Far East*

Brett, Lily

Lily Brett (b. 1946) is an Australian writer residing in New York who first made a name with *The Auschwitz Poems* (1986). Her parents are Holocaust survivors. She worked for the pop magazine *Go Set* in the early 1970s, and as both poet and fiction writer has achieved substantial success in working in urban Jewish storytelling. *Things Could be Worse* (1989), and *What God Wants* (1991) are short fiction; *In Full View* (1997) and *New York* (2001), non-fiction.

Brisbane, Katherine

The contribution to the development and maintenance of Australian theatre and especially Australian playwriting by Katherine Brisbane (b. 1932) and her husband Philip Parsons (1926–93) cannot be

overestimated. Brisbane was a highly influential drama critic for the *Australian* (1967–78) and elsewhere, and a founding member and continuous supporter of the National Playwrights' Centre and the annual National Playwrights' Conference, both of which nurtured many emerging talents. In 1971 she and her husband founded Currency Press, dedicated to publishing new Australian plays. Parsons also contributed significantly to the academic study of theatre through his teaching in the University of NSW School of Theatre and Film Studies.

Broderick, Damien

Stranger in a strange land, Damien Broderick (b. 1944) is more honoured for his science fiction overseas than in Australia. Books include *Transmitters*

(1984), *Striped Holes* (1988) and *The Sea's Furthest End* (1993).

Bronzed Aussies

The image of Australian masculinity before skin cancer was the surfer or surfie, looking healthy, on the beach. Also the acceptance of male athletes in coming third.
See: Golden Girls

Brown, Bryan

Very Australian film star Bryan Brown appeared in *Newsfront*, *Breaker Morant* and in teleflicks such as *A Town Like Alice* and *The Thorn Birds* – plus a Hollywood B grade or two (*Cocktail*). As producer he has put his money where his face is, for example *Dead Heart* (1996) in which he starred with Ernie Dingo as a cop probing a murder in central Australia.

The Lady's Alive: one of Carter Brown's 50 million pulps in print

Bob Skilton gets one of his three Brownlows at the MCG

Brown, Carter

Pulp fiction nom de plume of the prolific Alan G. Yates (1923–85) who wrote 150 Carter Brown books between 1953 and 1968, selling millions of copies. All the stories were set in the United States. Yates was born in London and after the war he worked as a sound recordist at Gaumont-British Films for two years then moved to Australia in 1948. In the same year he became an Australian citizen. In 1953 the first books appeared, among them: *Venus Unarmed*, *The Mermaid Murmurs Murder*, *The Lady Is Chased*, *The Frame Is Beautiful*, *Fraulein Is Feline*, *Wreath for Rebecca*, *The Black Widow Weeps* and *The Penthouse Passout*. They were slim, fast-paced paperbacks and always had a scantily clad dame on the cover.

Brown, Joe

From 1947 to 1981 Brown was the ABC's Melbourne racecaller. By the time he retired he was such a national racing institution that his final call was also relayed by the two main commercial racing stations.

Brownlow Medal

The biggest individual prize in Australian Rules Football, the Brownlow was introduced in 1924 to commemorate the services of Charles Brownlow to football. It is given to the fairest and best player in the league every year as decided by the field umpires who officiated each match. Only one vote was allocated per game until 1931 when a tie forced the introduction of the 3, 2 and 1 vote system in place today. The most prolific winners of the medal are Haydn Bunton Snr, Dick Reynolds, Bob Skilton and Ian Stewart, who each won the award three times.

Bruce, Mary Grant

The Billabong series of Mary Grant Bruce (1878–1958) is an Australian children's classic, which recreates the bush world of her childhood. In all, she wrote 37 children's books between 1910 and 1941, and much poetry, short fiction and journalism.

Bubonic Plague Cure

A little-known fact: the transmission of bubonic plague to humans from fleas found on infected rats was first demonstrated in Sydney. Proven by J. Ashburton Thompson and Frank Tidswell after an outbreak in Sydney in 1900, quarantine swiftly followed, with garbage, silt and sewerage

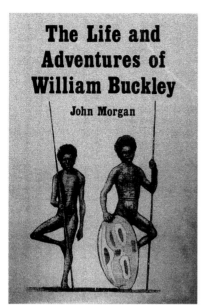

The cover of John Morgan's book on Buckley

The Bulletin celebrates its centenary

The Bulletin (1880), and right, a plague 'cure'

cleared from slum areas helping Australia to be free of the disease by 1906.

Buckley & Nunn

A Melbourne department store, but also a saying, as in you've got two chances: Buckley's (not good, see William Buckley, below) and none.

Buckley, Vin

A poet, editor, critic and academic, Buckley (1925–88) was very influential in Melbourne during the 1960s, especially with an emerging group of Catholic writers and thinkers.

Buckley, William

William Buckley (1780–1856) was transported to Australia for receiving a stolen bolt of cloth, arrived in Port Phillip in 1803, soon escaped and

nearly perished on the Victorian coast near Barwon Heads (*SeaChange* country). He was rescued by the local Aborigines and lived a tribal life for the next 32 years – one of the great sagas of early Victorian settlement. His sudden appearance at the camp of John Batman, dressed in animal skins and carrying spears and boomerangs, earned him the epithet of 'the wild white man'. Unfortunately his subsequent efforts to provide a link between the indigenous inhabitants and the new white settlers proved futile given the intransigence of the latter, and he died in Hobart, a disillusioned man.

Bulletin, The

The most important and well-known Australian journal and magazine, the *Bulletin* was founded on 31 January

1880 by J.F. Archibald and John Haynes. Anti-British, pro-Australian, often humorous, the *Bulletin* has always aimed to be distinctively Australian. Early contributors included A.B. 'Banjo' Paterson, cartoonists Lionel and Norman Lindsay and Henry Lawson. It encouraged local artists and writers and provided a regular outlet for their work. However its politics became conservative and its racial stance did not move for many years – 'Australia for the white man' was only dropped from the masthead in 1960 – and it ceased to be a literary publication at all, turning instead into a political news magazine in the 1960s.

Bunning, Walter

Bunning (1912–77) was an architect and town planner who did significant

B

Romantic Rupert Bunny

The Buntons at play

Suitably mysterious pic of Wilfred Burchett (top)

work for the Department of Post-war Reconstruction under 'Nugget' Coombs and whose book, *Homes in the Sun* (1945), was one of the first attempts to provide a rationale for house and urban design in an Australian context.

Bunny, Rupert

Rupert Bunny (1864–1947) was an Australian, rather romantic impressionist painter who mainly worked in Paris for 47 years and was highly regarded there. Bunny returned to Australia in 1933 and was involved with some of the emerging Australian expressionists such as Albert Tucker in the formation of the Contemporary Arts Society, set up to counter Robert Menzies' eventually failed attempt to establish a more conservative Australian Art Academy.

Bunton, Haydn Snr & Jnr

Father and son not only shared a name, they shared careers in football. Haydn Bunton Snr, regarded by many as the greatest footballer in the history of the game, took three Brownlow Medals and three Sandover Medals in his career. At Fitzroy 1931–37 and Subiaco 1938–41 he was a rover who could not be matched and his good looks made him an instant celebrity. His son, Haydn Bunton Jnr, proved himself a tough and talented rover in both South and West Australian leagues 1955–67. In 1962 he coached Swan Districts to the Flag and won the Sandover Medal himself.

Bunyip

Bunyips are large murky amphibious monsters who haunt the inland waterways of Australia and indiscriminately devour cattle, humans and other smaller animals. Although some people claim to have seen one, no one seems to have captured a specimen, either dead or alive, nor even captured its likeness on grainy out-of-focus film, so details about their habits, and even for that matter existence, remain sketchy.

Burchett, Wilfred

An experienced journalist of international standing, Burchett (1911–83) achieved notoriety in Australia through his close connections with the Communist world during the Cold War, and especially his visit to a POW camp in North Korea during that conflict. His big scoop was to be the first journalist to write about Hiroshima.

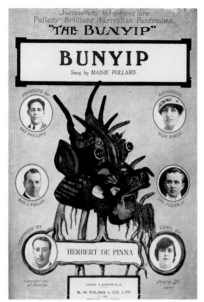

The poster for Herbert De Pinna's *Bunyip*

Burgess, 'Baby' John

TV personality and gameshow host extraordinaire, 'Baby' John Burgess tititlated the blue rinse set on the gameshow *Wheel of Fortune* for almost a decade. Controversially sacked from the show in 1996 for getting a little long in the tooth, he took many of his fans to the equally pedestrian gameshow *Catch Phrase*.

Burgess, Greg

Innovative architect (b. 1947) whose sweeping organic shapes and environmentally friendly designs – most notably for the Uluru-Kata Tjuta Cultural Centre near Uluru (Ayers Rock) and the Brambuk Living Cultural Centre at Halls Gap in the Grampians National Park in Victoria – have explored new directions in Australian architecture.

The Burke and Wills 'Dig Tree'

The Burke and Wills cemetery monument in transit

Burke (& Wills)

Doomed explorers Robert O'Hara Burke (1821–61) and William John Wills (1834–61) led the most expensive exploration of its time, costing £60 000 in 1860. Their aim was to be the first party to make a south–north crossing of the continent. Abundantly provisioned, they set out in August 1860 and arrived at the Gulf of Carpentaria in February 1861. Already weak, a heavily depleted group staggered back along their route to camp LXV, and famously arrived a day after the party sent to reprovision them had left. Instead of waiting, the remaining group set out for Mount Hopeless. They did not get beyond Cooper's Creek and by the time rescuers arrived only John King had survived. Icons of hopeless courage, their funeral was the largest event in Australia to that time.

The *Burke's Backyard Information Guide*

Mac Burnet working miracles

Jack Johnson in 1907, with his pal

Burke's Backyard

Long-running (since 1987) lifestyle program in which good-natured gardener Don Burke features anything likely to rate an audience if he can find even the slightest connection to gardening, most voyeuristically taking his cameras into backyards of well-known people.

Burnet, Sir Frank Macfarlane

Burnet (1899–1985) was one of Australia's greatest scientists, making significant contributions to the study of poliomyelitis, influenza and virology in general, and immunology, for which he shared the Nobel Prize for Medicine in 1960 with Sir Peter Medawar for their work on acquired immunological tolerance. He was Director of the Walter and Eliza Hall Institute from 1944 to 1965 and during his later years he used his considerable intellect and influence to contribute from a humanistic viewpoint to the debate about many broader medical and social issues, including the carcinogenic effects of tobacco, the hazards of radiation and the benefits of multiracial immigration.

Burns–Johnson Fight

The first ever black versus white world heavyweight title fight took place in Sydney, appropriately on Boxing Day 1908, between the reigning champion, Canadian Tommy Burns, and African-American challenger, Jack Johnson. Twenty thousand spectators saw Johnson humiliate Burns and become the first of an almost unbroken line of black world boxing champions.

Burrows, Don

Don Burrows (b. 1934) is an elder statesman of Australian jazz, who has performed with distinction all over the world (mainly on the flute and the clarinet), created many highly successful jazz recordings, most notably with guitarist George Golla (b. 1935), and taught many of the new generation of jazz musicians.

Burstall, Betty

A former high school teacher, Burstall (b. 1926) was the founder and for many years the driving force behind La Mama, the minuscule Carlton theatre that was the womb of the new Australian theatre movement of the late 60s and 70s. Although she has now passed on the reins to the equally capable Liz Jones, Burstall continues to take an active interest in

A romantic interpretation of the 'Bush'

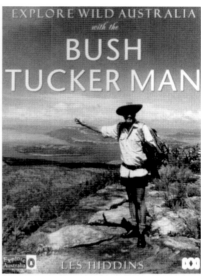
'All you can eat' says the Bush Tucker Man

the theatre. She is also a capable painter, exhibiting from time to time in inner-city galleries. Ex-wife of Tim. *See: La Mama*

Burstall, Tim
Pioneering film-maker of the 70s Australian cinema renaissance, Burstall's (b. 1929) later career was handicapped by flawed judgement. With *Stork* (1971) and especially the adolescent male fantasy *Alvin Purple* (1973) Burstall was the first filmmaker to demonstate that Australian films could do well at the box office. However, his later films such as *Jock Petersen* (1974) and *Eliza Fraser* (1976) failed to live up to earlier expectations. His two sons, Dan and Tom, continue to make significant contributions to the Australian film and TV industry.

Bush
Simply 'home' to the Aborigines, the Australian bush has always generated ambiguous feelings in European Australians, who have been both struck by its many beauties and at the same time spooked, even panicked, by its awesome alien-ness to the European race memory. The first European artists to arrive were totally unable to capture the ethos of the Australian bush on their canvases. 'Lost in the bush' became an enduring theme in Australian literature and art, most graphically in works by Frederick McCubbin.

Bush Tucker Man
A former army bush survival expert, Les Hiddins christened himself the Bush Tucker Man in a series of ABC documentaries (1988–91) which

attracted an audience of urban Australians still mesmerised by the idea that they were and still could be unrealised bushmen.

Bushfires
Bushfires have always been a normal part of summer in the Australian bush, whether ignited by lightning, or in the last 40 000 years, by Aborigines to flush out game, or in the last two centuries by European Australians through hubris and misadventure. Many Australian environments require a bushfire every so often to maintain their ecological balance and some plants only germinate after a bushfire has been through. However, the increasing encroachment of human settlement on the bush has meant that bushfires have become something to be feared

83

Tom Roberts' classic view of the Australian bushranger, in his painting, *Bailed Up*

B

by most of the populace. Australia has produced some spectacular conflagrations, usually named after the day of the week on which they occurred: Ash Wednesday (1983), Black Thursday (1851), Black Friday (1897 and 1939) and Black Sunday (1955). The early part of the week seems to be the safest. Every effort should be made to retain this excellent word which is in some danger of being ousted by the ugly Hollywoodesque Americanism 'wildfire'.

Bushranger

A simple combination of bush and ranger, bushranger originally referred to someone who had an official task in the bush, but soon mutated into a term which encompassed anyone skilled in 'bushcraft'. However, its most lasting definition refers to criminals attempting to survive and evade the law, in the bush. The classic bushranger operated from 1789 when the first-fleet convict 'Black Caesar' escaped into the bush and continued until 1880 when our most famous bushranger, Ned Kelly, was hanged in Melbourne.

based on the ABC television series

Harry Butler up to his neck in it

Ita following her *Passionate Life*

Alex Buzo up close in the 70s

Bussell, Grace

Grace Bussell (1860–1935) was the heroine of the sinking of the *Georgette* on rocks near Busselton in 1876. She repeatedly rode into the surf rescuing passengers until she and her horse were exhausted. Her story was featured in the *Fourth Victorian Reader* and she became a legend among Victorian schoolchildren.

Butler, Harry

Engaging bush naturalist who hosted a number of successful wildlife documentaries for the ABC. He has been criticised by environmentalists for acting as a consultant to mining companies, but his work on Barrow Island has demonstrated that it is possible for the two to work together. His nadir amongst former fans occurred when he seemed to agree

with Tasmania's Hydro Electric Commission that the south-west wilderness area, the subject of nationwide anti-dams protest, was apparently not of sufficient environmental value to preserve.

Buttrose, Ita

One of the best-known women in Australia and twice voted the 'Most Admired Woman in Australia', Ita Buttrose (b. 1942) and her trademark lisp have been making waves for years. The founding editor of *Cleo* magazine in 1972, a director of Australian Consolidated Press in 1974 and editor of its flagship *Women's Weekly* in 1975, she has left a heavy imprint on Australian publishing. She published her autobiography and has ventured into breathless bodice-ripping fiction.

Buvelot, Abram Louis

Louis Buvelot (1814–88) was a Swiss-born landscape painter who migrated to Australia in 1865, and worked as a photographer in Melbourne before touring country Victoria and painting the somewhat eerie works which made his name. He was an influence on the Heidelberg school of painters.

Buzo, Alex

Playright and author Alex Buzo (b. 1944) first made headlines when his play *Norm and Ahmed* (1968) was prosecuted for being 'obscene' in Melbourne and Brisbane. A satirist with a razor-sharp wit and an ear for dialogue, he has made another name as a student of tautology and a mordant writer about Australian places. Other plays include *Rooted*, *Macquarie* and *Makassar Reef*.

85

C

A souvenir cane toad, one that didn't get away

Cadbury ad from the 1940s

John Cain Jnr on the run

The centre of power in Canberra

Cadbury Chocolates

Australia had its own chocolate factory, long before any child of the 1950s heard of Willy Wonka. It is the Cadbury chocolate factory on the banks of the River Derwent in Hobart, and was the most dreamed-of and possibly accessible excursion or holiday, even after watching the Mickey Mouse Club and hearing about Disneyland.

Cain, John Snr & Jnr

John Cain (1882–1957) became John Cain Senior in 1982 when his son John (b. 1931) also became Labor Premier of Victoria. John Cain Jnr had the satisfying knowledge that his government replaced the Liberal Country Party which had retained power for the 27 years since his father had been defeated by Henry Bolte in

1954. Cain Snr was premier in 1943 (for four days), and 1945–47, and from December 1952–55, and had the misfortune to be in charge at the moment the Australian Labor Party split; he was leader of the factionalised and marginalised Opposition until his death in 1957. His two major achievements were attracting the Tattersalls operation from Tasmania to Victoria and being part of the successful bid for the 1956 Olympic Games. John Cain Jnr's time as premier, 1982–90, was beset by a number of financial problems – some would say scandals – to do with the State Bank, Pyramid Building Society, Tricontinental and the National Safety Council – not all of which could really be blamed directly on the government. But smeared with them Cain's government was. In parallel

with his father, the Cain government widened the gambling possibilities in Victoria and gave the former wowser state the best drinking laws in Australia, but failed to win an Olympic bid.

Canberra

Canberra is the capital of Australia, but it is also 'Canberra', the fount of power and authority in Australia, another word for The Government. Canberrans resent this, believing they are tarred with the Federal government brush when they are really a self-governing metropolis where ordinary people live. But people in other places know that Canberra is really stuffed full of fat cats, superduperannuants, pollies, pointy heads, pornographers, ackers and journos.

Still from Arthur Cantrill's avant-garde film classic *Harry Hooton*, 1970

Carbine, the 1890 Melbourne Cup winner

Cane Toad

The cane toad was introduced to Australia in 1935 to control the greybacked cane beetle in Queensland cane fields, but, like many similar measures, soon the cane toads themselves had become the problem. Even worse, there is no evidence that they had any impact on the beetles, as the cane toad outcompetes native amphibians and causes other predator numbers to decline due to the natural toxins it secretes. *Cane Toads: An Unnatural History* directed and written by Mark Lewis (1988) was a funny and perceptive 'mockumentary' which revealed the way the pest was introduced, and the 'fact' that some people used cane toad juice as a hallucinogenic. Tim Finn wrote a song for the film with the chorus:

Cane toads are coming, cane toads are coming,
Main roads are humming with the cane toad blues...
See: *Prickly Pear*

Cantrill, Arthur & Corinne

It's called the Australian Film Industry, and any filmmaker who isn't interested in the industry part has been doomed to a somewhat isolated experimentalism. That has been the lot of Arthur and Corinne Cantrill (b. 1938 and 1928). They have been making films together since 1960. After working in London for four years, they returned to Australia in 1969 and have worked solely in experimental filmmaking. *Expanded Cinema*, a multi-screen film-performance, was presented in 1971. The Cantrills have made more than

150 films including seven feature-length films. In recent years they have worked extensively in Super 8mm, in particular making a series of Super 8 films shot in Indonesia between 1990 and 1994. This material was used in a film-performance given at La Mama Theatre, Melbourne, in 1997, *The Bemused Tourist*.

Carbine

Carbine's breeder, the Earl of Glasgow, was so obsessed with improving the breed that he didn't sell his failures – he shot them. Thankfully, Carbine escaped the shotgun and won the 1890 Melbourne Cup, a victory considered that race's best – the horse was carrying a record 66.5 kilograms and beat thirty-six horses in the biggest field ever. Foaled in 1885, Carbine was not only one of

88

Peter Carey makes the cover of his own book

Australia's own car, the Holden, under the media spotlight in 1948

Australia's most famous horses, he was a success at stud, and his name is involved in the pedigrees of 51 Melbourne Cup winners.

Car Culture

Australian car culture revolves around the battle between the two tribes, Holden and Ford, and is played out in the gladiatorial contest at the Bathurst 1000 kilometre endurance race each October. These vehicles are more or less hotted-up production cars that any hoon or family man can buy. For the latter they recollect their former suburban youth. But are they lost tribes? Holden was perhaps once 'Australia's own car', and probably is considered still the more Aussie brand, but the motor industry is now completely internationalised, so under the bonnet a Holden is as

German or American as a Ford. Bathurst drivers enter the sporting pantheon as well: Peter Brock (Holden), Allan Moffatt (Ford).

Carey, Peter

Peter Carey (b. 1943), like Barry Oakley, Morris Lurie, Bryce Courtney and other Australian writers, began his career writing advertising. 'I can't get by without my Mum' was one of his award-winning lines for a female deodorant. He had a Sydney advertising agency named for him: McSpedden Carey. But after the publication of collections of fabulist short stories, *The Fat Man in History* (1974) and *War Crimes*, the outstandingly successful novels *Bliss* (1981), *Illywhacker* (1985) and *Oscar and Lucinda* (1988) eventually allowed him to write book-type fiction full

time. He lives in New York, writing about Australia from a considered but passionate distance. His Dickensian *Jack Maggs* (1997) was respectfully received in Australia and *True History of the Kelly Gang* (2000), an inner working of the Kelly myth, won the 2001 Booker Prize.

Carruthers, Jimmy

Boxer Jimmy Carruthers (1929–90) fought for Australia at the London Olympics in 1948, and was a bantamweight world champion in 1952 after defeating South African Vic Toweel. He retired as champion in 1954, but lost his unbeaten record with an ill-judged comeback in 1961.

Cars That Ate Paris, The

Advertised under the tagline 'they run on blood', *The Cars That Ate Paris* (1974)

Pat Cash wins Wimbledon 1987

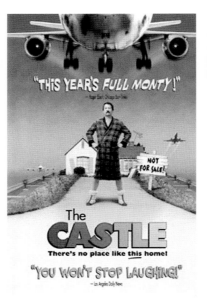
A Working Dog's *Castle*

Melbourne's Crown Casino on the Yarra

C

was co-written and directed by Peter Weir. It centres around the town of Paris, Australia that set up car accidents to salvage parts for resale. *See: Weir, Peter*

Cash, Pat

Pat Cash (b. 1965) was the saviour of Australian tennis in the 1980s. His powerful serve and immaculate net strokes saw him play an instrumental role in Australia's Davis Cup win in 1986. However, his greatest victory came in 1987 when he beat Ivan Lendl in the final at Wimbledon, securing one of the finest headlines ever to grace a sports page: 'Cash bounces Czech'. His climb into the stand to join family and supporters after the win is a major memory. Cash won a Master's title, defeating nemesis John McEnroe, in 2000.

Casino Culture

During Jeff Kennett's reign in Victoria, 1992–99, the government came to rely on the taxation income derived from gambling and gaming, especially the thousands of suburban and country poker machines, and the opulent casino on the south bank of the Yarra River. On the one hand this is a form of voluntary taxation, on the other it seems to attract those least able to resist it. Community projects – the new Museum of Victoria, Federation Square, the renovated State Library and National Gallery – were partly paid for by gambling revenue, attracting muted criticism. But Australia has always had a casino culture, relying on windfall profits from the gold rush of the 1850s to commodity booms such as in wool in the 1950s, to provide revenue. A

reliance on voluntary taxation might be unhealthy. Australia's casinos made a profit of $452 million in 1999–2000.

Castle, The

Breakout film from former D-Generation members, *The Castle* (1997) satirised suburban Australia with its portrait of a backwater family's fight to save their house from an airport redevelopment project. The result is a low-budget comedy rife with cliches, generally coarse, occasionally hilarious and hugely popular.

Cato, Ken

Ken Cato's career has seen him work in graphic design, interior design, environmental design and, recently, web design. He is a foundation

They're down in the Caulfield Cup, 1885 · Nick Cave in *Ghosts . . . of the Civil Dead*, 1988 · Roy Cazaly, above, and Ken Cato's hopeful logo (right)

member of the Australian Writers and Art Directors Association, a member of the American Institute of Graphic Arts, ICOGRADA, the Design Institute of Australia, the Australian Marketing Institute, the Industrial Design Council of Australia, the Australian Academy of Design and in 1980 he established Cato Design Inc. and has since helped it expand worldwide.

Caulfield Cup

The Caulfield Cup is a handicap over 2400 metres and was first run in 1879. It is the popular race to couple with the Melbourne Cup in a speculative 'double'. A jockey was killed in the 1885 Caulfield Cup, won by Grace Darling, when 16 of the 44 runners fell. It is the most exacting handicap south of the equator.

Cave, Nick

One of Australia's most influential and enduring rock musicians, Nick Cave (b. 1957) was lead singer of 1980s punk rock band The Birthday Party before leaving to form The Bad Seeds and then going solo. His back catalogue includes *The Birthday Party* (1980), *From Her to Eternity* (1984) with the Bad Seeds and *Murder Ballads* (1996) as a solo performer.

Cazaly, Roy

Cazaly (1893–1963) is a legendary figure in Australian football, after his name went into the language through the phrase 'Up There Cazaly', used by Fred 'Skeeter' Fleiter when he roved to Cazaly's ruck for South Melbourne in the 1920s. It was taken up by the South barrackers, and transferred itself to the AIF in the

Middle East in World War II as a kind of battle cry. Mike Brady revived Cazaly with the inspired anthem *Up There Cazaly* in 1979. As a footballer, Cazaly was a star for a number of teams. He was always on the move, playing for St Kilda 1911–20, South Melbourne 1921–24, Minyip 1925, South again 1926–27, Launceston 1928–30, Preston 1931, Newtown-Glenorchy 1934–36, playing coach of South Melbourne 1937–38, Camberwell 1940 (playing senior VFA footy aged 47), coached Hawthorn 1942–43, and captain–coach Newtown 1948–51. In this last stint he played a veterans game for Newtown in 1951, and then immediately turned out for the seniors as well – aged 58. No wonder he was a legend, he was – as Jack Dyer once noted of long playing Michael Tuck – 'an endurable'.

Rebecca Smart was *Celia*

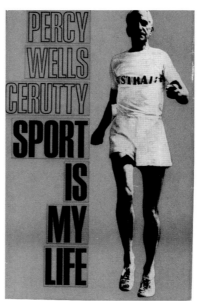

Percy Cerutty's training bible

Comte Lionel de Chabrillan, *pauvre homme*

C

Celia

Celia (1988) is a portrait of 1950s Australia which runs a discussion of Communism alongside a young girl's battle to save her rabbit, directed by Anne Turner.

Cerutty, Percy

Cerutty (1895–1975) was an eccentric coaching genius, whose pupil Herb Elliott was arguably the greatest middle-distance runner of all time – he won gold at Rome in 1960 and was never beaten. Cerutty trained his team up and down sand hills, and had them live and sleep in spartan conditions. He believed in going beyond the 'pain barrier'. He had eccentric ideas on diet and exercise, derived from a period of autodidactic study after 1939 when recovering from a nervous breakdown. His philosophy was Stotan, a combo of Stoic and Spartan: 'My Stotan philosophy is based on communication with nature. This communication takes place when the person sleeps under the stars at night, hears the birds in the morning, feels the sand between his toes, smells the flowers, hears the surf. Nature can bring the mind and body into perfect harmony and balance with the universe. This is one of the factors that allows the athlete to reach new levels of excellence.' It worked for him. He took up marathon running and retired at 55 as Victorian champion. He took up coaching at Portsea in 1959, eventually attracting for various periods of time John Landy, Betty Cuthbert, Russell Mockridge and Jimmy Carruthers as well as Elliott.

Chabrillan, Comte Lionel de

French consul in Melbourne during the 1850s, poor Lionel was married to the courtesan and writer Celeste (1824–1909) who scandalised Melbourne with her diary *Adieux Au Monde* and *The Gold Robbers*, finally published in English in 1970, originally as *Les Voleurs d'Or* (1857).

Chaffey Brothers

George (1848–1932) and William (1856–1926) were Canadian-born irrigation pioneers who had demonstrated the possibilities of the technology in California. They had already made Los Angeles the world's first completely electrically lit city and set up a huge fruit farming district in the Californian desert. Alfred Deakin, in the Victorian government, met them there in 1885, and invited the

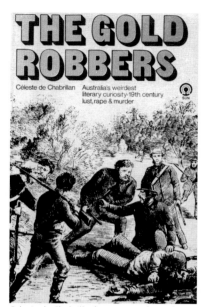

Celeste de Chabrillan's racy Australian tale

George Chaffey's Mildura memorial

Ian and Greg Chappell in younger days

brothers to make the desert around what became Mildura and Renmark bloom with water from the mighty Murray. They moved 3000 emigrants to the Mildura region and at first they used steamboats to power water pumps. Soon after, they designed a complex triple expansion steam engine – a design which the engine builder thought so ridiculous he refused to put his name to it. The first crop was a huge success, but then came trouble. The transport system broke down and food rotted. The town blamed the Chaffeys. The settlements ran into problems, and they were, after a Royal Commission, taken over by local Irrigation Trusts. George returned to California in 1897, but William remained in Mildura, becoming Mayor, and founded the vast Mildara winery. Hard done by at

the time, their monument is the great success of Mildura today, and the increasing environmental problems caused by over-irrigation and salination.

Chappell Brothers

Australian cricket's top trio of brothers, the Chappells have been at the forefront of change in Australian cricket since Ian (b. 1943) put on the baggy green in 1964–65. Ian's batting early on was modest, but his pugnacity and potential was great. In 1968–69 he found form against the West Indies, averaging 82. He was an aggressive hooker, safe in the slips and after becoming captain for the fifth Test of 1970–71, outstandingly successful. He had the benefit of the fiercely competitive larrikin cricketers Dennis Lillee and Rod Marsh to win 15

of his 30 Tests as captain. He was intimately involved in World Series Cricket, but played three final official Tests in the reconciliation season 1978–79. Ian was involved in a number of cricket controversies, best forgotten, but has been a straight-shooting commentator on Channel Nine. Greg (b. 1948) was the taller and more elegant batsman, whose characteristic shot was the on-drive rather than Ian's hook. He first played for Australia in 1970–71, and made a century on debut. In 1972 he and Ian became the first brothers to each score a century in the same innings. Greg took over the captaincy from Ian in 1975–76, scoring a century in each innings in the new job, against the West Indies. He lost the Ashes in 1977 in England as negotiations for World Series Cricket continued. Reinstated

Andrew 'Boy' Charlton – a great swimmer

Eddie Charlton – snooker whiz

The Chant of Jimmie Blacksmith

C

as Australian captain after WSC, he had a run of ducks in 1981–82 when he was batting okay, just getting out. He had seven ducks in 15 successive international innings. He retired in 1984, with a batting average of 53.86, and having won 20 of the 46 Tests he captained. He was a member of the ACB 1984–88, and has coached Queensland and South Australia. Trevor (b. 1952) played 88 first-class matches and three Tests in 1981 but will live in legend forever as the younger brother who was ordered by Greg to bowl underarm in 1981.

Charlton, Andrew 'Boy'
A born swimmer, Andrew 'Boy' Charlton (1907–75) swam for Australia in three Olympics: 1924, 1928 and 1932. He first came to national attention when he won the NSW

state championships in 1923, taking nineteen seconds off the world record for the 880 yards freestyle. However, 1924 was his greatest year. He won Olympic gold in the 1500 metres in Paris, but it was his series of races against Swede Arne Borg that same year which captured the popular imagination. Thousands of people edged the pool in Sydney's Domain – which now carries his name – to watch him thrash Borg. They say the crowd could be heard in Pitt Street. He was popular for his refusal to turn professional, and his last race was a win in the 1935 state championship.

Charlton, Eddie
A miner for fifteen years before taking up snooker, 'Steady' Edward Charlton (b. 1924) became a fixture in his chosen sport. Although he never

won a major ranking tournament, he holds a string of amazing records. He won the Australian Professional Championship in 1954, the year after he turned pro. He would repeat the feat, with one exception in 1968, for the next twenty years. His only defeat, at the hands of Warren Simpson, would haunt him again, when in 1970 Simpson beat him in the knock-out World Championships. Following that defeat he did not lose to an Australian on level terms for a decade. He was ranked number three in the world for five successive seasons and was runner up in the World Championships twice.

Chant of Jimmie Blacksmith, The
Based on the Thomas Keneally novel and directed by Fred Schepisi, *The Chant of Jimmie Blacksmith* (1978)

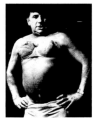

Ric Charlesworth carries the flag at Seoul

Elsa and Charles Chauvel, pioneer film-makers, and right, Gordon Chater dons a bra for his craft

was one of the films which helped establish the then-fledgling Australian film industry. The story centres around the life of a part-Aboriginal man unable to adapt to white culture and his subsequent violent collapse.

Charlesworth, Ric

Ric Charlesworth played in five successive Olympic hockey teams 1972–88, carrying the flag at Seoul, and represented Australia 234 times. He played cricket for WA, was Labor MHR for Perth 1983–93 and coach of the extraordinary Australian women's hockey team, which won back-to-back gold at Atlanta and Sydney.

Chater, Gordon

Gordon Chater (1922–99) arrived in Australia on four weeks de-mob leave

from the Royal Navy in 1945, and stayed. A very funny performer, he was in *Phillip Street Revue* and was a stalwart on TV in the *Mavis Bramston Show* in the mid 1960s. He confirmed that he was also a very considerable actor in Steve J. Spears *Elocution of Benjamin Franklin* in 1976, as the Double Bay transvestite, Robert O'Brien.

Chauvel, Charles

Charles Chauvel (1897–1959) was a pioneer in early Australian film. He believed in making films that were distinctively Australian, and after training in Hollywood returned to Australia to make *Moth of Moonbi* (1926). After marrying the lead in his next film, *Greenhide*, Elsa Sylvaney, they formed a remarkable filmmaking partnership. Together they would

make nine features, and are best remembered for the films *Forty Thousand Horsemen* (1940) and *The Rats of Tobruk* (1944).

Chauvel, Sir Harry

Harry Chauvel (1865–1945) was the revered commander of the Light Horse, the Anzac Mounted Division and other units in the Middle East in World War I. Chauvel's Anzacs were the first forces into Damascus in 1917, not Lawrence of Arabia.

Cheery Soul, A

The title of a Patrick White short story first published in 1962 and later included in his collection *The Burnt Ones* (1968). It was also a play first performed in 1963. The story follows Miss Docker, a tactless, invincible and eventually destructive do-gooder.

Chidley in his rational dress

Ben Chifley at the launch of the Snowy Mountains Scheme, and below, Chesty Bond

Chesty Bond

Created to promote Bonds singlets, Chesty Bond can be seen in animation, on posters and occasionally in the flesh (as portrayed by Paul Mercurio, among others) as a buff, bronzed Aussie encased in a skin-tight white singlet or T-shirt.

Chidley

Chidley was a Sydney eccentric and sex and dress reformer, and a kind of early feminist. He believed it was better for all concerned if the sexual act was performed with a flaccid penis, drawn in by some process, maybe love, rather than an aggressive act. He said so in public, often wearing his reformed form of clothing, a toga, and was arrested and driven further into eccentricity, perhaps madness. The subject of a

play by Alma de Groen, which was the first production of the Playbox, starring Peter Cummins, and directed by Garrie Hutchinson in 1976.

Chifley, Ben

Ben Chifley (1885–1951) was Prime Minister after John Curtin, from 1945 until he lost to the resurgent Robert Menzies in 1949, in the wake of bank nationalisation legislation. Under his

post–World War II administration such institutions as the Snowy Mountains Scheme, large-scale immigration and the nationalised Qantas appeared. To later generations his words to the NSW State Conference of 1949 still encompass what the Labor Party is, or should be, about. He said, 'I try to think of the Labor movement, not as putting an extra sixpence into somebody's pocket, or making somebody Prime Minister or Premier, but as a movement bringing something better to the people, better standards of living, greater happiness to the mass of people. We have a great objective – the light on the hill – which we aim to reach by working for the betterment of mankind not only here but anywhere we may give a helping hand.' Amen.

96

The emigrant's friend, Caroline Chisholm

Cinema Papers' Mad Max cover

Mark Brandon Read, aka Chopper

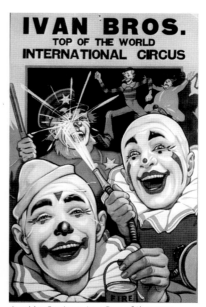

An older Oz circus: Ivan Bros of the 1920s

Chisholm, Caroline

Caroline Chisholm (1808–77) arrived in Australia in 1838 with her husband and family. Shocked by the treatment of emigrants and women on the boats from England, she set up a home for women and the Family Colonization Loan Society in 1849.

Chloe

The painting of a marble-smooth young girl by Jules Lefebvre has been a sensation since first exhibited in 1875. Showings in Sydney in 1879 and at the Melbourne Exhibition of 1880 were a scandal. Chloe was acquired in 1908 by Young & Jackson's hotel where she has been leered at since.

Chopper

Mark Brandon 'Chopper' Read (b. 1954), a vicious hitman, made the transition to media personality courtesy of Elle McFeast (Elspeth Gore), who generously but foolishly provided 'Chopper' with a 'slab' while he waited to come on her show. The resulting fiasco led to the termination of Gore's contract. Chopper was later portrayed by Eric Bana in an AFI award-winning biopic, from his strong-selling books.

Cinema Papers

Cinema Papers, edited in its heyday by Scott Murray, began in 1974, and was for 20 years or more the bible of Australian film culture. It rose in the renaissance of Australian film in the 1970s, but lost its way in the 1990s with the fragmentation – some would say disappearance – of film culture. It all but disappeared with management changes and a loss of Australian Film Commission subsidy in 1999. A new owner came to the rescue in 2000.

Circus Oz

Circus Oz was born in 1978 from a peculiar union of the Australian Performing Group's Soup Box Circus and Adelaide's New Ensemble Circus. The result was a contemporary, non-animal, non-star-based, acrobatic and musical circus which has been touring the world ever since.

Clarion, The

Literature and mining are not mutually exclusive, as the Melbourne monthly the *Clarion* proved from 1897 to 1909. Intellectually it promoted a message of white Australian, socialist republicanism. Its most notable features were covers by Will Dyson and cartoons by Norman Lindsay.

J.J. Clark's City Baths, Melbourne

The funny Clarke

The historical Clark

C

Clark, J.J.

James Clark, architect (1838–1915) worked in Melbourne, Brisbane, Perth, New Zealand and Sydney in government service and in private practice. Surviving memorable buildings include the Fremantle Town Hall, Melbourne Treasury Building at the top of Collins Street, red and white striped Melbourne City Baths, Melbourne Queen Victoria Hospital (one tower remaining) and the Brisbane Treasury.

Clark, Manning

Manning Clark's (1915–91) continuing claim to fame is that great personal work of literature, known as Manning Clark's *History of Australia*. It's not the kind of book you can look things up in; it is sometimes a bit loose with a minor fact and it is not very politically correct in its treatment of Aborigines or women, but it is one of the truly great works of literature. With C.E.W. Bean's Anzac volumes of the *Official History of World War I*, it is more honoured in the breach than in the reading. Charges of being a Soviet spy – he did write a credulous kind of travel book *Meeting Soviet Man* (1960) – made Clark something of a bête noire (a bête rouge) in death, for the conspiracy-hunting right. He stuck with the Labor Party through thin and thick, admired the saintly Curtin but not the compromising Hawke and stuck with the Carlton Football Club despite its administration. *A History of Australia* is one of the most passionately debated visions of our past, in which the struggle to realise an Australian nation is played out on an epic scale. Clark saw the process of change as driven by unceasing conflict between generosity of vision and inevitable human frailty. His Australians are people of great goodwill and deep sinfulness, of expansive ideas and small-mindedness, of patriotic independence and a fearful allegiance to Empire.

Clarke, John

John Clarke (b. 1948) has made a living making Australians laugh since arriving from New Zealand in 1977, where as the black-singleted, gum-booted Fred Dagg he had done the same to his fellow Kiwis. He was immensely popular, and loved by everyone it seems except the authorities of New Zealand broadcasting who couldn't find a way for him to capitalise on his success.

The bohemian Clarke

Marcus Clarke dressed up, 1874

Another Clarke: 1970s chef Peter Russell-Clarke

Not so in Australia, where Clarke has been welcomed as performer, writer, producer and actor, becoming – as Barry Humphries considers – the best humorist in Australia. His 2000 triumph was as the mock-Olympic organiser of the *The Games*. That followed his long run on television with dialogues between him and Bryan Dawe, where he would assume the identity of someone in the news without any make-up except words. His method of debunk: a *reductio ad absurdum*.

Clarke, Marcus

Marcus Clarke (1846–81) arrived in Melbourne in June 1863 and soon set to work earning a living as a journalist, quickly being published in *Melbourne Punch*. He was a terrific journalist, one of the first in a long

line of Australian writers who have mixed their media, Grub Street, theatre, fiction, criticism, publishing, anything and everything. Ian McLaren has described him as 'essentially the journalist. He was able to sense a story; he was aggressive and combative, ready to translate his thoughts into arresting words that caught the imagination of the public, or aroused antagonism to his views expressed so forthrightly'. He wrote extensively for the *Argus* and *Australasian*: editorials, literary articles and book reviews, plus the column 'The Peripatetic Philosopher' (1867–70), where he commented about 'everything'. His series 'Sketches of Melbourne Low Life', also in the *Australasian*, showed that he was an excellent investigative journalist. In fact his journalism (collected in the

splendid volume *A Colonial City*, edited by L.T. Hergenhan) demonstrate that Clarke's less literary writing is what resonates best today. Clarke had also been contributing to the *Australian Monthly* magazine, which soon became the *Colonial Monthly*. He was co-proprietor and editor for a time, during which his first novel, *Long Odds*, was serialised. Clarke then moved on to become co-proprietor and editor of the short-lived satirical magazine *Humbug*. Always in need of money, Clarke continued to contribute to newspapers for the rest of his life. His piece on the 1885 Melbourne Cup for the *Herald* was so popular that the newspaper had to be reprinted. In 1869 Clarke married Marian Dunn, a not very successful actress. Clarke's financial woes meant

The athletic Clarke

Frank Wilson and Jack Thompson in *The Club*

A Cobb & Co. coach

that he took a regular job as Secretary to Melbourne Public Library Trustees. Clarke's best-known work, *His Natural Life*, was published by George Robertson. It had been serialised in the *Australian Journal* between 1870–72. He loved the races, boozing, newspapers, and the bohemian life in Melbourne, but died in poverty aged just 35.

Clarke, Ron

Although he never won an Olympic gold medal, distance runner Ron Clarke (b. 1937) has gone down in Australian Olympic history as the white T-shirted boy who lit the flame in 1956. He was a world record breaker, making seventeen in 1967–68 over a variety of distances. His record in Olympic races was less impressive, not doing well in 1964 in Tokyo, and

while gallant in Mexico 1968 in the 10 000 metres, the altitude caused him to collapse and nearly die.

Club, The

The Club is supposed to be Collingwood, and the play of the same name by David Williamson, about a typical VFL club in the throes of social change in the early 1970s – drugs, professionalism, tradition ... Many of the stories in *The Club* were divulged to Williamson at a lunch one day in 1975 in the basement of the Grace Darling Hotel, the place where Collingwood was formed in 1892, told by Lou Richards and others.

Cobb & Co.

Established in Melbourne in 1853 by Freeman Cobb and three other Americans, the horse-driven coach

company Cobb & Co. grew steadily, changing hands three times before James Rutherford and partners bought it. Rutherford expanded the service to include NSW and Queensland. But in the end, the rise in popularity of motor vehicles doomed the service, and the last Cobb & Co. coach ran in Queensland in 1924.

Cole, E.W.

E.W. Cole (1832–1918) was a spectacular bookseller and publisher whose Book Arcade in the lost Eastern Market in Bourke Street, Melbourne was an Aladdin's Cave for decades after 1873. He published things like *Coles Funny Picture Book* in 1879 and it's still in print. He was a believer in world government and world religion.

John Coleman, the great full-forward

Bill Hunter and Toni Collette as Muriel

Bill Collins at the races, 1950s

Coleman, John

Perhaps the greatest full-forward ever, John Coleman (1928–73) kicked 537 goals in 98 games (1949–54) for Essendon. But an early death and a career-destroying knee injury embellish the legend, giving Coleman's life a mythic, heroic quality without peer in football. Mobile at ground level but even better overhead, springing to spectacular heights and marking surely. Ahead of his time, he was a courageous and direct runner at the ball, prepared to split opposing backmen with his speed to gain possession. Selected at full-forward against Hawthorn in the first game of 1949, he kicked twelve goals before going on to kick 100 for the season. He topped Essendon's goal-kicking in every year he played, including a personal record of 120 in 1950. He topped the League's goal-kicking 1949–50 and 1952–53. Suspension on finals eve 1951 cost Essendon a premiership. His career ended after he dislocated his knee against North Melbourne in 1954. He never played again, although he took over from Dick Reynolds as Essendon coach in 1961 and guided the Bombers to the 1962 and 1965 flags.

Collette, Toni

Actress Toni Collette (b. 1972) gained forty pounds in seven weeks for the lead role in *Muriel's Wedding* (1994). Her performance earned her an AFI award and took her to Hollywood where she garnered rave reviews for *Sixth Sense* (1999) and was nominated for an Oscar. She was also nominated for a Tony for *The Wild Party* (2000) on Broadway.

Collins, Bill

The Accurate One (1928–97) was a top racecaller for 3UZ in Melbourne, and HSV-7 personality, host of *Sunnyside Up*, from 1958.

Collins, Bill

Presenter of *The Golden Years of Hollywood* on Channels 7 (1966–75), 9 (1975–79) and then 10 (1980–93) for longer than most people thought possible. He now lectures on film and television for the Centre of Continuing Education at Sydney University.

Colonial Stadium

The short life of Melbourne's inner-city Colonial Stadium has been plagued with trouble. Trouble with the roof, trouble with the acoustics at concerts, trouble with the ground at

Mary Keneally, Rod Quantock, Henry Maas among the comedy revivalists

The Conscription vote, 1916

the football, trouble with ticketing at virtually everything, the stadium has been a nightmare for its owners. Nevertheless, like all new sporting arenas, it will no doubt eventually settle down.

Comedy

Comedy in Australia has typically been sardonic, beginning with Sir Joseph Banks' wry suggestion that Botany Bay was the ideal place for a colony! Although slightly more hospitable localities have since been found, dry humour has remained the European Australian's main defence against the vagaries of existence in a hostile continent, and later under a perverse political system, beginning with the 'tall tale', Dad and Dave and the *Bulletin* cartoonists and culminating in recent years in Paul

Hogan, Michael Leunig, Rod Quantock and John Clarke. At the other extreme we have produced a line of raucous over-the-top extroverts, from Roy Rene to Sue-Ann Post.

Comedy Company

In 1988, the Media Arts company was formed by Channel 10 to produce a new one-hour comedy show. Starring Ian McFadyen, Glenn Robbins, Maryanne Fahey, Russell Gilbert and more, it was an immediate success. The show was the number one rating show in the country for two years, knocking off *Sixty Minutes* in the same time slot.

Comedy Festival

Begun in 1987 in the heart of Australian comedy – Melbourne – the Melbourne International Comedy

Festival has been growing ever since. A grassroots organisation, it has become a festival of international renown, attracting acts from all parts of the globe.

Comic Australian, The

The *Comic Australian* magazine ran for about 80 issues between 1911 and 1913 and represented an early attempt to define the Australian identity through its humour. It featured the work of many then or later greats including Hugh McCrae, Hal Gye and J.C. Bancks, the eventual creator of Ginger Meggs.

Conscription

Due in part to the influence of the many political dissenters transported to Australia, partly to the bush ethos of the free individual and partly to

John Webber's portrait of Cook

Patrick Cook's take on the Australian home

the sense of security engendered by the country's geographical isolation, the whole idea of conscription for military service has been anathema to many Australians. Both Billy Hughes' referenda during the Great War were soundly defeated, and the introduction in 1964 of conscription to provide troops to join the United States' intervention in Vietnam was vehemently opposed.

Consider Your Verdict

Consider Your Verdict (1961–64) was Crawford Productions' and Australia's first tentative venture into television drama production. Only partly scripted and using both professional and non-professional actors, it was eventually superseded by more tightly scripted and professionally produced dramas, such as *Homicide*.

Continental

One of the key phrases needed to understand the 1950s and early 1960s. Something was 'continental' if it had spice or flavour, or was from an exotic part of the world, say Europe. Thus continental sausages and continental menus at continental cafes. Continental coffee in the decades before either instant or espresso machines was something made somehow from beans.

Cook, Captain James

Navigator and pioneer, Captain James Cook (1728–79) began his nautical career as a seaman in North Sea vessels before joining the navy in 1755. He became a master in 1759 and in 1768–71 he carried the Royal Society expedition to Tahiti to observe the passage of Venus across

the sun, during which time he circumnavigated New Zealand and 'discovered' parts of Australia. On his second voyage he sailed around Antarctica and 'discovered' several Pacific Island groups. But during his third voyage, which aimed to find a route around the north coast of America from the Pacific, he was forced to turn back and was finally killed by natives in Hawaii.

Cook, Patrick

Cook (b. 1949) has been a distinguished cartoonist and columnist, notably for the *National Times*, and has written extensively for television and theatre, including *The Gillies Report*, *The Big Gig*, *Kittson Fahey* and *A Night of National Reconciliation*. He is married to comedian Jean Kittson.

Coppin the Great

Some of the cast of *Cop Shop*

Peter Corrigan's Building 8, RMIT University

C

Cooper's Creek

Cooper's Creek skirts the eastern side of Queensland's Channel Country and runs through south-western Queensland and into South Australia. Featuring in much Australian legend and folklore, including the Burke and Wills expedition and 'Banjo' Paterson's *Clancy of the Overflow*, the river was also central to the country's pastoral expansion in the 19th century.
See: Burke (and Wills)

Coppin, George

George Coppin (1819–1906) had already performed extensively on the stage in England as a low comedian before emigrating to Australia in 1843, with his star turn, the endlessly extendible patter song *Billy Barlow*. He soon became a major player on the Australian stage in the mid-19th

century, both as a comedian and manager. Acts which toured under his management included Joseph Jefferson, Charles and Ellen Kean and J.C. Williamson (1845–1913) whose tour of *Struck Oil* in 1874–75 made both Coppin and Williamson a fortune, and founded the long running J.C. Williamson theatrical 'Firm'. Coppin built the prefabricated 'iron pot' Olympic Theatre, and the Theatre Royal, in Melbourne and many others around Australia. As a Victorian MLC he was responsible for the introduction of the freehold Torrens title system of land ownership to the State. Coppin was especially solicitous of old actors, and built two retirement villages for them. His other successful land developments included Sorrento, to which he ran his own steamer.

Cop Shop

Launched only a few years after other successful Crawford cop shows such as *Homicide* and *Division 4* had been axed, *Cop Shop* was a blend of both traditional cop drama and a soap opera. Screened on Channel 7, the show was a huge success, with 582 episodes screening between 1977 and 1983. The show starred Peter Adams as the tough and resourceful detective Jeffrey 'J.J.' Johnson and Paula Duncan as policewoman Danni Francis. Both won a few 'coveted' Logies for their performances.

Corrigan, Peter

Peter Corrigan (b. 1941) is an architect, with partner Maggie Edmond in Edmond and Corrigan, and theatre designer, who has worked with the Australian Opera on some Barrie

George Coulthard (right) with Ted Prevot

A couple of good sports, Molly Meldrum and Bob Hawke, *Countdown*, 1984

Kosky shows, and with the Australian Performing Group and successors. His best-known building is the jewel-like façade of Building 8 at RMIT University in Melbourne.

Corris, Peter

Peter Corris (b. 1942) is one of Australia's most popular crime writers. He began his career with the novel *The Dying Trade* (1980) but it was his fifth novel *The Empty Beach* (1983) which saw his career take off. His private detective, Cliff Hardy, is an Australian Philip Marlowe.

Coulthard, George

A genuine legend in pre-Federation Australian sport, George Coulthard (1856–83) was first and foremost a brilliant footballer for Carlton and was named Champion of the Colony

(the colonial equivalent of the Brownlow Medal) three times. He played in the first game under lights in 1879, kicking Carlton's entire score. However he was also a cricketer who both played and umpired a Test cricket match. In fact, he umpired his first Test in 1879 and became the first player ever to umpire a Test before playing in one – he did not make his playing debut until 1881–82. As a peculiar aside, his decisions as an umpire almost ended Test cricket. He gave local favourite Billy Murdoch run-out in a match between NSW and England in 1879, causing an immediate pitch invasion which saw the game postponed for a day and the second Test cancelled. The second umpire in that game would go on to become Australia's first Prime Minister – Edmund Barton.

Countdown

With Ian 'Molly' Meldrum up front, out there and quite often looking just a little bit 'under the weather', *Countdown* was Australia's first and biggest national music show. From 1974 to 1987 Australia poked fun at the ABC show and Molly's 'performances', but for twelve years the whole country still tuned in every week – its audience hitting three million at its peak. It brought international acts to Australia and Australian acts to the forefront, and although it was a stumbling, staggering, mumbler of a show at times, it occupies an unassailable position in Australian popular culture. The show returned from the dead in 1989 as *Countdown Revolution* but like all corpses, it stank and was quickly buried.
See: Johnny O'Keefe; rage

C

Margaret Court at home at Wimbledon

Ruth Cracknell in *The Singer and the Dancer*

Edith Cowan's stamp of approval

Court, Margaret

Blessed with a name custom-built for tennis, Margaret Court (nee Smith (b. 1942) dominated the women's game for most of the 1960s and early 70s and still holds the most impressive winning record in women's tennis. In singles and doubles she won an astounding 66 grand slam titles and in 1970 she completed the most prestigious of tennis achievements – the Grand Slam, winning the French Open, US Open, Wimbledon and the Australian Open in a single year.

Courtenay, Bryce

One of Australia's all-time best-selling writers, Bryce Courtenay (b. 1933) began life in marketing. He won many local and international advertising awards along with a gold medal for Best Documentary at the

1984 New York Film Festival. These skills served him admirably when at age 55 he turned his attention to writing blockbusters. His first novel, *The Power of One* (1989) sold over two million copies worldwide. It is the largest-selling book by a living Australian author within Australia, with over half a million copies sold.

Cowan, Edith

Australia's first female parliamentarian (and the second in the British empire), Edith Dircksey Cowan (1861–1932) fought for women's rights and social justice. She believed that better education and the breaking of various social taboos on certain issues was the key to effecting lasting social change. In 1919 she became the first female justice of the peace in Australia.

Cox, Paul

Dutch-born filmmaker Paul Cox (b. 1940) has made a substantial reputation for his series of sensitive films about Australian relationships: *Kostas* (1978), *Lonely Hearts* (1981), *Man of Flowers* (1983), *My First Wife* (1984), *A Woman's Tale* (1991), *Exile* (1994), *Innocence* (2000). Not loved enough in his adopted country.

Cracknell, Ruth

Actress and comedian Ruth Cracknell (b. 1925) made her debut on radio in 1945 and on stage in 1948, and hasn't stopped working since. A veteran of the performing arts, she is considered the doyenne of Australian theatre. Perhaps best known for her TV portrayal of the doddering Maggie Beare in *Mother and Son* which ran on the ABC between 1983 and 1993.

Crocodile Dundee promotes Japanese tyres

Cricket at the MCG in the early 1900s

Stan Cross 'For gor'sake stop laughing...'

CRAWFORDS
AUSTRALIA

She was named one of Australia's 100 living treasures in 1998.

Crawford Productions

Not only one of Australia's biggest and most resilient production companies, it is also this country's oldest. Founded in 1945 by Hector and Dorothy Crawford, it is responsible for shows such as *The Sullivans*, *Homicide*, *Cop Shop*, *The Henderson Kids* and more. Its dedication to making television shows for Australian audiences, set in Australia and starring Australians, marks it as an industry leader.

Cricket

The national summer game. The first game where teams represented Australia, or at least were seen retrospectively to represent Australia.

The first was the Aboriginal team which toured England in 1868, initially coached by Tom Wills. The second was the team which played the first Test at the MCG in 1877, for a result exactly duplicated in 1977's Centenary Test in Melbourne.

Crocodile Dundee

Crocodile Dundee is most definitely an Australian icon. Nobody can argue with that. However he's still a crass, slightly embarrassing icon you'd rather didn't come to the family Christmas BBQ. Played by Paul Hogan in three films, the first was for many years the highest-grossing local film ever made, clocking up $47 million dollars at the box office. Wearing a battered Akubra, its brim decorated with crocodile teeth, the character was the kind of rugged, Australian

larrikin that the rest of the world wanted to imagine.

Cross, Stan

Stan Cross (1888–1977) was born in Los Angeles, came to Australia with his parents in 1892, and became one of Australia's leading black and white artists. His 1933 *Smith's Weekly* cartoon, of the workers falling off a building, one hanging on to the other's trousers, saying 'For gor'sake stop laughing, this is serious' came to epitomise Australia's attitude to the Depression and other catastrophes. Cross also drew *Wally and the Major* and *Bluey and Curley*, which syndicated from the Melbourne *Herald* and were much loved especially during World War II, where Bluey and Curley's laconic exploits captured the Digger spirit.

Crowded House

Young Russell Crowe as The Man in John Tatoulis' *The Silver Brumby*, 1992

CSIRAC – CSIRO's first computer

C

Crowded House

An Australian band with an 'adopted' Kiwi lead singer in Neil Finn, Crowded House were one of the biggest and best rock/pop acts ever to pick up a guitar in Australia. Featuring the talents of Paul Hester on drums and Nick Seymour on bass (and occasionally Tim Finn on vocals), Crowded House formed from the wreckage of the band Split Enz in 1986, calling themselves The Mullanes, but quickly changed their name in tribute to their cramped living conditions during their first foray into America. Four hit albums followed, peaking with *Woodface* (1991). They broke up in 1996.

Crowe, Russell

Now one of the biggest 'properties' in Hollywood, Russell Crowe is yet another Kiwi. A great gladiator. By 2001 was seen hanging on the arms of real Hollywood actresses.

CSIRO

The antecedents of CSIRO (the Commonwealth Scientific and Industrial Research Organisation) go back to recommendations made in 1916 by Prime Minister Billy Hughes, but most directly to its own Establishment Act in 1949. Best known for myxomatosis, cloud seeding and wool research. Aerogard was invented by CSIRO chief entomologist Doug Waterhouse (1916–2000) in the early 1960s. The formula was acquired by the Mortein company in 1963 supposedly after Waterhouse was fly free at a Government House reception for the Queen in 1963, and Her Majesty was not. Twelve cans are alleged to have changed hands – as the CSIRO handed over its discoveries to industry for free.

Cultural Cringe

Critic A.A. Phillips' phrase, coined in 1950, to describe Australian subservience to all things in English, and later American, culture, notably but not exclusively literary. A species of the cultural cringe was that Australians had to go 'overseas' to prove themselves, especially in opera. Most obnoxious cringers are those who went and had some success, but still find it necessary to come back to Australia to demean and damn with faint praise – Clive James, Germaine Greer and Robert Hughes spring to mind. Once a mere description, in more nationalist times post 1960s it became an insult. Even

Bart Cummings points out another win

Australia's political saint, John Curtin

in the 21st century there is a feeling that unless a book is an international bestseller, or wins a prize such as the Booker, it isn't 'really' any good.

Cummings, Bart

Bart Cummings (b. 1927) was always the Cups King, but after Rogan Josh won his eleventh Melbourne Cup in 1999 Cummings assumed more god-like status. His other winners are Light Fingers (1965), Galilee (1966), Red Handed (1967), Think Big (1974, 1975), Gold and Black (1977), Hyperno (1979), Kingston Rule (1990), Let's Elope (1991) and Saintly (1996). He has triumphed over 1980s business problems and indifferent horses.

Currency Lad (& Lass)

Description of native-born people in the early 19th century. British-born were sterling, locals were currency. Also the name of a paper edited by Horatio Wills in 1832–33, father of the father of Australian football Tom Wills, whose motto was 'Arise Australia'. It was dedicated to the 'Genius of our native Hills'.

Current Affair, A

The most watched current affairs program in Australia, *ACA* ran originally from 1971–78 before being taken off air. In 1984 it returned with a new host, Mike Willesee, and a new name – *Willesee* – before reverting to *ACA* in 1988. Remarkable for its hosts (including Jana Wendt, Ray Martin and currently Mike Munro) and its style of journalism, the show has been a constant success. Lampooned by *Frontline*, it didn't change its style, still keeping the foot in the door.

Curtin, John

John Curtin (1885–1945), prime minister 1941–45 and a kind of political saint, albeit one who overcame all-too-human frailties in the national interest. Curtin is given credit for bringing our troops home to defend Australia when Churchill wanted to keep them to defend England, and with saying in a Christmas message in 1941 'Without any inhibitions of any kind, I make it quite clear that Australia looks to America, free of any pangs as to our traditional links or kinship with the United Kingdom.' The downside of this was coming too close to Douglas MacArthur's strategic view during World War II. Curtin represents what we don't have in politicians anymore – dedication, nationalism, selflessness, and dying in harness.

Dad tells it how it is in 1938

D-Generation at attention

Ross Wilson of Daddy Cool

Bill Hayden gives pre-election news, no dam for the Franklin

D-Generation

Loosely formed at a law revue in 1983, their first TV show was launched in 1987. Featuring the talents of Rob Sitch, Tom Gleisner, Santo Cilauro, Jane Kennedy, Tony Martin and Mick Molloy among others, the core group then worked in radio before returning for a few seasons on the ABC in 1992–94. *Frontline*, a satire of current affairs shows, followed, as well as the popular 'chat' show *The Panel* on Ten and the sentimental fishing show *A River Somewhere* and the films *The Castle* and *The Dish*.

Dad and Dave

The bumbling father and son of the Rudd family were born in the *Bulletin* in 1895 in the first of 'Steele Rudd's' rural sketches. Battlers and pioneers at first, they would later become comical figures, and then archetypes. They would star in a stage production, four movies (1932–40) a radio serial which ran for over 2000 episodes 1937–51 and a TV series. *See: Davis, Arthur Hoey*

Daddy Cool

A huge and almost accidental hit in 1970s Australian rock, Daddy Cool's debut single *Eagle Rock* (1971) and the album *Daddy Who? Daddy Cool!* (1971) were both the biggest selling records ever released up to that time. Formed for 'light' relief from the band's other endeavours as 'Son of the Vegetable Mother' by Ross Wilson, Ross Hannaford, Gary Young and Wayne Duncan, Daddy Cool soon eclipsed its parent and took over the shows. Another smash-hit album in 1973 saw their fame peak before studio difficulties led to the break up of the band in 1974, with only three songs on another album put to tape.

Dams

Damn those dams (and tunnels). The heroic achievement in multicultural work that saw the Snowy Mountains Scheme completed in 1974 (begun 1949) has been undermined somewhat by its malignant effect on the legendary Snowy and the mighty Murray. Talk of 'environmental flows' leached into political discussions in the late 1990s, as a Victorian independent pro-flow candidate was elected, helping cause the ejection of the Kennett government. Dam makers and politicians ought to remember the attempt to dam the Franklin River in Tasmania in the early 1980s, which led the incoming Hawke

William Dampier in extreme close-up

Les Darcy aims a sharp right to the jaw

Labor Government to increase federal powers, and the rise of Green political power in that state.

Damper
A traditional Australian bush 'delicacy', damper was popular amongst both Aborigines and early settlers. A type of bread, it is made by grinding seeds into flour and then mixing it with water and cooking it in the ashes of a campfire.

Dampier, Alfred
After emigrating to Australia in 1873, Alfred Dampier (1848–1908) formed his own provincial theatre company in 1877. His specialties were epic, nationalistic melodramas of which he co-wrote several, including the successful *Marvellous Melbourne* (1889) and *This Great City* (1891).

Dampier, William
Explorer and navigator William Dampier (1652–1715) published the book *A New Voyage Round the World* in 1697, which led to his commanding an expedition to further explore New Holland and New Guinea in 1699. He cruised the West Australian coast from Shark Bay to Roebuck Bay before 'discovering' New Britain.

Darcy, Les
The short life of boxer Les Darcy (1895–1917) was filled with controversy, peaked when he was crowned Australian Champion in 1915 (a title he defended successfully 12 times) and ended tragically when he died at age 21 from a suspected abscessed tooth. He had travelled to America in 1916 despite World War I and some claimed he was shirking his

duty to his country, but he said he needed the money. In his short career he went twenty rounds a dozen times and won 45 of his 50 fights. The only other boxer in Australia's history who comes close is Albert 'Young Griffo' Griffiths.

Dargie, Horrie
World-renowned harmonica player Horrie Dargie's (1917–99) first harmonica was apparently a boomerang. He began his musical career as a diatonica player and joined the Yarraville Mouth Organ Band, which practised in a shoe repairshop, before joining William Ketterer's 'Victorian Mouth Organ Band' which consisted of the most promising players in Victoria. In the early 1930s he took up the chromatic harmonica and won a variety

Jack Davey warms up the audience in the wartime Macquarie auditorium

William Dargie, war artist

Australia's victorious 1999 Davis Cup squad

competition on a local radio station in 1937. After the war Horrie formed a new group, The Harlequintet, which was to become recognised internationally. They were not so much a harmonica act, but an instrumental/comedy act using harmonicas as well as other instruments. He compered, presented and directed television shows, and made two instrumental albums, *Horrie Dargie Harmonica Spectacular* (1973) and *Harmonica Favourites* (1974). He composed and arranged music for radio, television and film. He supplied the harmonica music for *Crocodile Dundee II*.

Dargie, William

Born 1912, Sir William Dargie is a seven-time winner of the Archibald Prize, including once with a portrait of General Douglas MacArthur painted on a dunny door.

Davey, Jack

Australia's own 'Mr Radio', Jack Davey (1910–59) had an audience of five million Australians at the height of his career. In over six hundred shows a year he worked quiz shows, breakfast shows and straight comedy, and always lived beyond his means. When he died, he was penniless, despite an exorbitant salary for much of his working life.

Davis, Arthur Hoey

The man who defined an entire Australian subculture, Arthur Hoey Davis (1868–1935, aka Steele Rudd) was the son of a blacksmith who worked as a shearer and an under-sheriff before turning to writing. His original pseudonym 'Steele Rudder' comes from a combination of 'Rudder' for his passion for sailing and 'Steele' for a favoured British author. However by the time his first sketch was published, the surname was taken and he shortened it to Rudd. He was the author of the Dad and Dave books.
See: Dad and Dave

Davis Cup

Australia's victory in the centenary Davis Cup in 1999 not only broke a thirteen-year drought, it celebrated a legacy of Australian dominance in the event. In fact, Australia won 15 of 20 cups between 1950 and 1969. This cemented the competition's central place in Australian tennis and ensured its continued success. Australia lost to Spain in 2000 in the aggressive atmosphere of Barcelona.

Judy Davis in *Heatwave*, 1981

Neil Davis on the cover of *One Crowded Hour*

Rob de Castella's 19th-century family

Davis, Jack

Jack Davis (1917–2000), Aboriginal playwright and poet, was in his fifties when his poetry was published – *The First Born* – in 1970. In the 1980s his successful plays *The Dreamers*, *No Sugar* and *Honey Spot* were published. He became a member of the Aboriginal Arts Board of Australia in 1983 and was the creator and patron of Curtin University's Centre of Aboriginal Studies. He began a journal called *Identity* which offered hope to his people through literature and art and representations of dance. Through his great plays, beginning with *Kullark* in 1979, he advanced our understanding of the capacity of theatre to reach people, interpreting the Australian indigenous experience. His plays are frequently revived, and he remains an inspiration.

Davis, Judy

Australia's best-known leading lady, Judy Davis (b. 1955) dropped out of a convent in her teens to sing in a band before turning to acting. She drew huge critical acclaim for her performance in the lead of Gillian Armstrong's *My Brilliant Career* (1979) and Academy Award nominations for her roles in *A Passage to India* (1984) and Woody Allen's *Husbands and Wives* (1992). Fierce and often funny, Davis' independence and unwillingness to bend to the demands of Hollywood have not stopped her from carving out an enviable career.

Davis, Neil

Australian news photographer, Neil Davis was taken by many to be the inspiration of Christopher Koch's novel *Highways To War*. He worked in a heroic mould, and was the brave inheritor of the Damien Parer tradition in news picture gathering, and like Parer was killed in the line of duty in 1986 – this time in one of Thailand's coups – a particularly senseless death. His camera continued to film as he lay dying. Davis' biography, by Tim Bowden, was aptly titled *One Crowded Hour*.

De Castella, Robert

Affectionately known as 'Deek', Robert De Castella (b. 1957) is the only Australian to have placed in the top 10 at three consecutive Olympic games. Winner of the Boston Marathon in 1986 along with two consecutive Commonwealth gold medals in 1982 and 1986, he was named Australian of the Year in 1983.

D

114

Alfred Deakin, journalist and prime minister

De Groot arrested after opening the Bridge

Roy de Maistre, decor for Grace Brothers, 1927

De Groot, Francis
The official opening day of the Sydney Harbour Bridge on Saturday 19 March 1932 drew a crowd of over 300 000. The NSW Premier, Jack Lang, officially declared the Bridge open. However, the proceedings were enlivened when former cavalry officer Captain Francis De Groot (1890–1969) of the right wing para-military group, the New Guard, slashed the ribbon prematurely with his sword, prior to the official cutting. He declared the Bridge open in the name of the people of NSW, not Lang's 'socialist' government. He was fined and sent to a mental institution, and left Sydney in 1949. He died in Ireland.

de Maistre, Roy
In 1919, one of Australia's most controversial art exhibitions was held in Sydney. Called *Colour in Art*, it attracted a big crowd because of the furore surrounding the artists' use of colour. The two artists were Roland Wakelin (1887–1971) and Roy de Maistre (1894–1968), a young musician-turned-painter, who first used colour to soothe World War I shellshock patients. De Maistre abandoned colour-music ideas and took up the opposite – Max Meldrum's brown tonalism. He became more of a British 'cubist' painter after arriving in London in 1930.

Deakin, Alfred
Alfred Deakin (1859–1919) holds the peculiar honour of being Australia's 2nd, 5th and 7th prime ministers. When he was first elected to the Victorian Parliament, he resigned immediately because he believed that administrative bungling of the poll had given him an unfair advantage. In the subsequent by-election, the voters rewarded him by electing his opponent. A great proponent of Federation, he also campaigned for improved conditions for workers in factories and shops. During his prime ministership old age pensions were first introduced and Canberra was chosen as the capital city.

Demidenko, Helen
Briefly a member of the Australian literary scene, Helen Demidenko (or Darville, as was later revealed) found herself at the centre of a literary scandal when her book *The Hand that Signed the Paper* won the Australian/ Vogel Award, the Miles Franklin Prize and a Gold Medal from the Australian Literature Society in 1995. She had

Helen Demidenko/Darville before the scandal

C.J. Dennis at work

claimed that the book was the true story of her illiterate Ukranian parents and their involvement in the Holocaust, but it turned out she grew up in Brisbane. Worse, she later claimed that she had 'accidentally' copied whole slabs of work from other writers. She has since seemingly disappeared into the cultural ether.

See: Malley, Ern

Dennis, C.J.

Australia's 'laureate of the larrikin', Clarence Michael James 'C.J.' Dennis (1876–1938) published his first poem in a local newspaper when he was only nineteen. His first collection of poems *Backblock Ballads and Other Verses* (1913) was well reviewed but did not sell, but his next collection *The Songs of a Sentimental Bloke*

(1915) was a huge hit in Australia and also with homesick troops fighting overseas. *The Moods of Ginger Mick* (1916) was equally successful and Dennis had become Australia's most successful and best-loved poet, a position he has not strayed too far from ever since.

Denton Corker Marshall

Founded in 1972 and now an international practice with an enviable reputation, the architectural group Denton Corker Marshall is responsible for much of the current 'redesign' in Melbourne. They designed the first, ill-fated City Square but have been acclaimed for the Melbourne Exhibition Centre, the new Museum of Victoria, and sections of City Link.

See: Sheds

Depression, The

Jeff Kennett, after losing the premiership in Victoria, was appointed to head a depression taskforce. Paul Keating once told his fellow citizens that the series of non-growth months in the early 1990s was in fact the 'recession we had to have', being unable to utter the 'D' word. That was largely on account of the Great Depression of the 1930s, which so powerfully influenced the men and women of baby boomer Keating parents' generation. The Depression of the 1890s ended Melbourne's Land Boom Growth, and brought about the Labor Party. We will never have another depression, but we will have recessions, downturns, J curves, and slumps – and can still catch a cold when America sneezes.

A familiar sight during the Depression

Collette Dinnigan advertisement

Jack Hibberd's *Dimboola*

Dictation Test

A selectively applied test of the 1930s, used to deny entry to Australia of undesirable 'aliens'. In 1934 Egon Kisch, a Czech communist, was banned when he failed to take dictation in Scottish Gaelic. He appealed to the High Court and won on the grounds that Scottish Gaelic was not a European language. Kisch stayed, wrote a book entitled *Australian Landfall*, and left in 1935.

Dimboola

Victorian town made famous by Jack Hibberd's 1969 wedding reception play, and as the 1961 birthplace of football legend Tim Watson.

Dingoes

An Aboriginal name for wild dog, dingoes have a bad reputation in Australia. Seen as little more than vermin, they have been known to attack cattle and sometimes even people. So stealthy and cunning were these attacks on farms that 'dingo' was often used as an insult, implying cowardice and treachery. And a 'dingo took my baby', the cry of Meryl Streep as Lindy Chamberlain in *Evil Angels*, has gone into the international lexicon of mad Aussie sayings via Elaine in the US TV comedy *Seinfeld*. The Fraser Island dingo killing in 2001 confirmed the worst about the dogs.

Dinnigan, Collette

Collette Dinnigan launched her own label in 1990 and steadily worked her way to the top. In 1996 she was named Australian designer of the year and her work has been praised for both its Australian sensibilities and its international appeal. In 1995 she became the first Australian designer to launch a full-scale ready-to-wear parade in Paris.

Disasters

Australians both love and hate disasters. Despite the often tragic loss of life in bushfire or flood, cyclone or earthquake, a disaster also enables us to bring out our best in community spirit. Disasters in Australia are mostly natural disasters, and they have names – Cyclone Tracy (1974), Ash Wednesday (1983) – and they are also personal tragedies. Non-natural disasters are events with some kind of human intervention, like the Sydney to Hobart yacht race disaster in 1998, where heroism of a high order was evident.
See: Black Days

The real thing: Gough Whitlam listens to the proclamation of his dismissal, November 11, 1975

Bill Dobell in the 1940s

Dismissal, The

A 1983 TV mini-series featuring Max Phipps (1939–2000) as Gough Whitlam, John Stanton as Malcolm Fraser and John Meillon as Sir John Kerr. Directed by such luminaries as George Miller, Phillip Noyce, George Ogilvie and Carl Schultz, it marked the apogee of the mini-series genre's delving into recent Australian history. This retelling of the November 11, 1975 constitutional coup where the elected government was thrown out, more or less because Whitlam didn't know he was calling Kerr's bluff (egged on by Malcolm Fraser and, who knows, the CIA). There were many reasons why the Whitlam government would have lost the next scheduled election (incompetence being one of them), but few excuses for the precipitate action undertaken by Kerr.

Division 4

Some 300 episodes of *Division 4*, Nine's example of the Crawford cop show genre so popular on Australian TV, were made from 1969. *Division 4* notably starred Diane Craig, Terence Donovan, Chuck Faulkner, Ted Hamilton, Gerard Kennedy and Andrew McFarlane.

Dobell, William

Despite being one of the greatest painters this country has ever produced, the career of William Dobell (1899–1970) was dogged by scandal. When he won the Archibald Prize for his portrait of Joshua Smith in 1943, two unsuccessful artists took him to court claiming his painting was a caricature, not a portrait, and that 'when you look at a portrait you should feel that what you see is

human – not that you should send for the ambulance'. Thankfully, their objections were overturned. His greatest skill was the ability to adapt his style to the subject of his portraits, something not appreciated by Prime Minister Menzies, who sat for a *Time* magazine cover painted by Dobell and later refused to comment on the painting. Dobell would win the Archibald three times in his career, and in 1966 was knighted.

Dodson, Mick

Mick Dodson (b. 1950), Monash law graduate, director of Northern Land Council 1990–93, and former Aboriginal and Torres Strait Islander Social Justice Commissioner, ended his five-year term in 1997 questioning the Howard government's commitment to reconciliation. He

The dog sits on the tuckerbox

Once mighty Dollar Bill

Pat Dodson, working for reconciliation

Ken Done has it all wrapped up

remains a strong advocate outside the system calling for justice for the stolen generations and in 2000, even at the end of the ten-year reconciliation process, was resolute in calling for a treaty between the first people of Australia and later arrivals. He became Chairman of the Australian Institute of Aboriginal and Torres Strait Islander Studies in 2000.

Dodson, Pat

Pat Dodson (b. 1947), parish priest at Broome and Darwin to 1981, director of the Central Land Council 1987, resigned as Chairman of the Council for Aboriginal Reconciliation in 1997 after six years guiding the troubled process. On his resignation he said 'I despair for my country and regret the ignorance of political leaders who do not appreciate what is required to

achieve reconciliation for us as a nation.' His resignation followed the appearance of the Prime Minister John Howard at the Council's first national convention, when delegates turned their backs on the PM. Howard said Australians of this generation 'should not be required to accept the guilt and blame for past actions and policies'.

Dog on the Tucker Box

The original bullockies' song was about a place where 'the dog shits on the tuckerbox, 9 miles from Gundagai'. The statue, by one F. Rusconi, was unveiled by Prime Minister Joe Lyons in 1932 to commemorate the pioneers of the district. The dog still sits on that tuckerbox – but now it's 8 kilometres from Gundagai.

'Dollar Bill'

Dollar Bill was the star of the sales campaign in 1965–66 which heralded the switch from pounds, shillings and pence to dollars and cents in February 1966. Among the names rejected for the new dollar were the Austral and the Royal. One cent and two cent coins were withdrawn in 1992. The $1 and $2 notes were replaced by coins in 1984 and 1988.

Done, Ken

Wonderfully bright and breezy, painter and designer, Ken Done (b. 1940) sold a harbour-full of images that have best defined the Sydney/Oz spirit. Done (AM) is an Export Hero, and an accomplished painter, hung regularly in the Sulman, Wynne and Archibald shows. He is also heavily involved in the Ausflag campaign.

Graeme Blundell in *Don's Party*

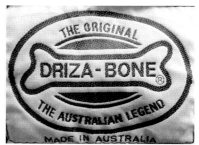

Still made in Australia

The Doug Anthony All-Stars in action

A contemplative Robert Drewe

Don's Party

A 'Don's Party' has gone into the language as the event held the night before an election. David Williamson's 1970 play was based around a night of disappointment for Labor supporters in 1969, and riotously directed by Graeme Blundell at the Pram Factory for the Australian Performing Group. It was his 'treatment' by the 'Carlton mafia' in this incredibly successful production that drove Williamson, world's tallest playwright, to wicked Sydney.

Doohan, Michael

One of the world's greatest motorcyclists, Mick Doohan (b. 1970) won the world championship from 1994–98 and then broke most of the bones in his body in the Spanish Grand Prix of 1999. He won 55 of his

first 136 starts, a record without peer. He later took to four wheels.

Doug Anthony All-stars

D.A.A.S., otherwise known as the Doug Anthony All-stars, were one of the funniest and most unusual comedy acts in Australia from their inception in the late 1980s to their eventual collapse in 1994. Featuring the talents of Tim Ferguson, Paul McDermott and Richard Fidler (who met in Canberra of all places) they were a huge success both nationally and internationally, touring Britain and America. A mix of outrageous, confrontational comedy and songs, they were fixtures on the ABC with the *Big Gig* and even had their own show for a while called *D.A.A.S. Kapital*. One of their best songs was *Camus Was a Whining Bastard*.

Drewe, Robert

Robert Drewe (b. 1943) began his career in writing as a journalist with the *West Australian* in 1961 and even after writing his first novel, *The Savage Crows* (1976), continued to work in the field. He has been rewarded with Walkley Awards in 1976 and 1981. His other novels are *A Cry in the Jungle Bar* (1979), *Fortune* (1986) and *Our Sunshine* (1991). His novel *The Drowner* (1997) was shortlisted for the Miles Franklin Award. His memoir of growing up Australian, subtitled 'memories and murder', *The Shark Net* (2000) was a critical and popular success.

Driza-bone

It began life aboard the early windjammers that plied the great southern oceans, and like all good

Drought, drovers and the drover's dog

Russell Drysdale at work

ideas, was born of necessity. When the sailors eventually went ashore they took their renowned wet weather coats with them. Once ashore, the coat was adapted to life on the land with a fantail to protect the seat of the horse rider's saddle, leg straps to keep the coat from taking off in high winds, and extra long sleeves. So effective were the coats that they eventually became known as Driza-bones, after the dried and parched bones of animals in the arid Australian outback. Made at Eagleby in Queensland, Driza-bones made an epic appearance at the Sydney Olympic opening ceremony on the men from Snowy River.

Drought

'I love a sunburnt country', said Dorothea Mackellar, and she loved 'droughts and flooding rains'. She must have been the only one. We put up with the sunburn, aware of skin cancer, and know that despite the fact that droughts seem to have occurred every decade, it's hard to love them. And what with climate change and everything, they seem to be becoming the norm rather than the exception.

Drovers

Drovers had the unenviable job of moving large groups of cattle over small distances – the short-range cousin of the overlanders. Their careers were romanticised in a variety of poems, plays, films and novels, including Henry Lawson's lonely *The Drover's Wife*, Louis Esson's one-act play *The Drovers* and Thea Astley's *The Droving Man*.

Drysdale, Russell

Most famous for his depictions of the 'harsh' Australian landscape, Russell Drysdale (1912–81) often portrayed the difficulties faced by settlers and Aborigines in the outback. He won the Wynne Prize in 1947, the Melrose Prize in 1949 and the Britannica Australia Award in 1965.

Dunlop, Weary

A surgeon and diarist, Edward 'Weary' Dunlop (1907–93) was on staff at St Mary's Hospital in Paddington when World War II broke out. In 1942 he was posted to Java where he established an Allied hospital at Bandoeng just before Java fell to the Japanese. He then became medical officer and commander of Allied prisoners of war in Japanese prison camps in Java and on the infamous forced labour

Weary Dunlop on duty near the Shrine

Don Dunstan, masked man

KEITH DUNSTAN

Cover by Cato, Hibberd, Hornblow & Hawksby

D

Burma–Thailand Railway, where he was seen as a miracle worker for his ability to work without proper instruments, medicines or facilities. Upon his return to Australia in 1945 he held honorary surgical posts at a number of Melbourne hospitals and was named Australian of the Year in 1976. The nickname 'Weary' comes, of all places, from Dunlop Tyres. (Tyres-tires-weary.) Weary Dunlop's tireless work on behalf of the POWs on the Railway during and after the war made him a hero to the men, and did much to restore the POWs' reputation as courageous Australians. A fellow Burma–Thailand Railway POW, Donald Stuart, said of him, 'When despair and death reached for us, he stood fast. Faced with guards who had the power of life and death, ignoble tyrants who hated us, he was

a lighthouse of sanity in a universe of madness and suffering.'

Dunstan, Don

As Attorney-General and Premier of South Australia, Don Dunstan (1926–99) is credited with changing the face of Adelaide. He was the driving force behind the expansion of the Adelaide Arts Festival, he took an active role in helping dismantle the White Australia policy, he pushed anti-discrimination legislation through parliament, expanded drinking hours, wore pink shorts to parliament, and once turned back a tidal wave.

Dunstan, Keith

Keith Dunstan (b. 1925) catalogued and dissected the goings-on in Melbourne in his column 'A Place In

the Sun' in the *Sun News-Pictorial* 1958–84, and was also a contributor to the anonymous columns about Melbourne in the Sydney *Bulletin*, under the nom de plume 'Batman'. His history of the MCG is an enduring classic, as are his accounts of Australian eccentricity in three books *Wowsers*, *Knockers* and *Sports*.

Dupain, Max

Max Dupain (1911–92) was born in Sydney and his images of sunbathers, women queuing for rations and the work of Australian architects have come to define his city and his country. In 1934 Dupain established his own commercial studio in Bond Street, Sydney and specialised in advertising, still-life and portraiture. In 1941 he commenced a partnership with the photo-engraving firm of

Fanny Durack receiving her gold medal in 1912

Slim Dusty, country music icon

Hartland and Hyde. During World War II Dupain served with the camouflage unit of the Royal Australian Air Force. The studio has run continuously from 1934 to the present, with Olive Cotton operating the studio for Dupain during the war years. In 1947 Max Dupain resumed commercial practice. Influenced by his war experiences, Dupain specialised in architectural and industrial commissions. Clients included designers Gordon Andrews and Douglas Annand and architects Harry Seidler, Douglas Snelling and Samuel Lipson.

Durack, Elizabeth
Elizabeth Durack (1915–2000) was the painter sister of Dame Mary Durack, brought up in *Kings in Grass Castles* country of the Kimberley. She gained recognition in the 1950s and 1960s using Aboriginal techniques in painting, and controversy arose in the 1990s when it was revealed that she had entered competitions under the name Eddie Burrup, posing as an indigenous painter.

Durack, Fanny
Sarah 'Fanny' Durack (1894–1960) won the 100 metres freestyle at the Stockholm Olympics in 1912, becoming Australia's first female gold medallist in the year swimming was included for the first time. She broke the world record in her first heat. To get to Stockholm she had to defeat a rule of the NSW ladies swimming association that women could not swim in front of male spectators! Once this change was achieved Fanny was supported by a fund established by the wife of the old Rushcutter's Bay boxing stadium, Mrs H.D. 'Huge Deal' McIntosh.

Durack, Dame Mary
Mary Durack (1913–94, DBE 1978) was a prolific author of children's books, many illustrated by sister Elizabeth, but is most famous for her family saga *Kings in Grass Castles* (1959) which told the Durack story to 1898, and its sequel *Sons in the Saddle* which took the story into Mary's father's time.

Durack, Terry
Food enthusiast and influential restaurant critic (b. 1949) first in Melbourne then Sydney, and in 2001 based in London, Durack is author of *Hunger* and *Noodle*, and with wife Jill Dupleix, *Allegro Al Dente*.

Bob Dyer in a clinch with rival Jack Davey

Captain Blood, Jack Dyer

Edward Dyson's Golden Shanty

Durex
In Australia a brand of condoms, in America a brand of sticky tape. Not a mistake you want to make.

Dusty, Slim
Australia's King of Country was born David Kirkpatrick at Kempsey in 1927. Changed his name to Slim Dusty at the age of eleven and had his big hit *The Pub with No Beer* in 1957. An enduring legend at the Tamworth (home of the Big Guitar) Country Music Festival.

Dyer, Bob
Bob Dyer (1909–84) was the Eddie Maguire of the 1950s and 1960s, an American vaudevellian stranded in Australia because of the war. He entertained the troops, and stayed, first hosting his quiz show *Pick A Box*

on radio in 1948. The Quiz King transferred to television in 1957 and was even more successful, bringing to life such wisemen as Barry Jones, and continuing in partnership with Dolly Dyer until 1971.

Dyer, Jack
The swashbuckling style of footballer Jack Dyer (b. 1913) earned him the nickname 'Captain Blood', after the Errol Flynn pirate movie. A feared ruckman and one of Richmond's greatest players, he played for 18 years and 312 games, was captain–coach 1941–49 and won two best and fairests. A fearless competitor, Dyer also built an impressive reputation as a language mangler on radio and TV, becoming a folk hero. Dyer is a more Australian candidate for legendary status than the saintly Don Bradman.

Dymock, William
William Dymock (1861–1900) was a Melbourne boy who began working for Sydney bookseller George Robertson in 1878. After a few years he started his own book business which was Dymock's Book Arcade in Pitt Street in 1884, moving to 428 George Street in 1890. Soon after he claimed that with over a million books he had the largest bookshop in the world, a claim disputed by E.W. Cole of Coles Book Arcade in Melbourne. Dymock was Australia's first native-born bookseller.

Dyson Family
Will Dyson (1880–1938) was one of eleven children of George Dyson who, as family tradition has it, was wounded at Eureka, and brought his family up with a healthy disrespect

Will Dyson's World War I illustration, *Outside the Pill Box*; 'Landscapes without colour as of an evil earth in the throes of its dissolution,' he wrote

for governments and authority – attitudes that served Will very well, becoming one of the greatest cartoonists in Australia and England. Will's elder brother Ted (Edward, 1856–1931) was already a prime Australian balladeer and writer by the time Will was 16, publishing *Rhymes From the Mines* (1896), and *Below and On Top* (1898). *The Golden Shanty* was the lead story in the *Bulletin*'s Christmas anthology of 1889. *Fact'ry 'Ands* (1906) was one of a series of novels he wrote concerning the larrikin life around Spat's Fact'ry. He wrote and published a magazine of his own, the *Bull Ant*, later the *Ant*,

1889–92. Ted is an unjustly neglected writer, not alone in his day, outshone by Lawson, Paterson and Dennis. The Dysons were part of the bohemian milieu of Melbourne and associated with the Lindsays to the extent that Will married Ruby Lindsay in 1909. Both were drawing for the *Bulletin*, but after marriage set sail for England where Will made a great name as a savagely radical cartoonist on the London *Daily Herald*, 1912–16. His most famous and tragically prescient wartime cartoon showed Woodrow Wilson, Lloyd George and the Italian President Orlando leaving the Versailles peace treaty looking

very pleased with themselves, while in the background a child labelled '1940 Class' wept. He became an Australian war artist and was wounded twice. He illustrated Ted's book of war poems *Hello, Soldier!* and worked for the *Daily Herald* again 1918–21. Ruby died during the great flu epidemic of 1919 while Will returned to Melbourne in 1925 and drew for the Melbourne *Herald*, then gathering many of the great black and white artists together. Other Dysons included Ambrose (1876–1913), who was also an illustrator for the *Bulletin*. Ross McMullin's 1984 biography of Will is a classic.

125

E

Edna Everage's first record, *Wild Life in Suburbia*

The children of East Timor, in Balibo school room, 2000

Pte Ball 5/7RAR and friends, Balibo 2000

East Timor

Australia's first excursion to East (formerly Portuguese) Timor was in the black days of 1942, when it was occupied by a handful of Australian commandos, 2/2nd Independent Company, together with the remnant of Sparrow Force which had withdrawn in the face of a superior Japanese invasion force to West (then Dutch) Timor. There were about 150 Australians, and they fought a vigorous and imaginative guerilla campaign against the Japanese for most of that year. They could not have survived without the support and sacrifice of the Timorese – each Australian had a mate to help, dubbed a 'creado'. After the Australian withdrawal in December 1942, Damien Parer's film shot earlier in the year was released, giving Australians the good news of a successful Australian operation. East Timor then disappeared back over the horizon until the Indonesian invasion of East (still Portuguese) Timor on 16 October 1975 and the killing by Indonesian special forces soldiers of five Australian journalists: Gary Cunningham, Brian Peters, Malcolm Rennie, Greg Shackleton and Tony Stewart. These murders and the festering outrage in Australia over the subsequent 25 years had much to do with the stone-in-the-shoe issue that Timor became for successive Australian governments. Few believed that governments did not know more about Indonesian intentions in 1975. Subsequent cosying up to the Suharto government, and the Timor Gap treaty dividing Timorese oil and gas between Australia and Indonesia, lent credence to the idea that at the least a blind-eye had been turned in 1975. Australia's lead role in securing East Timor's independence in the aftermath of the militia/military massacres and murders of 1999, following the referendum, was seen as repaying the debt owed the Timorese from 1942. But it also raised the same questions as in 1975, such as who knew what about the violence following the referendum. Most Australians, however, think our intervention on behalf of the East Timorese was a good thing, and that a cooling of relationships with Indonesia is not a bad thing. In hindsight some believe it might have been possible to find a way to deal with then Indonesian President B.J. Habibie, that might not have resulted in such haste and bloodshed.

A fab Easybeats cover

Easybeats

The Easybeats were Harry Vanda and George Young on guitar, Dick Diamonde on bass, Stevie Wright's vocals, and Gordon 'Snowy' Fleet on drums. Originally known as the Starfighters, they changed their name after the arrival of Fleet, who modelled their new style on that of the Liverpool beat groups of the period. They recorded six number one hits in Australia before moving to England where they released the smash hit *Friday on My Mind* (1966). Difficulties in the studio and gradual line-up changes put pressure on the band and in 1969 they split up, ironically just before their song *St. Louis* became a hit in America.

Eccles, Sir John

Rhodes scholar Sir John Eccles (1903–97) was Professor of Physiology at the Australian National University 1952–66 and later Professor of Physiology and Biophysics at the State University of New York, Buffalo,

Dorothy Brunton in an Efftee Production

1968–75. Along with two British scientists, he won the Nobel Prize in Physiology or Medicine in 1963 for 'their discoveries concerning the ionic mechanisms involved in excitation and inhibition in the peripheral and central portions of the nerve cell membrane'.

Sci-fi writer Greg Egan's *Axiomatic*

Efftee Productions

Efftee Productions was the film production company of Frank Thring (1883–1936) which produced its first talkie, *Diggers*, in 1931. It produced some of the hits of George Wallace, including *Harmony Row* and *A Ticket in Tatts*, as well as the 1933 version of *The Sentimental Bloke*. Efftee also became involved in theatre production with the long-running *Collitt's Inn*, *The Vagabond*, and *The Cedar Tree* from 1933 at the Princess Theatre in Melbourne. Efftee Broadcasters was the original licencee of radio station 3XY, in 1936.

Egan, Greg

The biggest thing to ever happen to Australian science-fiction writing, Greg Egan (b. 1961) shot to the top worldwide in the mid 1990s.

Eight Hour Day celebration in Melbourne

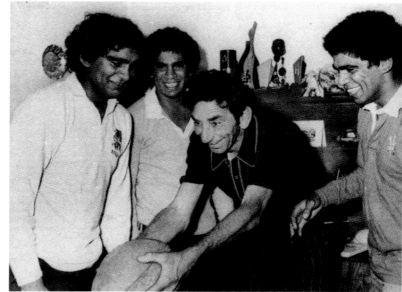
Ella brothers and Dad

Although his first novel was published in 1983, it was not until his second, *Quarantine* (1992), that he really hit his stride. A hard SF writer with a penchant for tackling big issues, he has won four Ditmar Awards, two Aurealis Awards and a John W. Campbell Memorial Award, among others. His short fiction has also been in high demand, featuring heavily in UK mag *Interzone* as well as many anthologies.

Egan, Ted
Ted Egan (b. 1932) has lived most of his life in the Northern Territory, and presently lives in Alice Springs. In his early career with the Department of Aboriginal Affairs he worked mainly in the bush as a patrol officer and reserve Superintendent. Later he was a teacher at bush schools. He was the inspiration behind the formation of St Mary's Australian football club in Darwin, and had a hit with his sung/spoken song *The Drover's Boy*. In the later 1990s he spent a good deal of time trying to raise the money for a feature film based on the song. He was awarded the Order of Australia (AM) in the 1991 Honours List for services to the Aboriginal people, and for an ongoing contribution to the literary heritage of Australia through song and verse. He was a foundation member of the Council for Aboriginal Reconciliation. He has been writing and recording songs since 1969, and has produced 25 albums.

Eight Hour Day
Melbourne stonemasons won the eight hour day as long ago as 1856, and it was the fundamental plank in the foundation of the industrial unions through to the 1890s, and equally important in the early Labor Party. Paradoxically, or perhaps not, a hundred years later has seen the working day increase in time, for largely un-unionised executives and knowledge workers, not to mention working women.

Ella Brothers
Known as 'The Invincibles', Mark, Glen and Gary Ella all played Rugby Union for Australia. Mark led the pack, playing 24 Tests and captaining the side before retiring in 1984 after the magical 1984 Grand Slam tour coached by the controversial Alan Jones. Mark Ella was one of the greatest five eighths ever. His brothers played 4 Tests each. The trio were role models for Aboriginal kids.

Breakfast of champions: young Herb Elliott with Percy Cerutty

Sumner Locke Elliott's 'Pip' reads to his aunt

Bob Ellis at the pulpit

E

Elliott, Herb

One of the best middle-distance runners ever, Herb Elliott (b. 1938) broke the four-minute mile 17 times during his career and was only ever defeated once over 1500m. He was trained from being a talent to an unbeatable running machine by Percy Cerutty. He won gold over 880 yards at the 1958 Commonwealth Games and gold over 1500m in the 1960 Olympic Games. After retiring from athletics he continued to be heavily involved in sport, both as an administrator and as head of Puma, and later as the athletes ambassador at the Sydney Olympics.

Elliott, Sumner Locke

Sumner Locke Elliott (1917–91) was the subject of a tug of war between competing aunts who wanted to

bring him up after his mother died soon after his birth. The question was not finally decided until he was ten years old, and forms the background for the autobiographical novel *Careful, He Might Hear You* (1963). It was made into a superior film by writer Michael Jenkins and director Carl Schultz in 1983. Elliott was a member of the Independent Theatre and his play *Rusty Bugles* was initially banned in 1948 for the salty language of its Digger protagonists, now it is a naturalistic classic. Elliott left for the USA that year, missing the play's success, but creating his own as the writer of a tremendous number of television plays in America. A visit to Australia in 1974 re-evoked the Australia of the 30s and 40s, resulting in such novels and TV series as *Water Under the Bridge* (1977). The ten-part

TV series (1980) was written by Michael Jenkins and Eleanor Witcombe, directed by Igor Auzins.

Ellis, Bob

Bob Ellis (b. 1942) has written for print, film, television and the stage, and has a reputation as fine writer with an enthusiastic appetite for controversy. Perhaps the best example of this is the successful law suit filed by Federal Treasurer Peter Costello for defamation in Ellis' book *Goodbye, Jerusalem*. His films include the award-winning *Fatty Finn* (1980) and his books include *First Abolish the Customer: 202 Arguments Against Economic Rationalism* (1998).

Ellis, Havelock

A pioneering modernist who reacted strongly against the 'proper morals' at

An original Esky (below), and with decor (top)

First extract your rabbit

Ballarat's evocation of the Eureka Stockade

the end of the nineteenth century, Havelock Ellis (1859–1939) wrote case studies of sexual behaviours which combined his own experiences with a naturalist-humanist philosophy. His years in Australia (1875–78) seem to have deeply affected him. His series *Studies in the Psychology of Sex* (1897–1910) made him one of the most controversial figures of his day. Ellis wrote a novel entitled *Kanga Creek* (1922) and had a vigorous correspondence with Australian sex reformer and eccentric Chidley.

Esky

A large, insulated box designed for keeping food and drink chilled, but often used to transport nothing but beer. The first portable Esky appeared in 1950 under the pseudonym 'car box'. Soon afterwards the name Esky

was adopted. Later the steel boxes became plastic boxes and a thousand imitators were produced. With the winecask, the Esky is tribute to Aussie drinkers' inventiveness.

Eureka Flag

On 29 November 1854 the Eureka flag was flown for the first time as a symbol of resistance against goldfield licensing. A white cross on a blue background, there are several theories about its origin. Some say a group of diggers on their way to the stockade looked up and saw the Southern Cross in the sky and gathered material to make it. Others say Canadian digger 'Captain' Ross designed it and commissioned miners' wives to make it. The tattered remains of the original flag is still kept in the Ballarat Fine Art Gallery.

Eureka Patent Rabbit Extractor

One of many curious devices invented in the war against the rabbit plague, the Eureka Patent Rabbit Extractor is a bizarre contraption designed to literally pluck rabbits from their burrows using a long, extendible arm with a claw on the end. Likely to fool the operator before the rabbit, it never saw widespread use.

Eureka Stockade

The pitiful events at Ballarat on the morning of 3 December 1854 have come to stand for the struggle for Australian independence and democracy, and in some eyes have constituted the required physical struggle and loss of life necessary for the satisfactory creation of a national identity. Gallipoli later provided the test of blood, but Eureka stood for the

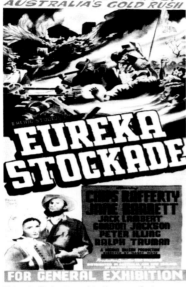

Chips Rafferty starred in the 1949 feature

What remains of the original Eureka Flag

Doc Evatt contemplates politics

American and French revolutions. While Eureka was the bloodiest event in European history on the continent, it was a curiously small and even genteel revolution. About 400 police and soldiers attacked 150 miners at the stockade they had built on the Ballarat goldfield, and five soldiers were killed, with about 30 miners. Some of these were bayoneted to death while lying wounded; 50 or 60 were wounded but escaped. Peter Lalor was one of the latter. The immediate issue was the introduction of the miner's licence which the miners regarded as being taxation before earning income. Plus, the enforcement by the police created ill-feeling in the community of multi-national deep-mine workers at Eureka. The immediate cause of the big demonstration was the killing

of miner James Scobie by the ex-convict publican James Bentley, whose pub, the Eureka Hotel, was a haunt of police. Bentley was found not guilty and the miners burned the pub down. Police started on a vigorous licence hunt on 30 November, and they were stoned by miners. Shots were fired and that night the miners were swearing allegiance to the newly stitched Eureka Flag at the stockade. It was a big demonstration, and many diggers hoped that Governor Hotham would back down and change the system. After the killings of Sunday, initial public support for the government quickly changed to massive approval of the diggers. Demonstrations in Melbourne followed, and when the 13 ringleaders, including Lalor, were tried in 1855, no jury would convict them,

and it didn't. By mid 1855 diggers got the vote, an export duty replaced the hated licence and elected courts were created so miners ran the goldfields themselves. Thus democracy came to Australia. The people showed they had to be taken into account.

Evatt, Herbert 'Doc'

A brilliant scholar and politician, Herbert 'Doc' Evatt (1894–1965) dabbled in state politics before becoming the youngest person appointed to the high court of Australia in 1930, at age 36. Ten years later he resigned the position to return to politics and was crucial in the formation of the UN and in championing Australia's involvement. In 1948 he was named President of the United Nations and, as he had in local politics, continued to fight for

Melbourne Exhibition Building, 1880

Eyre and Wylie

the rights of smaller nations. When new Prime Minister Robert Menzies was elected in 1949 and brought in legislation to outlaw the Communist Party of Australia, Evatt fought it in the High Court and found himself tainted by the accusation that he was 'soft' on communism. A proponent of free speech and civil liberties, Evatt became leader of the Labor Party in 1951 and found it impossible to hold it together after the Petrov business. Evatt, in the end, was perhaps a bit 'mad'.

Everage, Dame Edna
'Discovered' by Barry Humphries in Moonee Ponds, Edna Everage first made an appearance in a show called *Return Fare* at the Union Theatre at the University of Melbourne on 13 December 1955. According to Humphries, Edna arose at the suggestion of playwright Ray Lawler, of *Summer of the Seventeenth Doll* fame, and actor Peter Batey, as an expansion of a Humphries party turn. Edna next appeared in a Phillip Street revue in 1956. Since then she has conquered the world, including Broadway in 2000–01.

Exhibitions, Great
Great Exhibitions were held, importantly, in Sydney (1870, 1873, 1876, 1879) and Melbourne (1880–81, 1888–89). They established the Australian colonies as important places in the nineteenth-century economy, not only as sources of raw materials, but as markets for European manufactured goods, and shop windows for local inventiveness – in art as well as industry.

Eyre, Edward John
An early explorer, Edward John Eyre (1815–1901) migrated to Australia in 1833 and became a squatter in NSW, before overlanding stock to SA. Here he started exploration, leading forays to the Flinders Ranges and Eyre Peninsula in 1839. In 1841 he became the first-known European to cross the Nullarbor Plain, from east to west, in an epic of endurance and travail. His partner Baxter and one Aboriginal guide were killed, but Eyre and the other Aborigine, Wylie, helped by the French who happened to be at Albany, finally made it. He became a colonial administrator in the West Indies, brutally putting down a rebellion in Jamaica. Eyre inspired Patrick White (*Voss*), Francis Webb (*Eyre All Alone*) and Geoffrey Dutton (*The Hero as Murderer*).

F

Fatso shows us his better side

Bert Facey had a fortunate life

Polly Farmer vies with John Nicholls

John Famechon (left) wins in 1969; John Fairfax, right

Facey, Bert

Bert Facey (1894–1982) wrote the remarkable autobiography un-ironically called *A Fortunate Life*. Un-ironic because his 'ordinary' Australian life was filled with nearly a century of hardship, war and turmoil. It was in this way extraordinary. Facey, who taught himself to read and write, told how his father died before he, Bert, was two, how he began work at age eight, served at Gallipoli where his brother was killed, worked on the trams in Perth, was a soldier-settler, was knocked out by the Depression, had three sons join up in World War II, had one killed at the fall of Singapore . . . and came to write his book, which became a best-seller in 1981 – after which he died. Even in the TV series (1986) Facey's life was emblematic and inspirational.

Factor, June

June Factor (b. 1936) has been a student and collector of childhood language and lore, beginning with *Cinderella Dressed in Yella* (with Ian Turner), *Far Out, Brussel Sprout* (1983), *All Right, Vegemite* (1985) and a dictionary of children's language, *Kidspeak* (2000).

Fairfax, John

John Fairfax (1805–77) migrated to Australia after a libel suit forced him into insolvency in England. In 1841 he bought the *Sydney Herald* with Charles Kemp (renamed the *Sydney Morning Herald* in 1842). Fairfax bought out Kemp in 1853 and brought his sons in to management, and an Australian media dynasty was born, one almost lost in the 1980s by his strange descendent Warwick Fairfax.

Famechon, John

Champion featherweight boxer, Johnny entered the ring professionally at sixteen. He went on to win 62 of his 67 fights, including the world championship in 1969. He retired the year after.

Farmer, Graham 'Polly'

Despite a relatively short VFL career, Polly Farmer's impact on Aussie rules football was immense. In 101 games for Geelong from 1962–67 he virtually defined the handball as a weapon in the sport. His 30-metre handballs moved the ball like a rocket and changed forever the way it was used in the game. He had come to the VFL after a successful career in Western Australia where he had won the Sandover medal in 1956 and 1960, but he injured his knee on debut for the

Grant Featherston's Contour Chair

John Farnham, back in the 'Johnny' days

Miss Federation, 1901

Cats. The next year, however, he finished second in the Brownlow and never looked back.

Farnham, John
A pop singer virtually from birth, John Farnham (b. 1949) had the highest-selling Australian single of the 1960s with *Sadie the Cleaning Lady* while he was still a teenager. In 1969 he won the first of five consecutive King of Pop awards. He was briefly lead singer of the Little River Band (1982–85) but it was not until *Whispering Jack* (1986) that his solo career really took off. The album sold over one and a half million copies and remained at number one in the Australian charts for 21 weeks. He continues to record hit records and tour internationally with other entertainers like Anthony Warlow, Jimmy Barnes and Olivia Newton-John.

Farrelly, Midget
Surfer Bernard Farrelly (b. 1944) earned the nickname 'Midget' for his diminutive size and earned the respect of his peers as he became the first non-Hawaiian to win the international surfing championships at Makaha, Hawaii in 1963. He repeated the feat in 1964 by winning the first official World Surfboard-riding Championships at Manly.

Fatso
Fatso was the fat-arsed wombat, the star mascot of the Sydney Olympics. Invented by Roy Slavin and H.G. Nelson on their hit late-night show during the Olympics, Fatso out-rated any of the official Olympic mascots, perhaps because there was only one of him and he was not for sale. Fatso was a gold medallist in the diving.

Featherston, Grant
A designer and innovator, Grant Featherston designed remarkable chairs from the late 1940s on, including the 'Relaxation Series' (1947–50) and his most famous and popular creation, the 'Contour Series' (1951–55). He described the Contour Series as 'a negative of the human body' and produced them by cutting and bending plywood.

Federation
The joining together of the six Australian colonies in 1901 has been described by historian John Hirst as the making of a 'sentimental nation' because Australia was made not

Edward VII Federation Arch, Melbourne

German Citizens' Federation Arch, Sydney

The modern Federation Arch, Melbourne 2001

through war, revolution or economic necessity but because the people wanted it. The politicians and poets wanted it: there was a growing belief that 'for the first time in the world's history, there will be a nation for a continent and a continent for a nation', in the words of first prime minister, Edmund Barton. Henry Parkes, whom Geoffrey Blainey has described as the 'grandfather of Federation' was wont to express the same idea, that Australians had 'one destiny', formed from the 'crimson thread of kinship'. Boosters of the Australian national code of football noted (incorrectly) we had 'one nation, one people, one code of football'. There was a certain amount of popular enthusiasm for Federation; it was the proper course of progress in the colonies where many of the

Edwin Flack, our first gold medallist

Flemington Racecourse hosted the running of the first Melbourne Cup, in 1861

social virtues were being expressed. The franchise, state education, even the voting for Federation conventions: these were all expressions of progress. But there was not a riot of enthusiasm for Federation. 'Inexorability' and 'proper process' were its watchwords. Celebration of the centenary of Federation had at least one virtue, that it was not a load of pomp or the misplaced razzamatazz that there was for the Sydney Bicentenary. The centenary of a constitution put in place by a meeting of wise representatives is, in the Australian way, best celebrated in the breach.

Firsts

Australians love being first, and hate coming third. Bronzed Aussies are not only surf lifesavers, but also the unsatisfactory crop of bronze medallists, say the swimmers in the wake of Kieren Perkins in his pomp. This might be thought of coming from two sources or traditions. One goes back to the First Fleet, which brought the First Europeans and all the other 'improvements' that followed: First Sheep, First Gun. The second is the Gold Rush, where Australians first learned that gold was the route to success. Another notable first for Australia was Henry Sutton, who invented TV in the 1880s.

Flack, Edwin

Winner of Australia's first Olympic gold medal, Edwin Flack (1873–1935) was also our first and only representative at the 1896 Olympics in Athens, Greece. He won the 800 metres and 1500 metres athletics events and received a wreath for his efforts. Legend has it that at the awards ceremony, the Austrian flag was raised and the Austrian anthem played, although this cannot be verified.

Flags, Swim Between The

Not only the lifesaver's lament, but a metaphor for Australia, in the Pacific somewhere between Europe and America, but not quite in Asia. In Japan, swimmers learn to swim outside the flags.

Flemington Racecourse

Opened in 1861, Flemington Racecourse is the oldest official race track in Australia. While the first 'official' race meeting was held in 1838 at Batman Hill, it was transferred two years later to 'Saltwater Flat' on

Matthew Flinders surveys his street and station

Flying Fruit Fly Circus jumps through hoops

the Maribyrnong River, on land owned by farmer Robert Fleming and his wife. The site became known as Fleming Town and later Flemington Racecourse, when it passed into the hands of the government. Dubbed 'Australia's International Racecourse', it is a spacious pear-shaped course with sweeping turns and long straights, and also boasts an integrated 1200-metre straight course, often referred to as 'the Straight Six' (because of the old six-furlong measure). It has hosted the Melbourne Cup since 1861, when Archer won. Over 72 000 spectators saw Phar Lap win the Cup in 1930, while other famous winners include Carbine and Peter Pan.

Flinders, Matthew

In 1795–99 and 1801–03, Matthew Flinders (1774–1814) circumnavigated both Australia and Tasmania, making invaluable charts and maps. He is also said to be the first person to notice and correct compass errors caused by iron ships. He wrote *A Voyage to Terra Australis* (1814). *See: Australia*

Florey, Sir Howard Walter

Sir Howard Florey (1898–1968) studied pathology at Adelaide University before working at Oxford where he was primarily responsible for discovering penicillin, for which he shared the Nobel Prize for Medicine in 1945.

Flying Doctors, The

Beginning as a six-show mini-series, *The Flying Doctors* became an ongoing series, dubbed into four languages and broadcast in fifty countries. The show detailed the tribulations of the flying doctor service in the fictional outback town of Cooper's Crossing. It ran for 221 episodes (1986–90).

Flying Fruit Fly Circus

Australia's youth circus, the Flying Fruit Fly Circus, was set up in 1979 by the Murray River Performing Group as an initiative during the International Year of the Child. It features performers exclusively between the ages of 8 and 19. The group now tours internationally, with many of its graduates going on to feature in other troupes such as Circus Oz.

Flying Trapeze Café

A Fitzroy-based avant garde cabaret show and theatre restaurant, The Flying Trapeze was the spiritual

Flying Trapeze Cafe, a pioneer comedy venue

Errol Flynn (left) and his father (right) study aboard Errol's boat *Zaca*. Marine biologist Carl Hobbs, centre

F

birthplace of comedy in Melbourne. It saw the debut of many Australian comics including Captain Rock and most of the cast of *Australia, You're Standing In It*. Run by John Pinder, it was the predecessor to The Last Laugh Theatre.
See: Quantock, Rod

Flynn, Errol

The swashbuckling Hollywood film star Errol Flynn (1909–59) was born in Hobart. As befitted a bloke who played the pirate Captain Blood and the outlaw Robin Hood, his mother was a descendent of a *Bounty* mutineer – and Errol played Fletcher Christian in Charles Chauvel's *In the Wake of the Bounty* (1933). Chauvel had seen him in a film shot in New Guinea where Flynn was mucking about in boats – his boat was used

and sunk during the Battle of Milne Bay in 1942. Flynn wrote for the *Bulletin* from New Guinea and his autobiography *My Wicked, Wicked Ways* was published shortly after his death. Flynn has gone into the language, as in 'in like Flynn', and in song, *Oh Errol*, by Australian Crawl.

Flynn, John

Founder in 1928 of the world's first flying medical service, the Australian Royal Flying Doctor Service, Reverend John Flynn (1880–1951) had earlier established The Australian Inland Mission. Driving a ute, wearing a suit despite the temperature and smoking a pipe, Flynn became a regular sight for isolated communities. Nicknamed 'Flynn of the Inland' he helped establish fifteen country hospitals and bring medical care to people who

would otherwise need to travel for hours to reach a doctor.
See: Flying Doctors, The

Footy Show, The

In the 1990s when Seven had the exclusive rights to screen AFL football action, Nine began a Thursday night variety show that took advantage of not having any actual football to show. Hosted by the ubiquitous Eddie McGuire, it named the teams for the following round of games and surrounded this with comment and comedy featuring current-day or recently retired players, and love-him-or-hate-him personalities such as John 'Sam' Newman. It rated its head off, especially with the broader reaches of the football market, and Seven never recovered. The game was not the same, whoever was showing it.

For the Term of His Natural Life

Four Corners logo from the 1960s

Some of the Forty Thousand Horsemen

Miles Franklin by Norman Lindsay

Ford

Ford cars have been distributed in Australia since 1925 with the imported Model T, but Australian manufacture really began with the Falcon in 1960. Ford boast that it is the longest surviving 'badge' in Australian motoring, at least Australian from the sketch book to design and manufacture. Since 1960 over 2.5 million Falcons have been sold.

For the Term of His Natural Life

First a novel by Marcus Clarke published in the *Australian Journal* 1870–72 and titled *His Natural Life*, it has since been made into two films (1908 and 1927) and a TV series (1982). It is the story of Rufus Dawes and his transportation to Australia for a crime he did not commit. Much of the book details his experiences at Macquarie Harbour, Port Arthur and Norfolk Island. It is the most important 19th-century Australian novel and is blacker than Dickens would be about convict life.

Forty Thousand Horsemen

Directed by Charles Chauvel and written by Elsa Chauvel, *Forty Thousand Horsemen* (1940) is a seminal early Australian film. It broke box-office records in Australia and was a similar success overseas. Starring Chips Rafferty and Harvey Adams, it tells the story of three members of the Australian Light Horse during the desert campaigns of World War I.

Four Corners

Australia's longest-running current affairs show, *Four Corners* was first aired in 1961 when Michael Charlton interviewed American astronaut Scott Carpenter. It has since won virtually every award Australia has to offer, from Walkleys to Logies along with (among others) a UN Media Peace Prize. The ABC show's list of reporters is a who's who of Australian journalism, including luminaries such as Kerry O'Brien, Marian Wilkinson, Mike Willesee, Ray Martin, Chris Masters and Paul Barry.

Franklin, Miles

Miles Franklin (1879–1954) was a remarkable woman in Australian colonial society. Not only for her list of publications, which included the autobiographical *My Brilliant Career* (1901) and *All That Swagger* (1936), but also for her progressive views on the role of women in society and her

Dawn Fraser shows gold, 1960

Susannah York as Eliza Fraser – shipwrecked!

Furphy Water Tank, an uncommon invention solved a common problem

F

rejection of the idea of a male-dominated society. She also wrote under pseudonyms, the most successful of which was 'Brent of Bin Bin'. Despite the fact that one of Australia's biggest literary prizes is now named in her honour, some twenty of her plays and novels remain unpublished.

Fraser, Dawn

'Our Dawn' (b. 1937) took up swimming when she was eight to help her asthma. She was the first swimmer to take the gold medal in the same event at three consecutive Olympics, winning the 100 metres freestyle in 1956, 1960 and 1964. She also broke 27 world records during her career, and was the first woman to swim under a minute over 100 metres. Controversy caught up with

her in 1964 when she stole a flag from the emperor's palace in Japan for a prank and was banned for a decade, although she still managed that same year to be named Australian of the Year.

Fraser, Eliza

Fraser Island, the largest sand island in the world, near Hervey Bay in Queensland, is named after shipwreck victim Eliza Fraser. When the *Stirling Castle* hit the Great Barrier Reef in 1836, only Eliza Fraser would live to tell the tale. Fraser and the other survivors were captured by the local Aborigines and spent two months in forced labour, during which time a pregnant Fraser gave birth, although the baby later died. Upon her rescue and return to Australia (and then England) she wrote about her ordeal

in the distractingly titled *The Shipwreck of Mrs Fraser, and the loss of the* Stirling Castle, *on a Coral Reef in the South Pacific Ocean*. Tim Burstall's feature film *Eliza Fraser* screened with moderate success in 1976, starring Susannah York as the heroine.

Fraser, Malcolm

Malcolm Fraser (b. 1930) has undergone a remarkable transformation from the man who was assisted by Governor-General Sir John Kerr to become prime minister in 1975 during the Dismissal. Now he and Gough Whitlam are the best of mates, agreeing on more than they disagree, except over 1975. Fraser became a critic of the later Liberal Government of John Howard over such matters as reconciliation and refugee policy. He earned praise as

Cathy Freeman – a national hero

A couple of New Guinea veterans calculate the odds on the 1943 Melbourne Cup

head of CARE Australia during the crisis in Kosovo in 1999 when CARE employees were arrested as 'spies'.

Freeman, Cathy
When Cathy Freeman, clad in virginal silvery-white, rose from the water and lit the flame at the Sydney Olympics opening ceremony, she became something more than a dual world champion or Olympic gold medallist. She was widely seen to have singlehandedly become the symbol, the end-point, of the reconciliation process. This might have been overstating the case, but it was definitely the most powerfully emotional moment for black and white relationships in Australian history. For the first time millions of Australian television viewers had taken an Aboriginal person to their hearts as the symbol of what Australia was (or was to become). There was something transient about this, but it was a more potent moment than Freeman's previous move in Australian symbolism – the donning of Aboriginal and Australian flags after international race victories.

Furphy
A furphy in Australian slang is a rumour or false report and the term is believed to have originated during World War I. Diggers would congregate to gossip around the water-carts which were known as 'furphies'. Ironically, the pen name of Joseph Furphy, 'Tom Collins', had been used to mean the same thing – and Joseph Furphy's older brother, John Furphy, invented the water-cart, furphies ever since.

Furphy, Joseph
Generally ignored during his lifetime, Joseph Furphy's (1843–1912) only published novel was *Such Is Life: Being Certain Extracts From the Diary of Tom Collins* (1903) under the pseudonym Tom Collins. He wrote two more novels, *The Buln-Buln and the Brolga* and *Rigby's Romance*, but due to the poor sales of his first book, neither was published until after his death. His career was 'rediscovered' in the 1940s however and has been the subject of continual praise and scrutiny ever since.

Fuzzy Wuzzy Angels
A term of affection, which is also patronising, for the World War II carriers in Papua New Guinea more or less press-ganged into carrying supplies along the Kokoda Track.

G

Mad Max and the Feral Child, from *Mad Max II*

Gallipoli, the film

Gallipoli, looking towards the Sphinx and the Nek, Canterbury Cemetery below

Gallipoli

Directed by Peter Weir and written by Weir and David Williamson, *Gallipoli* (1981) served to reinforce an already potent chapter of Australian cultural myth. Following two Australian sprinters after they are sent to fight the Turkish army at Gallipoli and starring Mel Gibson, it is a stand-out Australian film. The international tagline went: 'From a place you've never heard of, comes a story you'll never forget.'

Gallipoli

Gallipoli is perhaps the only battlefield where both the winning and (one of) the losing nations have situated their national stories. For Australia the 8587 dead and 19 367 wounded were the first casualties of the newly federated Australia. It was the first time Australians had fought together as Australians, rather than colonials in the British Army, as they had in the Boer War of the 1890s. While Gallipoli was also a terrible campaign for other nationalities, such as the British and French, their casualties were subsumed in the even bigger slaughter of the Western Front. And while Australians also died there, Gallipoli was our first battle. For the Turks it was also a first, when Mustafa Kemal, later Ataturk, the Turkish commander at Anzac Cove, rallied his troops to defeat the attacking Anzacs on the hill Chunuk Bair, ordering them not to defend but to die. In this battle Ataturk's Turkish republic was formed. He said in 1934 when the Gallipoli peninsula was declared a national park, 'Those heroes that have shed their blood and lost their lives ... you are now lying in the soil of a friendly country. Therefore rest in peace. There is no difference between the Johnnies and the Mehmets to us where they lie side by side here in this country of ours ... having lost their lives on this land they have become our sons as well.'

Garner, Helen

Controversially dismissed from her first job as a secondary school teacher for answering students' questions about sexual matters, Helen Garner (b. 1942) then turned to journalism and fiction. She is the author of *Monkey Grip* (1977) which won the National Book Council Award, and the bestseller *The First Stone* (1995), a work of non-fiction about sex and power on campus at Ormond College in Melbourne.

G

Andrew takes it to the hoop under the gaze of father Lindsay

George Giffen in his whites

Gaze, Lindsay & Andrew

Lindsay Gaze and his son Andrew have been the heart and soul of Australian basketball since Lindsay first played for Australia at the Rome Olympics in 1960. He also played in 1964 and 1968, and coached the Australian team in 1972, 1976, 1980 and 1984, when Andrew first played for the Boomers aged 19. Andrew has played in every Olympic tournament since, and carried the Australian flag at the Sydney Olympic Opening Ceremony.

Ghan, The

The central Australian train that runs between Adelaide, Port Pirie and Alice Springs, named for the Afghan camel drivers who worked the inland, opened in 1929. The slow narrow-gauge *Ghan* was replaced by a standard-gauge track in 1980.

Gibson, Mel

Australia's premier acting export, Mel Gibson (b. 1956) shot to stardom in *Mad Max* (1979) and has since become one of the hottest properties in Hollywood. He learnt the trade at NIDA in NSW where he shared a room with Geoffrey Rush and worked with Judy Davis, among others. The star of all four *Lethal Weapon* movies as well as other huge hits such as *Braveheart* (1995) and *The Patriot* (2000), he is the definition of a 'bankable' star. Voted numerous times into *People* magazine's 'world's 50 most beautiful people'.

Giffen, George

George Giffen (1859–1927) was a leading colonial cricketer, an all-rounder playing 31 Tests for Australia between 1881 and 1896, best with the

bat 161, and with the ball 7/117. Appropriately his classic account of contemporaries and predecessors was entitled *With Bat and Ball* (1898).

Gilbert and Sullivan

The comic operas of Gilbert and Sullivan have been hugely popular in Australia for over a hundred years, mostly due to the efforts of theatre baron J.C. Williamson. He was so impressed by *H.M.S. Pinafore* in America in 1878 he decided to tour the production in Australia and New Zealand. Written by William Schwenck Gilbert (1836–1911) and Arthur Seymour Sullivan (1842–1900) the production was a huge hit in 1879 and their works have been in production in Australia ever since, with only momentary lapses.
See: Williamson, J.C.

Max Gillies out of character

The Ginger Meggs billycart derby, from the 1982 feature film starring Paul Daniel

Gillies, Max

Actor, comic and impersonator Max Gillies (b. 1941) first came to notice at the Pram Factory in the early 1970s, especially in Barry Oakley's *The Feet of Daniel Mannix*, as a character called 'Santa', and in Jack Hibberd's *A Stretch of the Imagination*. He achieved a wider public with impersonations on the satirical *Gillies Report* and *Gillies Republic* on ABC TV 1983–86. In 2001 he was back at his wicked best with a stage show called *Your Dreaming*.

Gilmore, Dame Mary

From 1908 to 1931, poet Dame Mary Gilmore (1865–1962) edited the Women's Page of the Sydney *Worker* and filled its pages with campaigns for the welfare of the sick and helpless and constant attacks on privilege and corruption.

Giltinan, James

Professional Rugby League was founded in 1907 as a revolt by Rugby Union players over out-of-pocket expenses for injured players. They used to get together for grumbling sessions at Test cricket legend Victor Trumper's sports store. Leading light among the revolutionaries was J.J. Giltinan, who organised a professional series against a New Zealand team in that year.

Ginger Meggs

Jim Bancks' comic character Ginger Meggs first appeared in 1921 in the *Sydney Sun*, and was taken up almost immediately around Australia as the quintessential charming larrikin Australian boy. He had to battle the dark side of childhood, the loutish Tiger Kelly and had his moments with

Mum and Dad. Ginge's girl was Minnie Peters, a good girl, who wouldn't let him get away with anything. Ginger Meggs represents that innocent inner-suburban Australia of backyards and adventure that perhaps never existed but surely should have.

Goanna Oil

A universal healing compound, 'the Australian bush remedy' for everything from eczema, sores, nasal catarrh, lumbago, sciatica to dandruff, piles and contracted sinews. Made in Bulimba, Queensland, not from boiled goannas as some children used to think, for a hundred years.

Gold

Gold got Australia going in the 1850s, drawing adventurers, diggers and

Marjorie Jackson, Golden Girl

Evonne Goolagong bends for a volley

Adam Lindsay Gordon, poet

G

their necessary trading supporters first to NSW after the Ophir find in 1851, and dubbed a second California. The 1848 California rush had shown that there was money to be made by individuals. James Edmonds found paydirt at Clunes in Victoria in 1851, and other strikes were made at Ballarat and Mount Alexander (Bendigo). By year's end half the men of Melbourne were at the diggings. Over 342 000 people came hoping to strike it rich.

Golden Girls

Betty Cuthbert, Marjorie Jackson and Shirley Strickland were the great gold-medal winning girls of the 1950s. Unsurprisingly, women have won, proportionately, more medals than men at the Olympics.
See: Bronzed Aussies

Good News Week

Based on the British TV show *Have I Got News For You*, hosted by Paul McDermott and featuring Mikey Robbins, Julie McCrossin and a rotating cast, *Good News Week* is yet another ABC ratings success to jump ship – this time to Channel 10. Half pretend gameshow, half stand-up comedy, in *Good News Week* the points are rigged, there are no prizes and the funniest answer is always the right one. Originally aired for a few episodes in 1996, in 1997 the ABC brought the show back in and saw its ratings soar, then lost the show to Channel 10 for two seasons in 1999.
See: Doug Anthony Allstars

Goolagong, Evonne

The second Australian woman and first Aboriginal woman to win the

Wimbledon singles final, in 1971, Evonne Goolagong was named Australian of the Year that same year. Amazingly, she retired to have her first child, then came back and won Wimbledon again in 1980.

Gordon, Adam Lindsay

Banished in 1853 by his parents in Bengal to South Australia, Adam Lindsay Gordon (1833–70) immediately joined the mounted police. Already notorious for his 'escapades', he resigned two years later and used the money from his parents' estate to buy property and support his poetry. His two best-known works are *Sea Spray and Smoke Drift* (1867) and *Bush Ballads and Galloping Rhymes* (1870). The day after the latter's publication, Gordon committed suicide.

John Gorton, surprise prime minister in 1968

Percy Grainger at the piano

Shane Gould, Olympic heroine

Gorton, John

Prime minister from 1968–71, the political career of John Gorton (b. 1911) was filled with intrigue. He achieved the top job by default when Harold Holt disappeared in the surf off Cheviot Beach, and he was later deposed by Billy McMahon in a party-room coup in 1971.

Gould, Nat

Writing sometimes under the pseudonym 'Verax' but generally under his own name, Nat Gould (1857–1919) wrote over a hundred novels generally revolving around crime and horse racing in Australia. He was the most popular 'pulp' writer of his day. His non-fiction work *On and Off The Turf* is an illuminating look at Australian racing in the 1890s. Novels include *Jockey Jack* (1892).

Gould, Shane

Auspiciously, Shane Gould (b. 1956) was born the same year that the Olympics came to Melbourne and in 1972 she dominated the Munich Games aged only 15. In fact, from 1972–73, she was untouchable in the pool and in one eight-month period she held every women's freestyle world record from 100 to 1500 metres

Grainger, Percy

Concert pianist and ratbag Percy Grainger (1882–1961) was famous not only for his music, but also for his peculiar beliefs and attitudes. His belief in the superiority of the Nordic race saw him invent his own language which expunged all ethnic words. Hugely successful overseas, he tried to express an unique 'Australianness' in his music, which he

thought was based around an 'Australian democratic principle' – a belief which saw him refuse every award, honour and doctorate offered him. His habit of walking long distances between concert engagements saw him arrested at least three times on suspicion of being vagrant.

Grand Prix

From 1985–95 the final race of the Formula One season took place in Adelaide until it was 'stolen' by Melbourne in 1996 and became the first race of the carnival. The move was one of the Kennett government's 'great' sporting initiatives, but divided the community when the residential inner suburb of Albert Park and its peaceful lake was chosen to host the race, now a fixture in Melbourne.

St Luke's Church by Francis Greenway

Walter Burley Griffin's Capitol Theatre

Granny Smith Apple

Granny Smith (1801–70) accidentally invented the world's most popular sweet yet tart green apple in 1868 when she noticed that some Tasmanian apple cores thrown in the backyard had turned into something new. The Granny Smith was propagated by her sons.

Great Ocean Road

Built as a 1930s Depression make-work project, and winding from Torquay to Portland near the SA border, the Great Ocean Road is now the centre of surf culture manufacturing and SeaChangers.

Greenway, Francis

Born into a family of stonemasons and builders it was no surprise when Francis Greenway (1777–1837) became an architect. However disaster struck in 1812 when he was found guilty of forgery and was transported to Australia for 14 years. His qualifications earned him an early ticket of leave and he set up an architectural practice in Sydney. Governor Macquarie appointed him Sydney's first civil architect in 1816 and his first project was building the lighthouse at South Head. This success led to a free pardon in 1819 and more work – the new Government House, Hyde Park Barracks, the Female Factory at Parramatta and the Conservatorium of Music. Greenway was sacked by Macquarie in 1822 allegedly after trying to charge exorbitant fees; he turned to private practice but could not find much work. He died at his property in the Hunter.

Greer, Germaine

Expatriate intellectual, author and feminist, Germaine Greer (b. 1939) is best known for her book *The Female Eunuch* (1970). Both lauded and attacked, Greer advocated sexual freedom, renounced marriage, and adopted a unique combination of intelligent, progressive and somewhat eccentric ideas. *Life* magazine called her 'a saucy feminist that even men like'. *The Whole Woman* was published in 1999, and created a controversy over female circumcision, of which Greer appeared to approve.

Griffin, Sam

Australia's best-known poster model, Sam Griffin was supposedly a regular at McVeigh's Upper Yarra Hotel in the Yarra Valley in the 1890s. A passing

Australia's most popular poster model

Rachel Griffiths on stage in *A Doll's House*

Clarrie Grimmett sends one down

artist dropped in for a drink at the pub and saw Sam as he stopped for his regular drink. A quick sketch was later sold to Carlton Brewery as a full-sized poster, accompanied by Sam's famous phrase – 'I allus has wan at eleven'. This was soon parodied as 'I allus have eleven at wan' but the poster remains one of the most reproduced in Australia.

Griffin, Walter Burley
In 1914 Walter Burley Griffin (1876–1937) moved from America to Australia after winning the international competition to design our new capital city, Canberra. Collaborating with his wife, Marion Mahony Griffin, until 1935, he introduced the ideas of his previous collaborators, such as Frank Lloyd Wright, to Australia. His surviving

work includes several incinerators, a couple of suburbs, Melbourne University's Newman College, and the stunning Capitol Theatre ceiling. He died in India.

Griffiths, Rachel
Rachel Griffiths (b. 1968) won an Australian Film Critics Award and an AFI Award, both for best supporting actress, in *Muriel's Wedding* (1994). Her individual style is probably the result of not being trained at any Australian acting school. Her career peaked in her Academy Award nomination for *Hilary and Jackie* (1998). She also paraded topless through the city of Melbourne wearing a crown of thorns to protest against Crown Casino. Asked why she replied: 'If I didn't flash my tits, you wouldn't put me in the paper.'

Griffiths' Tea
Griffiths Brothers began selling tea in the 1890s in Melbourne, and their Signal brand was famous among train travellers into the 1960s, when old signs could still be seen beside the tracks indicating that it was, say, 80 miles to the next station, and Griffiths Brothers Tea. These days, such signs indicate the next occurrence of those inescapable fast food outlets.

Grimmett, Clarrie
Clarence Victor Grimmett (1891–1980) became one of Australia's greatest ever leg-spinners, but it wasn't an easy journey. The Victorian selectors gave him only five matches in six seasons, prompting Grimmett to accept an offer to play for Adelaide in 1924. A prodigious wicket taker, he was the first Australian to take ten

Reg Grundy's first national quiz show, *Concentration*, with Philip Brady

Norman Gunston was a winner

G

wickets in a match on debut, in the fifth Test against England in 1924–25. He took only 17 Tests to snare 100 wickets and in 1935–36 became the first bowler to take 200. Grimmett's chief quirk, aside from taking wickets, was wearing his cap while doing it.

Grollo Brothers

Controversial property developers Bruno and Rino Grollo built Melbourne's tallest building, the Rialto, in the 1980s, and in the 1990s further astounded the country with a bid to build the world's tallest building in Melbourne's re-developing Docklands area. Regarded as a folly shaped like a phallus, it was only in the new millennium that the great erection turned flaccid. While waiting they began building the world's tallest apartment tower.

Grundy, Reg

Reg Grundy (b. 1923) is an Australian TV quiz show, soapy, serial and television producer who made a packet with *Wheel of Fortune* and pioneered the international sale (and later production of foreign replicas) of Australian serials such as *Neighbours*. Grundy worked as a sports commentator and for a time salesman with Sydney radio station 2CH. He hosted a radio quiz show in 1957 which he subsequently took to television TCN 9 in Sydney in 1959. Reg Grundy Enterprises became the leading producer of game shows in Australian television, expanding into production of drama serials, from 1973, including *The Young Doctors*, *The Restless Years*, *Prisoner* and *Neighbours*. Grundy relocated to Bermuda in 1982 and sold the

television company to Pearson Television, United Kingdom, in 1995. The name is also immortalised in rhyming slang for underwear – grundies: Reg Grundys=undies.

Gulgong

An old gold-mining town in NSW conserved by the National Trust, and preserved – with nearby Hill End, NSW – by the photographs commissioned by Bernard Holtermann. Henry Lawson set some stories in Gulgong, and some of the buildings were pictured on the original $10 note.

Gunston, Norman

'The Little Aussie Bleeder' was a character first created for actor Garry McDonald on the ABC. Norman Gunston appeared in his own show in 24 programs for the ABC 1975–77, and

Alex Gurney's classic characters Bluey and Curley in a strip titled *Down Under*

eight shows for Seven 1978–79. Gunston was an edgy mock *Tonight* show host, lusting after Logies and personalities, dressed in a lurid sparkling blue jacket and with bits of tissue on shaving wounds. He became a legend through fronting innocent real personalities at press conferences and elsewhere, the joke being the slow realisation that Gunston was not really real.

Gurney, Alex

English-born Alex Gurney (1902–55) was brought to Tasmania as a toddler by his widowed mother, and worked for the Hydro until he was 20 while studying at Hobart Tech. He sent cartoons to various publications, and worked in Melbourne and Sydney in the 1920s, creating the cartoon strips *Stiffy & Mo* and *The Daggs*. In 1933 he drew Ben Bowyang for C.J. Dennis' column in the Melbourne *Herald*. He created his most famous strip, about the larrikin soldiers Bluey and Curley, in 1939. The strip moved to the *Sun*

Hal Gye

News Pictorial in 1940, and was a much-loved institution through war and peace until Gurney's sudden death in 1955. Bluey and Curley lived, drawn by others, until 1975.

Gye, Hal

During his life Hal Gye (1888–1967) pursued three distinct artistic careers. He was the illustrator on the original edition of C.J. Dennis' *The Songs of a Sentimental Bloke* as well as an illustrator for the *Bulletin*. Under the name 'James Hackston' he wrote the 'Father' series of short stories for the

Bruce Gyngell, the first image on TV

Bulletin from 1936 and published two collections, *Father Clears Out* (1966) and *The Hole in the Bedroom Floor* (1969). Finally, as the poet 'Hacko', he wrote verses which appeared on the Aboriginalities page of the *Bulletin* in the 1940s and 1950s.

Gyngell, Bruce

Bruce Gyngell (1929–2000) made media history in 1956 with the first words on Australian TV: 'Good evening ladies and gentlemen, welcome to television'. He was a big man in the local and UK TV business.

H

Bert Hinkler and his aircraft, an Avro Baby

Bushranger Ben Hall

Ken Hall during filming

Deborah Halpern's *Angel*

Hall, Ben

Ben Hall (1837–65) was a bushranger in the Kelly tradition, forced into a life and death of crime by forces beyond his control. A stockman, he was arrested and acquitted of armed robbery in 1862, but then rearrested and again released for the Eugowra gold escort job. When he returned to his run, it had been burned and his animals killed. This caused Ben to take up the bushranging life, specialising in holding up coaches on the Sydney–Melbourne road near Goulburn. For the next two years his gang was successful, but killed two policemen. Hall was betrayed, ambushed and killed in 1865.

Hall, Ken G.

Ken Hall (1901–94) was a pioneer filmmaker and won a documentary

Academy Award for *Kokoda Frontline* (1942) filmed by Damien Parer. He began his career as a cadet reporter on the *Evening News*, and in 1917 joined the film industry as an assistant in the publicity department of Union Theatres. He visited Hollywood in 1925 when he worked for First National Pictures' Sydney Office. He had his first taste of production when he reconstructed the German feature film *Exploits of the Emden* in 1928. In 1929 he supervised the publicity campaign for the opening of the State Theatre in Sydney. He established Cinesound Studios in 1932, and went on to produce and direct 17 commercially successful feature films, including *On Our Selection* (1932) and *Dad and Dave Come to Town* (1938). His last feature was *Smithy* (1946). He established one

of Australia's long-running sound newsreels, *Cinesound Review*, which ran from 1930 until 1956. He managed Australia's first television station (TCN9) from 1956 until 1965 and made it a market leader. Hall was a man of extraordinary energy and versatility, and he has left a legacy of feature films that have helped shape the Australian identity.

Halpern, Deborah

Deborah Halpern (b. 1957) is an Australian sculptor with an international reputation. Her most visible work in Melbourne is the *Angel* bicentennial commission (1987–89) which towers above the moat outside the National Gallery of Victoria. Her sculpture *Ophelia* was chosen in 1996 to be the new 'face' of Melbourne.

Neil Harvey, bareheaded as usual

Lawrence Hargrave's flying machine

Hardy, Frank

Author Frank Hardy (1917–94) left school at thirteen to work a variety of menial jobs, from fruit picking to road construction work. After a stint in the army and some time as a journalist, he collected material on John Wren, which would become the basis for his first and most famous novel, *Power Without Glory* (1950). He was sued but acquitted of criminal libel. A long-term member of the Communist Party, his agitation and writing on behalf of Vincent Lingiari and the striking stockmen at Wave Hill over land rights was perhaps his finest non-fictional moment.

Hargrave, Lawrence

Australia's pioneer aviation inventor and theoretician, Lawrence Hargrave (1850–1915) created a body of knowledge about manned flight which was used by later aviators. His experiments with model aeroplanes in the 1880s were not followed up, but his lightweight radial rotary internal combustion engine was the beginning of the dominant aircraft engine until the 1920s. And his work on box kites gave the wing-form for the earliest aircraft. He did not patent any of his inventions, believing that they should be for the benefit of all. He flew briefly in a box kite, but not with an engine.

Harris, Rolf

Notorious oddball Rolf Harris (b. 1930) grew up in Perth but thankfully now lives in England where his wobbleboard can threaten Australian children no longer. As an entertainer he had hits with the remarkably twee and tuneless songs *Tie Me Kangaroo Down Sport* and *Two Little Boys*.

Harvey, Neil

Neil Harvey (b. 1928) was the stylish young left-hander on the 1948 Invincibles tour. He ran five to bring up his first Test century, at 19 years and 121 days (then the youngest player to do so) against India in 1947–48. He was aggressive but graceful, and had the champion's average of 48.41 from 79 Tests. He captained Australia in a single Test in 1961, for a win. *The Times* said of him, 'He will be remembered always as a player who never grew old.'

Hawkes, The

Bob Hawke (b. 1929) Rhodes Scholar, modernising ACTU President 1970–80, and populist Prime Minister 1983–91

Ivor Hele sketching during WWII

Streeton painting in the bush near Heidelberg

was, in his time, the ultimate larrikin – but a teetotal, consensual larrikin. Large numbers of Australians loved him, or seemed to. He lost some of his gloss after leaving office, and Hazel. Hazel Hawke (b. 1929) has retained a dignified presence as a low-key mother of the nation. Son Steve (b. 1959) wrote a terrific biography (1994) of pioneer Aboriginal footballer Polly Farmer.

Heidelberg School

Heidelberg was the bushy outer suburb of Melbourne where a group of painters and mates used to paint in the 1880s. Charles Conder, Frederick McCubbin, Tom Roberts and Arthur Streeton were the leaders of the first distinctive 'school' of painters. Their controversial exhibition of small impressions of Melbourne and

Melburnians in 1889 was called *Exhibition of 9 x 5 Impressions*, and was so named because most of the paintings were done on cigar box lids which measured 9 inches by 5 inches (20.7 cm x 11.5 cm).

Hele, Ivor

Ivor Hele (1912–93) was the first official war artist appointed in World War II; when serving as a private he was commissioned in the field by General Blamey. He served in such diverse theatres as North Africa, New Guinea and Korea. Not only was he Australia's longest-serving official war artist, Hele won five Archibald Prizes. His paintings and drawings in the Australian War Memorial, especially those from New Guinea around Kokoda, Lae, Salamaua and Shaggy Ridge, are extraordinarily powerful.

Helfgott, David

Eccentric West Australian pianist David Helfgott (b. 1947) came to popular attention after the movie *Shine* (1996). At twelve Helfgott was the youngest player ever to enter the ABC WA state Instrumental and Vocal competitions, which he went on to win six times, and at 19 was assessed in London as a 'near-genius' talent. However, after a performance of Liszt's *Piano Concerto in E Flat Major* at the Royal Albert Hall in front of 8000 people, he suffered a serious nervous breakdown. On his return to Perth in 1973, he was admitted to hospital and ten years of psychiatric and drug treatments. Asked to fill in for a sick pianist at Riccardo's restaurant in 1983, his performance launched his career again – and the huge success of the film based on his

Herald 1920s delivery truck outside the newspaper's old Flinders St building

Joy Hester (left) with Sunday Reed

life only cemented his position as one of the most successful and celebrated classical musicians of modern times.

Helpmann, Robert
Ballet dancer, choreographer, director and actor Sir Robert Helpmann (1909–86) worked in virtually every dramatic art conceivable. He toured Australia with Anna Pavlova's company in 1926 before joining J.C. Williamson's troupe. A devotee of Shakespeare, he adapted several works for the ballet as well as performing in various productions as an actor. In 1965 he became co-artistic director of the Australian Ballet, a position he held until 1976.

Henley-on-Todd
In 1962 a rowing and sailing regatta was launched in Alice Springs – 930 miles from any significant body of water. To parody the annual rowing regatta at Henley-on-Thames, they named it Henley-on-Todd. Watching seemingly sane people race in bottomless vessels through the deep coarse sand of the Todd River provides a unique spectacle amongst world sporting events. The multi-event program attracts participants who often finish up on world TV news paddling canoes with sand shovels and in 'land lubber' events like filling empty 44 gallon drums with sand.

Herald, The
An early Melbourne newspaper was the *Port Phillip Herald*, first published in 1840. It became the *Morning Herald* in 1849, and then the evening *Herald* in 1869. A broadsheet that appealed to a wide cross-section of Melburnians (and journalists) for over a hundred years, it was only occasionally challenged, and never successfully, as the evening paper, with late news and the day's sporting results. It took television and a decline in the public transport market nearly 40 years later to kill it off. The *Herald* merged with its morning stablemate the *Sun* in 1992, to form the morning tabloid the *Herald Sun* – spawning the nickname 'The Hun'.

Hester, Joy
Artist Joy Hester (1920–60) decided early in her career to draw and not paint. She tried to catch fleeting expressions and was heavily influenced by the forms of expressionism adopted by friends such as Sidney Nolan and Albert

Dorothy Hewett in repose

Daryl & Ossie in a Logie moment

Roy Higgins in his racing gear

Tucker (to whom she was married for several years). Her work has an intensity of emotion and a sense of anguish that sets her apart.

Hewett, Dorothy

Poet and dramatist Dorothy Hewett (b. 1923) was heavily involved with the Australian Communist Party from the 1940s through to 1968, and it is reflected in much of her early work. Her first poetry collection *What About the People!* (1961, with Merv Lilley) was followed by four more, although she has become better known for her drama and autobiographies. *The Chapel Perilous* (1972) is her most produced play.

Hey Hey It's Saturday

Running from 1971 to 1999 on Channel 9, *Hey Hey It's Saturday*

began life as a Saturday morning kids' show but soon graduated to an early evening adults variety show. Presented for the entire run by Daryl Somers, his long-running sidekick was a talking ostrich puppet 'Ossie Ostrich' who lived from 1971–94 with the help of puppeteer Ernie Carroll. Other cast members included Molly Meldrum and his music segment, Red Symons, Russell Gilbert, Dicky Knee (voiced by John Blackman), Wilbur Wilde, Denise Drysdale , Jacqui McDonald and Plucka Duck. Popular segments included 'Red Faces', which allowed amateur performers from all over the country to humiliate themselves for money, and the almost gameshow Pluck-a-Duck. Virtually every celebrity to set foot in Australia was also on the show, if only for a few minutes.

Hibberd, Jack

Jack Hibberd (b. 1940) wrote the meditative 'monodrama' *A Stretch of the Imagination* which, when performed by Peter Cummins in 1972, instantly achieved the status of a classic. His popular wedding reception play *Dimboola* (1969) was for many years the most-produced work in Australia. Hibberd's ear for our language and eye for the essence of Australia make his best work the best we have. He is an acerbic critic of the state of the theatre, culture and football in Australia.

Higgins, Henry Bournes

Victorian and Federal member of Parliament, H.B. Higgins (1851–1929) was Attorney General in the shortlived Watson Labor Government in 1904, the same year he was

Lance Hill with his hoist

Hoges before Dundee went big

Holt and step-daughters, swimming

H

President of the Carlton Football Club. Higgins was appointed to the High Court in 1906, and was President of the Conciliation and Arbitration Court, 1907–20. From this bench he handed down the Harvester Judgement in 1907, establishing the principle of the basic wage – then seven shillings a day.

Higgins, Roy

The Professor, Roy Higgins (b. 1938) was Australia's top jockey of the 1960s and 1970s, and won two Melbourne Cups – on Light Fingers in 1965 and Red Handed in 1967.

Hill, Clem

An attacking number three batsman, Clem Hill (1877–1945) was cursed with appalling luck. He once scored 99, 98 and 97 in consecutive innings against

England (1901–02) and was the first person to score 500 runs in a Test series without notching up a century. One of the 1911 'standouts'.

Hill's Hoist

The popular myth is that the Hill's Hoist was created by Lance Hill in 1945 in his backyard, and that he set up a business soon after. While Mr Hill made a fortune selling his hoists, there is some argument concerning the design's origin. A rotary clothes line was patented in America in 1890, but the all-metal hoist with its crown-and-pinion winding mechanism had been designed, manufactured and widely advertised in Australia in the early 1920s by Gilbert Toyne. 'Toyne's All-Metal Rotary Clothes Hoist' was a success before Hill's first was ever built, but

legend has attributed the design to Lance Hill and the resultant success of his design enshrined it.

Hinkler, Bert

Record-breaking aviator of the 1920s, Bert Hinkler (1892–1933) set an England–Australia record in 1928 when he made the first solo flight in 15 days 2 hours 15 minutes in an Avro Avian. Ross and Keith Smith's first-ever flight took 27 days 20 hours in a Vickers Vimy in 1919. Hinkler died in an attempt to break the England–Australia record in 1933 when his Puss Moth crashed in the Italian Alps. He is buried in Florence.

Hogan, Paul

The face of Australia to most Americans in the 1980s, Paul Hogan's (b. 1940) bronzed and weather-beaten

Australia's own car, the Holden

Ben Chifley watches the first Holden

The original *Homicide* team

face threw more shrimps on the barbie in the name of Australian tourism than any other. As the star of one of this country's highest-grossing film franchises, *Crocodile Dundee* (1986, 1988, 2001), he both laughed at and helped cement the image of Australians as bushmen and larrikins. Originally a rigger on the Sydney Harbour Bridge, he was discovered on *New Faces* before appearing regularly on *A Current Affair* (1971), then his own series of the *Paul Hogan Show* (1977–81), but since the second Dundee flick he has basically disappeared, and several attempts to revive his film career have been less than successful. Strewth!

Holden

On 29 November 1948 Prime Minister Ben Chifley officially launched Australia's own car, the Holden 48-215, the country's first locally produced vehicle. During the following 50 years Holden has acquired a significant national status as a symbol of Australia. The company grew out of the saddlery company established in Adelaide by James Alexander Holden.

Holt, Harold

22nd prime minister of Australia, Harold Holt (1908–67) was elected under US President Lyndon B. Johnson's slogan 'All the Way with LBJ'. On 17 December 1967 he disappeared in the surf at Cheviot Beach near his home on the Mornington Peninsula in Victoria and was never seen again. A massive search was mounted but his body was never recovered and theories abound on his eventual fate. Was he eaten by a shark? Did aliens abduct him? Did the FBI assassinate him? Or did he just drown, a scenario which seems likely, considering he had had to be helped from the surf only seven months earlier while snorkelling.

Home and Away

Since 1988 *Home and Away* has had the unenviable position of going up against the grand-daddy of Australian soaps, *Neighbours*. Surprisingly, the show has garnered its own group of hardcore fans and despite occasional flirtations with a breed of peculiar product-placement advertising within the show, has seen much success. Created by Alan Bateman, the show revolves around the Fletcher family, their many foster children and their caravan park.

A.D. Hope, concerned

Tempe Hoysted outside the family home, about 1908

H

Homicide

Arguably the most important and influential TV series ever made in Australia, produced by Crawfords for twelve years between 1964 and 1975. Incredibly, it generally rated in the forties and low fifties (by comparison, today's best-rating shows often only manage to hit 20–30) and most importantly, it kick-started continuous Australian TV production which had previously been sporadic. Hector Crawford was so adamant the project would succeed (despite almost universal opposition) he funded the project himself. Starring Terry McDermott as Det. Sgt Frank Bronson, John Fegan as Inspector Connolly and Lex Mitchell as Det. Rex Fraser, it took a year to sell the pilot. When HSV-7 finally picked it up it took 107 episodes for Crawfords to

recoup their losses, but they persevered for three reasons: to show that Australians were capable of producing a quality drama series, to answer criticism of local actors and writers, and to show that Australians will watch, and would prefer to watch, programs produced by Australians for Australians. A spiritual successor to the radio serial *D24*, it continued that series' involvement with police who vetted script, lent props and occasionally 'extras'.

Hook, Jeff

Geoff 'Jeff' Hook (b. 1928) began his career as a cartoonist on the Hobart *Mercury* and became a full-time cartoonist on the *Sun News Pictorial* in Melbourne in 1964, infesting every image with his trademark fish hook. He semiretired in 1993.

Hope, A.D.

One of Australia's finest poets, Alec Derwent Hope (1907–2000) was recognised internationally for the rich, authoritative and mythic qualities of his poetry, and won major prizes in Europe, America and Australia. He published eleven volumes of poetry during his life including *The Wandering Islands* (1955), *A Late Picking* (1975) and *The Tragical History of Dr Faustus* (1982). He also published three selected works, one collected works, several volumes of criticism and a play.

Horne, Donald

Donald Horne (b. 1921) was an editor 1954–76, working on magazines like *Weekend* (1954–61), the *Bulletin* (1961–62, 67–72) and *Newsweek International* (1973–76), as well as

Billy Hughes, the Diggers' friend

Hughes auditions for Charlie Chaplin by Low

writing many articles and books of social and political criticism. His books include *The Lucky Country* (1964), an account of the Whitlam dismissal *The Death of the Lucky Country* (1976) and a striking and critically acclaimed autobiography.

Howard, John
John Howard's (b. 1939) Prime Ministership (1996–) has been highlighted in his view by the introduction of a new tax, books included, but also by, in his first term, the guns buy-back, and in the second by the successful support of East Timorese independence.

Howard, John
Actor, most famous for his 'sorry' speech delivered on John Clarke's Olympic Games send-up, *The Games*,

in 2000. Many regarded it as a speech the other John Howard should have made. Played Bob Jelly in *SeaChange*.

Howard, Ken
Racecaller famous for such expressions as 'London to a brick on'.

Hoysted Family
Since Frederick Hoysted's arrival in 1859, over 25 descendants of his family have been involved in horse training and over 15 members have been professional or amateur riders. Racecallers, bookmakers, clerks of the course, saddlers, farriers and course secretaries have all been 'Hoysted'.

Hudson, Peter
One of the best full-forwards of all time, Peter Hudson (b. 1946) averaged 5.59 goals per game – the best

average the VFL/AFL has ever seen, including a huge 150 goals in the 1971 season. A tragic knee injury in 1972 almost finished his career, but he returned in 1977 and kicked 110 goals that year. His ability to read the game was legendary throughout his 129 games for Hawthorn, where he won the best and fairest in 1968 and 1970. Proof of his status could be found outside a church in his team's home suburb. The sign read: 'What would you do if Jesus Christ came to Hawthorn?' The graffito reply: 'Move Hudson to half-forward'.

Hughes, Billy
His tour of the Western Front in 1916 earned Billy Hughes (1862–1952) the nickname 'the Little Digger', and his fifty-one years in politics earned him a reputation as a divisive figure, a

163

Robert Hughes' eagle eye

Humphrey B. Bear salutes his fans

Barry Humphries enjoys a cuppa

H

loveable larrikin and the quintessential little Aussie battler, who thumped hard to get Australia a place at the Versailles peace conference in 1919. Labor prime minister in 1915, he divided Australia over the conscription issue. He was a strong supporter of White Australia and Imperial duty. Popular with the AIF, it was ironic that the Diggers mostly wanted to retain an all-volunteer army. Hughes was forced out of the Labor Party, surviving as a nationalist prime minister at the 1917 elections. His posturing at Versailles after the war made him the butt of jokes back home, and a book, *The Billy Book*, by Low. He was re-elected in 1922, but was replaced by S.M. Bruce as PM. In Parliament until 1952, a wicked-tongued old larrikin – and quintessential Labor rat.

Hughes, Robert

An enfant terrible of Australian culture and art critic for *Time* magazine in America since 1970, Robert Hughes (b. 1938) is the only art critic to win America's most coveted art critic award, the Frank Jewett Mather Award, twice, in 1982 and 1985. Author of the controversial history of Australia *The Fatal Shore* (1987), which was a best-seller. He is also the writer and presenter of various TV series on art, including *The Shock of the New* and *American Visions*. Most recently, he found himself in court after a serious car accident, while making a TV series about Australia. The series, completed after the prang, was not well received by local literati, and Hughes's comments during subsequent courtcases lost him many admirers.

Humphrey B. Bear

Mute, seven feet tall and covered in fur, Humphrey B. Bear has been amusing Australian children since 1965 and his TV show on Channel 9 has never been off-air. He first spoke to his fans via the internet in 2000, furiously typing away despite the obvious difficulties.

Humphries, Barry

The man 'inside' such creations as Dame Edna Everage and Bazza McKenzie, Barry Humphries (b. 1934) is one of the world's most successful comic performers. Humphries established himself in the 1960s with a series of one-man shows in Australia, and translated that success overseas in the 1970s. Since then his savage portraits of Australian stereotypes, and his parodies of our

Michael Hutchence in full cry

Hutton's advertisement

A handful of Bazza's: Barry Humphries as Dame Edna and Barry Crocker as Barry McKenzie

social structures, have found large audiences in Britain and Australia, and in 2000 even in America. Humphries is a passionate conservationist and Melburnian, and remains much loved in his home town. As a 'serious' writer his autobiography *More Please* is as evocative of a different young suburban life as *My Brother Jack*.

Hunters & Collectors

Formed in 1981, Hunters & Collectors comprised Mark Seymour (vocals), Doug Falconer (drums), John Archer (bass), Geoff Crosby (keyboards), Greg Perano (percussion) and Martin Lubran (guitar). Although their work possessed a unique, gritty and Australian sound from the beginning, it was not until *Human Frailty* (1986) that they found commercial success.

Hurley, Frank

Frank Hurley (1885–1962) was photographer on Douglas Mawson's Antarctic expedition of 1911–13, and Ernest Shackleton's heroic Trans Antarctic Expedition 1914–16, and was an Australian official war photographer 1917–18. He accompanied Ross and Keith Smith on the first flight between England and Australia in 1919, then 'settling down', photographing in New Guinea, Antarctica again and at Ken Hall's Cinesound 1932–36, before filming with the AIF in the Middle East in World War II.

Hutchence, Michael

Frontman for 1980s rock sensation INXS, Michael Hutchence (1960–97) had a stage presence which led to comparisons with Mick Jagger and

Jim Morrison. His work with INXS was his main focus, but his private life often received more press than his music in the 1990s, and his high-profile relationships with pop singer Kylie Minogue and supermodel Helena Christensen filled many a tabloid. He had a child in 1996 in a relationship with Sir Bob Geldof's soon to be ex-wife Paula Yates, but depression and creative difficulties had set in. He hanged himself in a Sydney hotel room in 1997, causing surprising grief and unsurprising speculation around the world. Yates died in 2000.

Hutton's

The 'Don't Argue Hutton's is the Best' was derived from comedian Mel B. Spurr's handbill, 'Don't Argue Go and See Mel B. Spurr' in 1904. Spurr died in Melbourne.

He sat on his chair and thought "I'm sitting on an icon; the chair, in its functional simplicity, is truly a great icon."

He sipped his tea and thought "A cup of tea is a great icon also"

He looked out the window and thought, "What a wonderful icon is the common domestic window"

And out there, through the window, the world was full of icons. "The world is one big icon" he thought.

And then he thought, "I used to be ironic and laconic but now I'm...... ...I'm ICONIC!

"◎#✳!!", he said to himself; and no sooner had the word left his lips than he realised what a great icon it was — this amazing word.

Leunig

Leunig on Icons

Ion Idriess, popular author

The original INXS line-up; Sir Isaac Isaacs, first Australian-born Governor-General, right

Idriess, Ion
Better known as Jack Idriess 'in the bush', Ion Llewellyn Idriess was the author of 52 books over the period from 1927 to 1969 at an average of one new title every ten months. He travelled extensively around Australia, including the Torres Strait Islands, and his writing drew on his own experiences as a prospector, traveller and 'bushman'.

Imbruglia, Natalie
Cementing an Australian tradition of soap opera stars turned pop stars, Natalia Imbruglia (b. 1975) seems unusual in that unlike almost all the rest, she might actually stick it out for a second album. Her first, *Left of the Middle* (1997), was surprising not only for its catchy singles, but also for the fact that she wrote it.

Inglis, Ken
Historian and academic Ken Inglis (b. 1929) was Vice-Chancellor and Professor of History at the University of Papua New Guinea and has been involved in teaching and research everywhere from ANU to Brown, Harvard, Cork, Hawaii, Cambridge and Rutgers universities and is the author of nine books, including the award-winning *Sacred Places: War Memorials in the Australian Landscape*.

In-Vitro Fertilisation (IVF)
Dr Alan Trounsen and Dr Linda Mohr developed a technique which allowed the world's first frozen embryo baby to be born in 1984. This Melbourne team, including Professors Carl Wood and John Leeton, racked up other firsts, including the first IVF twins in 1981 and first triplets in 1983. In 1991 a team led by Wood developed a technique for freezing mature eggs for use at a later date.

INXS
INXS was Garry Beers, Andrew Farriss, Jon Farriss, Tim Farriss, Michael Hutchence and Kirk Pengilly. Formed in 1980, their early albums were fad chasers, imitating British New Wave acts such as XTC. *Shabooh Shoobah* (1982) was their first internationally released album, but it was not until *Listen Like Thieves* (1985) and *Kick* (1987) that they became a truly international act.

Isaacs, Sir Isaac
Sir Isaac Isaacs (1855–1948) was a Victorian and Federal politician and was the first Australian-born Governor-General, from 1931 to 1936.

J

Marjorie Jackson, the Lithgow Flash, won gold in the 100 and 200 metres at the 1952 Helsinki Olympic Games

Daryl Jackson's perspective of the Great Southern Stand, MCG, 1990. The perhaps doomed Members' Stand is on the far side. And right, a Jason ad

Jackeroo (Jilleroo)

Originally a term for a young man, usually direct from England, who was working as a station hand (and sometimes paying for the privilege) prior to taking over his own station. Another word for it, although it lacks the same ring, was 'colonial experiencer'. The term is still used and is now accompanied by 'jilleroo', a word appearing in World War II when women worked as station hands to replace the men away at war.

Jackson, Daryl

One of Australia's most influential architects over the last thirty years, Daryl Jackson (b. 1937) set up his architectural practice with Evan Walker in 1965. Best known for the popular and effective Great Southern Stand at the MCG, and hopefully for the completion of its circle, announced by the MCC in 2001.

James, Clive

Another 1950s expatriate, Clive James (b. 1939) is a poet, author and critic with an acerbic wit and a deadpan delivery which has made him a huge hit in both Australia and his new home, England. Best known for his three volumes of unreliable memoirs, his ten years as TV critic for the *Observer* (later collected in three books) and his regular TV series, James has proven himself an intelligent and often hilarious social commentator.

Jason Reclina-Rocker

Based on the American La-Z-Boy, the Jason Reclina-Rocker became the beau ideal of Australian living-room comfort from 1961 when it was first manufactured. Rich houses had one for mum as well.

Jedda

The last film made by Charles Chauvel before his death in 1959, *Jedda* (1955) starred Robert Tudawali and Ngarla Kunoth, who were the first Aboriginal actors to share top billing in a movie.

Jennings, Paul

Funny, smart and without a trace of condescension, it isn't too hard to see why Paul Jennings (b. 1943) has become one of Australia's best and most successful children's authors. Don't agree? Jennings is the highest-selling author in the country, having sold 2.35 million books across his first nineteen titles in Australia alone.

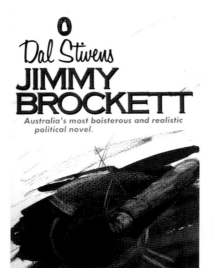

Dal Stivens' legendary *Jimmy Brockett*

George Johnston (right) yarning in a Sydney pub, 1964

From the publication of his first book, *Unreal!* (1985), Jennings was a bestseller and has gone on to write or co-write 29 more, gathering dozens of awards along the way. Jennings' books are generally collections of quirky short stories, packed with surreal twists and snappy dialogue. The successful TV series *Round the Twist* was also based on his books.

Jimmy Brockett

Dal Stivens' (1911–97) 1951 novel has some of the same concerns as Frank Hardy's *Power Without Glory* but is set in Sydney. Stivens' character Jimmy Brockett makes a bitter fortune from boxing, newspapers and racehorses – and the book is more entertaining and carries less baggage than Hardy's. It's more Keith Murdoch than John Wren.

Jindyworobak Movement

Rex Ingamells named the society of Australian poets he founded in Adelaide in 1938, and which continued until the mid-1940s, after a term in the glossary of James Devaney's *The Vanished Tribes* (1929). He claimed it meant 'to annex, to join', which was perhaps a misinterpretation, but as a title for a patriotic literary group devoted to promoting Australian poets it seems entirely suitable. The Jindyworobaks tried to free themselves from all alien (non-Australian) influences and believed that Aboriginal culture showed the ideals of art – the practice of associating everything to nature.

Johnston, George

George Johnston's (1912–70) novel *My*

Brother Jack (1964) is for many Australians (of a certain, baby-boomerish age) a favourite novel, a window on Australia between the wars. It is a detailed evocation of growing up in Melbourne in the after-light of Gallipoli, of being a working-class boy at the high-toned newspaper the *Argus*, and of the war in New Guinea. In many ways it is an exploration of Johnston's own life and memory, growing up in Melbourne, becoming a successful journalist and Australia's first appointed war correspondent who, disillusioned with war and journalism, takes a sabbatical on a Greek island that lasted ten years (the Greek idyll was the background to the novel *Clean Straw for Nothing*). A wartime affair with Charmian Clift scandalised the *Argus* after the war, and they had to

George Johnston in the Middle East in WWII

Publicity for the the inventor of talkback radio in Australia, Barry Jones

move to Sydney, then London and the Greek island of Hydra (1954–64). Johnston developed tuberculosis in 1959, and after moving back to Australia in 1964 enjoyed the success of *My Brother Jack*, and working on *Clean Straw*. The final book in the trilogy *A Cartload of Clay* was nearly finished when he died. Charmian Clift committed suicide in 1969. Their son Martin (1947–90) was a fine poet and translator who also died too young.

Jolley, Elizabeth

Acclaimed as one of Australia's best writers, Elizabeth Jolley (b. 1923) began life as a nurse during World War II before moving to Australia in 1959. Upon arrival Jolley had numerous jobs before taking on a part-time tutoring job at the Fremantle Arts Centre, where she remained until 1985. She wrote for twenty years before her first novel was published, although her short stories had begun appearing in journals in the mid-1960s. Her first collection, *Five Acre Virgin* (1976), started a stream of praise and critical attention, which has garnered her three *Age* Book of the Year Awards, a Miles Franklin Award for *The Well* (1987) and a Booker nomination. Thematically, her deviation from the historical/biographical style of earlier female writers and her confident presentation of women and the world they inhabit has ensured her a unique place in Australian literature.

Jones, Barry

Barry Jones (b. 1932), leading Australian brain, entered parliament in 1977 after working as a school teacher, pioneering the first Australian two-way public affairs radio program and becoming Australian Quiz Champion (1960–68) on Bob Dyer's *Pick-A-Box*. During his parliamentary career, Jones was Minister for Science from 1983 to 1990 and chaired the OECD Meeting of Science Ministers in Paris in 1987. He was a popular co-chair with Ian Sinclair of the 1999 Constitutional Convention. He was ALP National President 1992–2000. Jones' books include the farsighted techno-vision of *Sleepers, Wake!*

Jones, David

David Jones (1793–1873) set up shop in George Street, Sydney in 1838, at the place where the emporium bearing his name still trades. He retired from management in 1856.

K

Ned Kelly

Kakadu traditional owner Big Bill Neidjie

Nonda Katsalidis' Republic Tower

Kakadu National Park

Kakadu is listed on the World Heritage Register for its extraordinary natural and cultural values. Indigenous people have occupied the area continuously for at least 50 000 years, and believe that they were placed in this land at the time of the first people by creation figures such as the Rainbow Serpent – regarded as being still active today. These creation figures gave the people laws and a way of living that are still followed. They also provided the rich heritage of indigenous art and archaeological sites found throughout the park. Kakadu National Park covers an area of almost 20 000 square kilometres in the tropics of northern Australia. Kakadu was proclaimed a National Park in three stages from 1979 to 1991. Since 1979, it has been managed cooperatively by the traditional (indigenous) owners and Parks Australia (Australian Government). Since 1987 there has been joint management, with traditional owners having a majority on the Board of Management. From its inception, Kakadu National Park has been designed to protect its universal cultural and natural values while allowing for the potential development of pre-existing mineral leases in exempted areas at Ranger, Jabiluka and Koongarra. The Ranger uranium deposits were discovered in 1969, and the mine commenced production in 1980. All developments on Aboriginal land, both in the park and on exempted lease areas, require the permission of traditional owners and their agreement on sacred site protection. This permission for Jabiluka was given in 1982 and re-confirmed in 1991. After a three-year environment impact assessment process, the Jabiluka project is now subject to more than 70 stringent conditions that protect associated cultural and natural values. Many people still find this situation paradoxical, to say the least.

Katsalidis, Nonda

Nonda Katsalidis (b. 1951) was one of the architects who changed the face of Melbourne through the 1990s. He professes to be just a commercial architect, but his projects (including the Eureka Tower, Republic and the Ian Potter Gallery at the University of Melbourne) have added new angles, sculptural forms and planes to the formerly blade- and shard-riddled architectural scene.

173

Paul Keating plays Placido Domingo to Bob Hawke's thin Pavarotti, by John Spooner, 1999

Another Aussie star, Annette Kellerman in 1905

Keating, Paul

Paul Keating (b. 1944) was Prime Minister of Australia from the end of 1991 to 1996. Along the way he dealt with aspects of the big picture he had for Australia. He was briefly a minister in the dying days of the Whitlam government in 1975, having been elected to Federal parliament in 1969. As Treasurer (1983–91) he floated the dollar and opened up the economy to global competition, and began the sale of government-owned assets. He famously said the recession of the early 1990s was one 'we had to have'. Keating was enthusiastic about Asia, the High Court decisions in the Mabo and Wik cases and the arts – as well as antique clocks. He won the 1993 election against the odds, for the True Believers.

Kelly, Edward 'Ned'

One of Australia's core legends, the story of Ned Kelly (1855–80) and his family details the last stand of the famous bushranging gangs. The son of an Irish ex-convict, Ned was involved in various petty crimes prior to 1878, but he was also persecuted by police. In 1878 Constable Fitzpatrick went to the Kelly home to arrest Dan Kelly for horse theft, and although the exact events are unknown, he claimed that Ned shot him – despite Ned almost certainly not being there at the time. Dan and Ned went into hiding, but their mother Ellen Kelly was sentenced to three years hard labour for her part in the attempted murder. The Kelly response was swift – they surprised a police camp at Stringybark Creek, killing three officers. Immediately outlawed, the

gang still avoided capture for almost two years, until June 1880 when a local schoolmaster warned the train crew of plans to derail a special police train. In the shootout the rest of the gang, including Dan Kelly, was killed and only Ned in his home-built metal armour was taken alive. Sentenced to death and hanged on 11 November 1880, some record his last words as 'Such is Life'. There are many reasons for his subsequent popularity in Australian myth: he was a brilliant bushman, loyal to his mates, brave to the last and although he was something of a larrikin, he was 'driven' to his crimes by the incompetence and corruption of the authorities. Sid Nolan's Ned Kelly is an essential Australian image – Kelly with the black letterbox helmet, sometimes with the eyes looking out

174

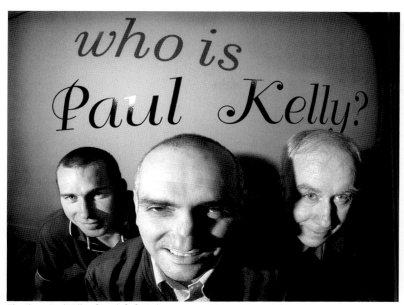

The three Paul Kellys: from left, footy hero; songwriting genius; weighty writer

A stern Henry Kendall

at us, in accusation, perhaps; sometimes with an empty space in the letterbox slit, as if we are looking at Australia through the mind of Kelly. As well as the historians Ian Jones and John Molony, the Kelly story has attracted the poet / playwright Douglas Stewart (*Ned Kelly*, 1942), novelists Robert Drewe (*Our Sunshine*, 1991) and Peter Carey (*True History of the Kelly Gang*, 2000). Carey had nurtured a love of Kelly's own Jerilderie Letter, which is written in a Joycean–Dickensian rapture of justification, and a romantic desire for a Republic of North East Victoria. Kelly's skull reappeared and his armour was reassembled in 2000.

Kellys, The Three Paul
No name is more distinguished in Australian life and letters than Paul Kelly. The name Paul Kelly resounds in all fields of cultural endeavour – publishing, sport and music. In order of seniority, Paul Kelly (b. 1947) has been a leading political journalist and commentator, first for the *Australian* in the tumultuous Whitlam Years in 1974–75, then at the *National Times* 1976–80, the *Sydney Morning Herald* 1981–84, and since 1988 at the *Australian* again, with stints as Editor in Chief, and latterly at his favourite trade, writing, as International Editor. Books include *The Dismissal* (1983) *The Hawke Ascendency* (1984) and *The End of Certainty* (1992). The musician and songwriter Paul Kelly (b. 1955) is the only one in Australia who has had his *Lyrics* (1993) published. One of the world's best urban angst writers, his bands include Paul Kelly and the Dots, Coloured Girls and Messengers. Paul

Kelly, footballer (b. 1969) is the courageous heart and soul of the Sydney Swans Australian football team, who won the Brownlow Medal in 1995. Along with Tony Lockett, Paul Kelly ensured the survival of the Swans in the 1990s.

Kendall, Henry
Throughout a life troubled by alcoholism, Henry Kendall (1839–82) still managed to become one of Australia's most respected early poets, publishing *Poems and Songs* (1862) and *Leaves from Australian Forests* (1869). His sympathetic portraits of Australian outback types are seen as a precursor to other poets such as Lawson and Paterson. The most substantial poet of the colonial period, he has since drifted into relative obscurity.

K

Gra Gra, the early 60s sex symbol

A startled young Tom Keneally

Sir Sidney Kidman on his estate

Keneally, Thomas

A passionate republican, Tom Keneally (b. 1935) was made famous by Steven Spielberg's movie adaption of his book *Schindler's Ark* (1982) which had won the Booker Prize that year. His first taste of success was winning the Miles Franklin for his book *Bring Larks and Heroes* (1967). The Irish Australian history *The Great Shame* (1998) was a successful return to non-fiction storytelling.

Kennedy, Graham

Graham Kennedy (b. 1934) became the King of Television when his show *In Melbourne Tonight* was the top-rating tonight/variety show on Australian TV in the late 1950s and 1960s. Kennedy, a four-time Gold Logie winner, was the cheeky and sometimes blue (he was once in hot

water for an expletive-like imitation of a crow) host, sending up live commercials with his sidekick Bert Newton. Gra Gra was so popular they even watched him in Sydney when his slot was known as the *Graham Kennedy Show* in the 1970s. He had a new lease of life on the quiz comedy show *Blankety Blanks*, where he tested the censors once again. Perennially disillusioned with TV, Kennedy has had a career as a film actor (who better to play a character like himself?) in such Australian works as *Don's Party*, *The Odd Angry Shot* and *Travelling North*.

Kidman, Nicole

Before her marriage breakup in 2001, Nicole was authentic Hollywood royalty. Nicole Kidman (b. 1967) was not only 'Mrs Tom Cruise' but a

talented actress with huge box office appeal and a price tag to match. She started out in films like *BMX Bandits* (1983), before graduating to top-notch performances in films such as *Dead Calm* (1989) and *To Die For* (1995). Her latest film, *Moulin Rouge*, was the most expensive Australian film ever, costing over $50 million.

Kidman, Sir Sidney

Known throughout Australia as the 'Cattle King', Sir Sidney Kidman (1857–1935) owned a vast pastoral empire of more than a hundred properties. The world's largest cattle station, Anna Creek in SA covering some 30 000 square kilometres, is still owned by his descendants. To celebrate his 75th birthday, his employees held a rodeo in Adelaide with an attendance list of around 50 000 people.

A not so busy and not so seedy Kings Cross in 1931

Crossing Eora Creek on the Kokoda Track

Kings Cross

'The Cross' is a bohemian icon in Sydney, with a reputation for exciting nightlife, restaurants and dance spots. The 'sin centre' of Sydney, it has also garnered a reputation for its strip joints and brothels, and its drug culture. This somehow works most of the time, providing a brilliant cross-cultural extravaganza most nights and weekends.

Kingswood Country

Spun out of a recurring sketch in *The Naked Vicar Show* specials, *Kingswood Country* was launched in 1979 starring Ted Bullpitt (Ross Higgins). The show was conceived by Gary Reilly and became a huge success, playing off the 'traditional' Aussie bloke and his love of beer, sport and his Holden Kingswood.

Kngwarreye, Emily Kame

Emerging in the 1990s as one of Australia's leading painters, Emily Kame Kngwarreye (1910–96) was only introduced to acrylic on canvas when she was 78. Growing up in the Northern Territory in crippling poverty, she worked from 1977 with other artists on batik which was exhibited internationally. Her painting style was bold and individual, combining traditional dot painting methods with her own custom brushes and techniques. A prodigious talent, in the last eight years of her life she produced over 3000 works on a variety of media.

Kocan, Peter

Peter Kocan (b. 1947) was sentenced to life imprisonment and restricted to a mental hospital for trying to assassinate Labor Party leader Arthur Calwell in 1966. While serving ten years he proved himself an intelligent poet and novelist, winning the NSW Premier's Award for *The Cure* (1982).

Koch, Christopher

Christopher Koch (b. 1932) has won the Miles Franklin Award on two occasions: in 1985 for *The Doubleman* and in 1996 for *Highways to a War*. His novel *The Year of Living Dangerously* was *Age* Book of the Year and was filmed by Peter Weir (1983).

Kokoda Track

Epic defensive battle fought by young Australians July–November 1942. They stopped the Japanese advance outside Port Moresby before fighting back up the Track, and finally defeating them at Buna and Gona in December.

L

The Australian Lighthorsemen, first into Damascus, 1918

La Mama poets, 1969

George Lambert at work

John Landy (right) on the track, 1954

La Mama

Opened on 30 July 1969, La Mama aimed to help foster Australian theatrical talent in a climate where the performance of Australian productions was almost non-existent. Inspired by and named after a similar off-off-Broadway venue in New York, La Mama was launched by Betty and Tim Burstall. The first play performed there was Jack Hibberd's *Three Old Friends*.

La Trobe, Charles Joseph

Notorious for his decision to make money on the backs of goldfield prospectors via a monthly licence fee during his term as lieutenant-governor of Victoria (1851–54), Charles Joseph La Trobe (1801–75) began his career in Australia as superintendant of the Port Phillip District in 1839.

Victoria's third university is named in his honour, and he departed these shores in 1854.

Labor/Labour

Labor is the Party since 1891, Labour is the movement, since the 1840s. The spelling is a convenient point of difference, or equally a note of fraternity, depending on the circumstances.

Lambert, George Washington

A cartoonist and illustrator of poems for the *Bulletin* from 1895, George Washington Lambert (1873–1930) travelled to England in 1900 on a scholarship where he worked as a portrait painter. He won the 1899 Wynne Prize for his painting *Across the Black Soil Plains*. He later became an AIF war artist, 1917–20.

Lamington

Small squares of plain sponge cake, dipped in melted chocolate and sugar and coated in desiccated coconut. Said to have been named after Baron Lamington, a popular governor of Queensland from 1895 to 1901.

Landy, John

Gentleman John Landy (b. 1930) is best remembered as the man who stopped during the 1956 National Mile Championship after Ron Clarke tripped, helped him up, and went on to win the race anyway – a remarkable display of speed and sportsmanship which has cemented his place in Australian folklore. He has since been involved with many notable distance runners, coaching Robert de Castella and Steve Moneghetti. He became Governor of Victoria in 2001.

Fred Lane clambering out of the water

Utopian William Lane

Jack Lang on the Sydney Harbour Bridge

Lane, Don
At the end of 1964, American Don Lane was hired to fill a six-week gap as presenter on a 'tonight' show on Channel TCN-9. The six weeks turned into seven years and Lane became an Australian TV staple. He could tell a joke, he could sing and his easy demeanour won him fans. He returned to America in 1972 but was lured back to Australia to perform at the Sydney Opera House in a benefit for Cyclone Tracy victims. Some club work followed, and when Graham Kennedy resigned from GTV-9, Lane agreed to fill in for a few weeks – and ended up staying permanently.

Lane, Fred
Freddie Lane (1880–1969) won two gold medals for Australia at the 1900 Paris Olympics, where he was the sole Australian representative. One was in the 200 metres freestyle and the other in the 200 metres obstacle race, held in the River Seine, and which involved swimming over and under rowing boats. Lane's participation meant that Australia is one of just three nations to have competed at every Olympic Games.

Lane, William
William Lane (1861–1917) was originally a charismatic utopian socialist and writer who led the New Australia colony in 1893 and then the Cosme colony in 1894, both in Paraguay. He left Cosme in 1899 and became a conservative journalist in New Zealand. His novel *The Workingman's Paradise: An Australian Labour Novel* was an explication of his early views, published in 1892.

Lang, Jack
Jack Lang (1876–1975) was twice Labor premier of NSW, 1925–27 and 1930–32. His second term ended when NSW Governor Sir Philip Game sacked him as a result of his economic plan, the Lang Plan, to deal with the Great Depression. The conservative Federal Government elected at the end of 1931 wanted to confiscate NSW revenues, and Lang did his best to avoid this but was dismissed. Lang was an incorrigible controversialist inside and out of the Labor Party, and was expelled in 1946. But by 1971 when he was re-admitted, he had become something of a hero to many, including the young Paul Keating. He died on 27 September 1975, aged 99, and before he would have drawn some grim satisfaction from the Whitlam Dismissal on 11 November.

An early poster for The Last Laugh

Harry Lasseter MIA

A familiar shot of Rod Laver in action

Larrikins
Ratbag gangs of young men (and women – larrikinesses) who wore ostentatious clothing, often tight pants and hats, and who picked on the respectable in Melbourne and Sydney in the 1890s and early 1900s. Given to causing trouble when organised in gangs or 'pushes', they inhabited public places, and were the predecessors of youth phenomena such as the bodgies and widgies of the 1950s, mods, jazzers and rockers of the 1960s and goths and skateboarders of the 1990s.

Lasseter's Reef
A mythical, or maybe not, cave or reef of gold somewhere south-west of Alice Springs, found by Harry Lasseter (1880–1931) some time between 1897 and 1911, or so he said. Lasseter died trying to find it again during a large expedition in 1931. The King Solomon's Mine of Australia.

Last Laugh, The
According to ABC TV, 'New York has the Met, London has Covent Garden, Sydney has the Opera House and Melbourne has The Last Laugh.' In 1976 the old Forrester's Lodge was turned into the first large-scale comedy venue in Australia, masterminded by John Pinder and Roger Evans, graduating from the Flying Trapeze Cafe. The opening show was a combo of the Razzle Dazzle Revue and the Busby Berkeleys, other acts included Circus Oz, Los Trios Ringbarkus, and the Doug Anthony Allstars. Upstairs at Le Joke, many standup comics pioneered their work. The venue closed in 1989.

Laver, Rod
Tennis star Rod Laver (b. 1938) is considered by many to be the greatest tennis player ever to lift a racquet. He is the only man to have won the Grand Slam twice (1962, 1969) amidst his 20 total Grand Slam titles, and he was the first tennis player to have earned a million dollars in prize money, passing the mark in 1971. He was also a member of the undefeated Davis Cup side of 1959–62. His career is also unique in that it straddled the switch from amateur to professional tennis, with Laver himself turning pro following his first Grand Slam in 1962, a move that saw him unable to play in the major tournaments, which were still strictly amateur. He won the US Pro five times and the London Pro four times, proving himself the best player alive.

Two Burstalls at work filming D.H. Lawrence's *Kangaroo*

A sketch of Henry Lawson

Lawler, Ray

Ray Lawler (b. 1921) left school at thirteen to work in a foundry, where he spent ten years before an interest in theatre saw him join the Nation Theatre Company in Melbourne. In 1955 his play *Summer of the Seventeenth Doll* shared first prize in the newly formed Elizabethan Theatre Trust's search for its first staging of an original Australian play. The play changed the face of modern Australian drama with its natural language, and inspired a new generation of dramatic realism.

Lawrence, D.H. (Kangaroo)

English novelist D.H. Lawrence (1885–1930) visited Australia with wife Frieda in 1922, first to Perth, where he collaborated with Mollie Skinner on the novel *The Boy in the Bush* (1924).

Lawrence then travelled to Sydney and rented the house Wyewurk at Thirroul on the NSW coast, where he wrote the novel (Lawrence described it as a 'thought-adventure') *Kangaroo* (1923) before departing for the United States in August. It seems he had some contact with the local Fascists, prefigurations of Eric Campbell's New Guard of the 1930s.

Laws, John

The Golden Tonsils, Sydney's lucratively rewarded radio host, became enmeshed in the 'cash for comments' affair of 2000. Laws turned out to be a paid spruiker for various companies and organisations, with the result that it was difficult to tell what was advertisement and what was editorial comment. Laws' defence was that he was a mere

entertainer, not a journalist, and anyway everyone knew. This event soured the cosy relationship Laws had with politicians of both sides of the fence, who loved to appear on his influential show in order to reach 'ordinary' Australians. The Australian Broadcasting Authority inquiry did little to dent his popularity.

Lawson, Henry

Bush balladeer and short story writer Henry Lawson (1867–1922) occupies an enviable position in Australian letters. Although some claim his work to be a collection of artless yarns, his insightful portrayals of bush life have entertained readers since their publication over one hundred years ago. His first short stories were published in the *Bulletin* (1887–88), and his first collection in 1894,

The influential Louisa Lawson

Percy Leason (in porthole) bids farewell to Australia

followed by his best prose collection *When the Billy Boils* (1896) and the verse collection *In the Days When the World Was Wide* (1896). The final twenty years of his life saw Lawson in and out of prison for drunkenness and arrears of maintenance, and also periods in mental or 'convalescent' hospitals. However, when he died, he became the first Australian writer to be given a State funeral.

Lawson, Louisa
Henry Lawson's mother, Louisa Lawson (1848–1920) was a prominent figure in early Australian feminism and publishing. In 1887 she took over the radical monthly magazine the *Republican* and founded the *Dawn*, Australia's first feminist journal, the following year. She published Henry Lawson's first collection *Short Stories*

in *Prose and Verse* (1894), although the book's poor production contributed to their estrangement. She also published a novel herself, *Do*, in the 1890s and a book of poetry, *The Lonely Crossing* (1905).

Leak, Bill
Growing up in the 1950s in Sydney's North ('the dullest place on earth'), Bill Leak began drawing subversive cartoons as a means of self-defence. Somehow that became a career and along the way Leak became one of the best political cartoonists on earth. He started out trying to make it as a painter, but when the *Bulletin* bought one of his cartoons he found himself hooked. Over more than twenty years has worked for the *Sydney Morning Herald*, the *Financial Review* and, currently, the *Australian*.

Leason, Percy
Percy Leason (1889–1959) was apprenticed at the same Melbourne lithography studio as was George Johnston a generation later. But Leason was a country boy, born in Kaniva, and while Johnston wrote about Melbourne life between the wars, Leason drew it, and country life as well. Leason was the master draftsman among black and white artists of his generation. When hired by Keith Murdoch for the Melbourne *Herald* he was said to be the highest paid cartoonist in the world. His elaborate bird's-eye perspectives of Australian sport, suburban streets and happenings in the mythical town of Wiregrass are as evocative today as they were in the 1920s and 1930s. He illustrated many Australian writers, from Henry Lawson's selected poems

Leichhardt's expedition members

Ben Lexcen in an Elton John moment

The much-loved Leyland P76

A wry Michael Leunig

L

to C.J. Dennis' column in the Melbourne *Herald*. He also painted an extraordinary series of portraits of Aboriginal people from Lake Tyers in Victoria, which were a revelation when re-exhibited in 2000. He left Australia for the United States in 1939, drawing once for the *New Yorker*.

Leichhardt, Ludwig

Ludwig Leichhardt (1813–?48) came to Australia in 1842 to study natural science in a new and unexplored environment. In 1844–45 he led an expedition overland from Brisbane to Port Essington and in 1848, after an abortive attempt to cross the continent east to west, he set out from the Condamine River – and disappeared. Nine major searches over almost a hundred years found nothing and his disappearance

remains one of the great mysteries of the Australian bush.

Leunig, Michael

Australia's best-loved cartoonist, Michael Leunig's (b. 1945) whimsical, insightful views on life were first published in *Newsday* and *Nation Review* in the early 1970s and then in the *Age*. His characters and drawings evoke some twisted world that is a recognisable Australian universe but is also somehow symbolic of a dadaesque heaven. He is not afraid of unintended controversy, at one time suggesting that women should stay home to mind the children – even men took offence!

Lexcen, Ben

Ben Lexcen was born Bob Miller (1936–88) and gained immortality as

the designer of the winged keel with which *Australia II* won the America's Cup in 1983. Toyota named a car model for him.

Leyland Brothers

The Leyland brothers (and their four-wheel drive) and their endless TV request to 'ask them' something, were a staple of the 1980s.

Leyland P76

Manufactured by British Leyland in Sydney 1973–74, the Leyland P76 has somehow gained itself a devoted fan base – as being the Edsel of Australia, the ugliest lemon ever produced.

Liberal Party

The first Liberal Party was the title by which the Fusion Party of 1909 was generally known – a conglomerate of

Cheong Liew (left) and Tim Pak Poy at work

Still from a Life. Be In It ad by Alex Stitt

The charge of the Light Horsemen

LIBERAL

parties led by Alfred Deakin, Joseph Cook and John Forrest. It became the Nationalist Party in 1917. The later Liberal Party of Australia was formed by Robert Menzies from the ashes of the United Australia Party in 1945. Menzies was parliamentary leader from 1945 to 1966, and the Liberals governed from 1949–72, 1975–83, and from 1996 under John Howard.

Liew, Cheong
Cheong Liew (b. 1950?) came to Melbourne from Malaysia in 1969 and worked at Spencer Street Railway station as a short order cook while studying. He later moved to Adelaide, and worked and learned at a classically inclined Greek restaurant, before moving to some of Adelaide's gastronomic temples of the 1970s and 1980s – Kitcheners, Moos, Neddy's. As the head chef at the Hilton Hotel's Grange Restaurant he is widely regarded as one of the top two or three chefs in Australia. His secret is to 'follow the flavours'. He claims never to have cooked a classical dish correctly.

Life. Be In It
An animated 1970s get-fit advertising campaign featuring a slob Norm and the activities of other non-Norms – brilliantly designed by Alex Stitt.

Light Horsemen
Mounted units of the colonial and then Australian Army, most famously in the Middle East in World War I. By the outbreak of war there were 9000 Light Horsemen in eight regiments based in each state. During the war the Light Horse was led by the great commander General Harry Chauvel. The 3rd Brigade fought dismounted at Gallipoli. It was the 3rd who were slaughtered at the Nek, made famous in Peter Weir's film, *Gallipoli*. The Light Horse formed the bulk of the Desert Mounted Corps, led by Chauvel, who fought the decisive battles at Beersheba (the last charge of a light brigade), at Amman, Damascus and Aleppo – where they forced the Turkish victor at Gallipoli, Mustafa Kemal, to retreat. It was the Light Horse that liberated Damascus, not Lawrence of Arabia, who turned up later. The Light Horse also helped put down a revolt in Egypt, in 1919–20, earning the emnity of locals.

Lillee, Dennis
Dennis Lillee (b. 1949) took more Test wickets than any other Australian

185

Dennis Lillee in mid-stride

Bobby Limb at the mike

Walter Lindrum watches someone else try

bowler – until Shane Warne came along. Had his World Series Cricket Test scalps been added he would have remained in front. With Jeff Thomson he formed one of the most lethal fast bowling duos in cricket history. After he returned from a back injury in 1974–75 he was not quite as quick, but twice as smart. Overall he took 355 wickets at 23.92, his best haul being 7/83.

Limb, Bobby

Bobby Limb (1926–2000) was posthumously awarded the AO for services to Australian entertainment and charity work, especially for diabetes. He won eleven Logies for his shows which included Australia's first national television show, *The Bobby Limb Show*, in the late 1950s. *The Sound of Music* first beamed into our

households in 1963, and was the country's top-rating show for nine years. Limb was a great advocate for Australian content on TV when the battle raged in the 1970s. Former Labor minister Mr Doug McClelland said Limb was to the entertainment industry what Don Bradman was to cricket, Charles Kingsford Smith to aviation, Joan Sutherland to opera and Victor Chang to surgery.

Lindrum, Walter

The man who could not be beaten, billiards guru Walter Lindrum (1898–1960) established 57 world records, none of which have ever been broken, except by himself. Naturally right-handed, a childhood accident saw him switch to his left for billiards, and between 1929 and 1933 he could not be touched, conceding up to 7000

point starts to his nearest rivals. His record break of 4137 made in 175 minutes consisted of about 1900 consecutive scoring shots without a mistake. The rules were changed on several occasions to try and stop him, but his cannon-style play could not be curbed, and it is unlikely his ability will ever be matched.

Lindsay Family

A remarkable artistic and literary family originating from Creswick near Ballarat. Leader of the Lindsays was Norman (1879–1969) whose buxom beauties and bacchanalian scenes excited many a young person's interest in Australian art, but is better known as the author of the best Australian kids' book ever, *The Magic Pudding* (1918 and in print ever since). Another novel *Redheap* (1930) was

A signed portrait of Ruby Lindsay

A pensive Norman Lindsay

The Little Boy of Manly

banned in Australia, which means it must also have been good. Other books worth reading again include *A Curate in Bohemia*, *The Cousin from Fiji* and the other two books in the Redheap trilogy, *Saturdee* and *Halfway to Anywhere*. Brother Daryl (1890–1976) was an artist and director of the National Gallery of Victoria (1942–55). His wife Joan (Weigall) Lindsay (1896–1984) was related to the Boyd dynasty and wrote the classic *Picnic at Hanging Rock* (1967). Lionel Lindsay (1874–1961) was the elder brother and a painter and illustrator. His wife Joan was a Dyson, sister of Will and Ted (qv). Lionel was a stern critic of modern art and published *Addled Art* as late as 1942. Sister Ruby Lindsay (1887–1919) married Will Dyson. Brother Percy Lindsay (1870–1952) was also a

painter and illustrator. The next generation included Jack Lindsay (1900–90), son of Norman, who went to London in 1926, taking the press he founded in 1923, Fanfrolico Press, with him. He converted from Nietzsche to Marx in the 1930s. Jack Lindsay was a formidable biographer, critic and historian and author of 150 books.

Lindsay, Ruby

Painter and illustrator Ruby Lindsay (1887–1919) (also known as Ruby Lind) was sister to Percy, Lionel, Daryl and Norman Lindsay. She contributed drawings to the *Lone Hand*, but died in the 1919 flu epidemic.

Lindwall, Ray

Great Australian fast bowler, and partner of Keith Miller, Ray Lindwall (1921–96) was perfection and lethal

grace in action. He took 27 wickets in the 1948 Invincibles Tests, including 6/20 in the Fifth. In all he took 228 wickets at 23.03, and whacked two Test hundreds.

Little Boy of Manly

The creation of Livingston Hopkins in the 1885 *Bulletin*, the Little Boy of Manly was the personification of NSW, and after Federation, of the whole of Australia. Dressed in a sailor suit, he was also drawn by artists like David Low and Norman Lindsay. and influenced Jim Bancks' Ginger Meggs.

Little, Jack

American-born gravel-voiced Australian TV personality of the 1960s and 1970s, most famous as the host of the real Australian *World Championship Wrestling* on Nine from

Jack Little, wrestling host

Jeannie Little and her trademark squeal

Glenn Shorrock fronts the Little River Band

1962 to 1978, featuring legends such as Killer Kowalski of the dreaded claw hold, Mark Lewin with the sleeper hold, Andre the Giant, and good guys such as Mario Milano and Domenic Denucci. At the end of each show, Little's tag-line was 'That's all there is, there isn't any more.' He was initially brought to Australia in 1958 as a newsreader at GTV-9 in Melbourne as a double act with Eric Pearce.

Little, Jeannie
Supposedly mistaken for a drag queen on her first television appearance, Jeannie Little began her career on TV in 1975 as a guest on the *Mike Walsh Show*. Her trademark nasal, whining voice and 'ooooOOO darlings' won her the Gold Logie in 1976 and has kept her on TV ever since. Most recently she found

international success with her one-woman show *Marlene*, a tribute to Marlene Dietrich.

Little, Jimmy
In a career spanning four decades in the entertainment industry, Jimmy Little (b. 1937) was Australia's first black pop star. In the 50s he was a hillbilly singer before a contract switch from EMI to Festival Records saw him polish his sound and achieve huge mainstream success. In 1963 his cover of *Royal Telephone* went to number 3 in Australia, and he was named pop star of the year in 1964 by *Everybody's Magazine*. He continued to release albums and work clubs until the 1980s when he seemed to disappear before making a welcome comeback with the hit album *Messenger* in 1999.

Little Nippers
Kids in general, more particularly a program designed for kids between the ages of 5 and 13 years. Little Nippers (or more correctly 'Surf Life Saving Junior Activities') aims to teach kids basic surf skills, and outposts can be found in many Australian coastal regions.

Little River Band
One of Australia's earliest internationally successful rock bands, the Little River Band evolved in the early 1970s from another Australian band called Mississippi. Guitarist/vocalist Graham Goble, guitarist/vocalist Beeb Birtles and drummer Derek Pellicci called on singer Glenn Shorrock to found the new band, and their debut album won an ARIA for album of the year.

Reg Livermore, hear him roar

Every actor's dream . . . a Logie

The *Lone Hand* flies the flag

Livermore, Reg

Reg Livermore (b. 1938) is an actor, a singer, a dancer and a female impersonator who has been entertaining Australian audiences since the 1960s. His greatest creation is 'Leonard', originally a tribute to Roy 'Mo' Rene, who quickly morphed into an opinionated, philandering one-man show of his own in the Betty Blokk Buster Follies, in the mid 1970s.

Logies, The

A part of Australian TV culture since their inception in 1958, the Logies were initiated by Melbourne's *TV Week* magazine. Originally known as the *TV Week Awards*, Graham Kennedy (who won the first 'Star of the Year' award) renamed the award after the middle name of the inventor of television, John Logie Baird. Kylie

Minogue made Logie history by winning four on a night (including the prestigious Gold Logie) in 1988, and Kennedy still holds the record for Gold Logies, with six, although Lisa McCune is fast catching him, winning four from 1997–2000.

Lollies

What other nations call sweets. Aussie favourites include Polly Waffles, Choo Choo Bars, Lifesavers, Minties, Jaffas, Fantales, Freddo Frogs.

Lone Hand

Planned by J.F. Archibald, the *Lone Hand* was an illustrated magazine based on the *Strand* magazine in London and was published in two series in unbroken sequence, 1907–21. Under the control of the *Bulletin*, it actually carried the name Archibald

had wanted to give its parent. Its innovations and contributions to journalism included the beauty contest and columns by famous people. It was an also an important forum for longer investigative pieces, and creative writing and criticism.

Longford, Raymond

Raymond Longford (1878–1959) was born John Walter Longford but adopted Raymond after Raymond Hollis. He served in the Boer War before turning to acting, performing with various companies in both Australia and New Zealand. He later became one of Australia's most innovative directors, beginning with the feature film *The Fatal Wedding* (1911) and continuing through over thirty other silent films. Sadly, only his adaptations of Steele Rudd's *On Our*

Raymond Longford, and left, Louie the Fly

David Low as drawn by David Low

Lenny Lower shows some teeth

L

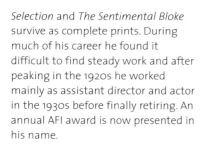

Selection and *The Sentimental Bloke* survive as complete prints. During much of his career he found it difficult to find steady work and after peaking in the 1920s he worked mainly as assistant director and actor in the 1930s before finally retiring. An annual AFI award is now presented in his name.

Louie the Fly
A longtime star of Mortein bug spray commercials, Louie the Fly was devised by none other than best-selling author Bryce Courtenay during his early forays in advertising.

Low, David
One of the most important cartoonists in the last century, Sir David Low (1891–1963) was a staff artist on the *Bulletin* after leaving his

homeland of New Zealand for Australia. He created the character Colonel Blimp and later *The Billy Book* which parodied then-prime minister Billy Hughes, before moving to England where he found fame as a political cartoonist working on such papers as the *Star*, *Evening Standard* and the *Manchester Guardian*.

Lower, Lennie
After some early work as a journalist, Lennie Lower (1903–47) published the acclaimed comic novel *Here's Luck* (1930). He continued to work as a columnist, including a stint at the *Australian Women's Weekly* which ended when he was dismissed by Frank Packer, allegedly for insulting Noel Coward. He continued to publish collections of his humorous columns throughout his career, including

Here's Another (1932) and *Lennie Lower's Annual* (1941), which were filled with his trademark slapstick cynicism, chauvanistic males, nagging wives, conformist suburbanites and his hatred of 'wowsers'. Barry Dickins' play (1982) was nicely sentimental.

Lucky Country
Coined by Donald Horne for the title of his book, *The Lucky Country* (1964) it has since become an expression buried deep in positive mythology. However, Horne intended it to be exactly the opposite: Australia is 'a lucky country run by mainly second-rate people who share its luck . . . it lives on other people's ideas, and, although its ordinary people are adaptable, most of its leaders (in all fields) . . . lack curiosity about the events that surround them.'

The Luna Park in Melbourne is a real mouthful

Australia's first female film star, Lottie Lyell

Lukin, Dean
Years of hauling blue fin tuna off the coast of South Australia was good training for Dean Lukin (b. 1960), the 'nice man' of weightlifting, whose easygoing personality seemed at odds with his ability to hold huge weights above his head. Winner of the Olympic gold medal in the super-heavyweight division in 1984, Lukin lifted 15 kilos more than his closest rival in the clean and jerk, and well above his personal best, to pull out one of Australia's greatest wins at an Olympics.

Luna Park
Australia's oldest theme park and the first of seven 'Luna' Parks was opened in Australia in 1912, a descendant of the oldest theme park in the world, the Luna Park on Coney Island, USA.

Visitors enter through the open mouth of a clown and the desire of the builders was to make people believe the park was, in fact, on the moon (hence the name). Today, only Melbourne remains, Sydney having closed in 2001. Sir John Monash, engineer and soldier, was a director of Melbourne.

Luhrmann, Baz
Beginning his career on the stage, Baz Luhrmann (b. 1962) wrote and directed the stage production of *Strictly Ballroom* in 1986, a show which he would reinvent for the big screen to international critical acclaim in 1992. His next film in 1996 was just as huge, a hip reinterpretation of Shakespeare's *Romeo and Juliet*. His third feature, *Moulin Rouge*, was released in 2001,

starring the former Mrs Tom Cruise, Nicole Kidman.

Lyell, Lottie
Lottie Lyell (1890–1925) was Australia's first female film star, remembered in association with Raymond Longford, acting together in *Captain Midnight* in 1911, and then 20 films between 1911 and 1919, including the haunting classic version of *The Sentimental Bloke* (1919) directed by Longford, for which she also wrote the sceenplay. Lyell co-produced many of these films, and co-directed at least one. Her acting owed something to her luminous beauty and athleticism, but she was accomplished in all areas of the new medium. The only visual evidence left of her brilliant career, cut short by TB, is *The Sentimental Bloke*.

M

Nellie Melba as Cleopatra

John Macarthur, merino pioneer

Camden Park, designed by John Verge, completed in 1835 after John Macarthur's death

Mabo, Eddie

Eddie Mabo was born on the remote Torres Strait Island of Mer (Murray Is.). His surname has become a household word throughout the length and breadth of the country. Mabo (1936–92) believed he and his family had traditional title to a relatively small patch of land on Mer and in 1982 he took his case to the Queensland courts. Until then the received wisdom was that, because Australia was 'terra nullius' (empty land) before European settlement, since annexation by Britain all lands were the property of the crown. Mabo's case dragged on through the court system for many years and finally reached the High Court of Australia in 1991, but Mabo himself died of cancer before their decision had been reached. Five months after

his death the country's highest court found 6 to 1 in his favour. The idea of 'terra nullius' had been discarded and the legal standing of native title to land (albeit in certain limited circumstances) had been established. The Mabo judgment had a profound effect, both real and symbolic, on the rights and self esteem of indigenous Australians, and despite scare campaigns by a succession of mean-minded reactionaries, continues to point the way for most Australians towards full reconciliation between settlers and traditional owners in a multicultural community.

Macarthur, John

Macarthur (1767–1834) first leapt to fame as a leader of the 1808 'Rum Rebellion' against the notorious Governor Bligh, but his motivation in

this, as in all his activities, was purely and simply self interest. An officer in the New South Wales Corps, he had already begun a second career as a sheep grazier when he was sent back to England for duelling and flouting the Governor's authority. England at the time was in need of a major supply of fine wool, so instead of punishment, Macarthur received a further grant of land, some Spanish sheep and official support to promote wool production in New South Wales. After unsuccessful forays into politics and trade he returned to sheep farming and became a leader of the ultra-right grazing interests in the colony, until he went mad. The title 'Father of the Wool Industry' should be 'Mother' and belong to his long-suffering wife, Elizabeth, who actually managed the family estate.

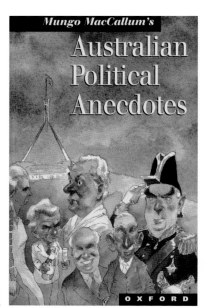
Mungo McCallum, a collector of political wit

Bruce McAvaney at the track

Garry McDonald as Ginger Meggs' Dad

M

McAvaney, Bruce

A leading Australian sports presenter and commentator, McAvaney (b. 1953) won a Logie for his coverage of the 1992 Olympic Games. McAvaney's prodigious memory served him well though his somewhat mannered enthusiasm and predilection for happenings to be 'special' made him the butt of criticism.

MacCallum, Mungo

The first Australian Mungo MacCallum, Mungo William MacCallum (1854–1942) came to Sydney University in 1887 to take up the chair in modern literature. He eventually rose to become Vice Chancellor (1925–27), Deputy Chancellor (1928–34) and Chancellor (1935–36). His son, Mungo Lorenz MacCallum (1883–1933), was a

lecturer in Law at the University and a leader writer for the *Sydney Morning Herald* (1919–32). His son, Mungo Ballardie MacCallum (1913–99) was a freelance writer and critic and a producer, announcer and interviewer for radio and television, mainly the ABC. His son, Mungo Wentworth MacCallum (b. 1941), is a journalist mainly famous for his acerbic descriptions of political life in Canberra, first for the *Australian* (1965–71), then for the *Nation Review* (1971–78) and *Mungo: The Man Who Laughed* (2001).

McCune, Lisa

Lisa McCune (b. 1971) graduated from the WA Academy of Performing Arts and appeared in TV commercials (many for Coles) before shooting three TV pilots for Channel 7. One, co-starring Rob Sitch, never got off the

ground, in another her part was recast and the third was as Maggie Doyle in *Blue Heelers*. As *Blue Heelers* continued her role grew until it became little more than a star vehicle for 'Our' Lisa. The show earned her four consecutive Gold Logies (equalling Ray Martin's record) before she bowed out in early 2000 to pursue other options. Lead roles in a stage production of *The Sound of Music* and the telemovie *The Potato Factory* followed and she continues to be a hot property on Australian screens.

McDonald, Garry

A talented actor, Garry McDonald (b. 1948) suffered the fate that is every actor's nightmare – his screen persona, Norman Gunston, became more recognisable, more real even,

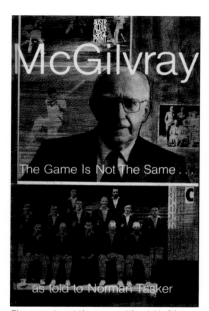

The game is not the same without McGilvray

Eddie McGuire meets the press

H.V. McKay puttering up Wheelers Hill

than he was. As Gunston, the totally gauche and inept television interviewer, McDonald created many of Australian TV's finest moments as he ambushed unsuspecting celebrities for excruciatingly embarrassing encounters. He recovered from Gunston enough to create a second successful TV career as Ruth Cracknell's long-suffering son in Geoffrey Atherden's sit-com *Mother and Son*.

McGilvray, Alan

When he retired as ABC cricket commentator in 1985 a song was written which noted, 'The game's not the same without McGilvray'. Alan McGilvray (1909–96) was the voice of Australian cricket for 50 years, making his Test debut in 1935. He called the 'synthetic broadcasts' in 1938,

devising commentary from ball-by-ball telegrams.

McGuire, Eddie

Working-class boy from Broadmeadows, who touched a seam of gold with Nine hosting the *Footy Show* during the 1990s, and segueing this role into an immensely successful business and television career. Hosted *Who Wants to be a Millionaire?*, became President of the Collingwood Football Club and created, with another medium media mogul Steve Vizard, an Internet content empire. Nine's acquisition of the AFL TV rights from season 2002 makes him uniquely prominent.

McKay, H.V.

Hugh Victor McKay (1865–1926) was the founder of Australia's first great

manufacturing success story – the Sunshine Harvester Works in the outer western suburbs of Melbourne, which was for many years the largest factory in Australia, in its heyday employing 2500 workers. Contrary to the myth he later promulgated, McKay did not actually invent the combine harvester, but he did make a very efficient prototype. His success was based partly on his own energy and great entrepreneurial and management skills, partly on the fiercely Protectionist stance of early colonial and federal governments, which McKay supported in order to keep at bay his main overseas rivals, Massey Harris in Canada and International Harvester in the US, and partly on his determination to keep workers' wages at a minimum and oppose unionism. This latter led to

Elle 'the Body' MacPherson

Dorothea Mackellar in portrait

Billy McMahon jumps for joy

M

Justice Higgins' famous 'Harvester judgment' in 1907 which held that even a successful industrialist like McKay should not be exempt from paying his workers a minimum wage for an eight-hour working day. The business continued to flourish until McKay's death from cancer in 1926. His younger brother Sam (1871–1932) took over the reins and in 1930 the company merged with former rival Massey Harris to become H.V. McKay Massey Harris, with McKay's son Cecil (1899–1968) in charge from 1937. The McKay part was dropped in 1955 when the remaining family interests were bought out.

Mackellar, Dorothea
A poet of modest achievement, Dorothea Mackellar (1885–1968) will live forever in the memory of Australians on the basis of one poem she wrote when she was nineteen. The beginning of the second stanza of *My Country*: 'I love a sunburnt country, a land of sweeping plains . . .' is arguably the best-remembered line of Australian verse.

McKern, Leo
Rotund Australian actor Leo McKern (b. 1920) went to England after the war like so many of his contemporaries and gradually progressed to lead roles with the Royal Shakepeare and Old Vic companies. He achieved lasting fame as Rumpole, the phlegmatic barrister in John Mortimer's long-running TV series *Rumpole of the Bailey*, and appeared in some local features including *Travelling North* (1987) and *On Our Selection* (1999).

McMahon, Billy
Billy McMahon (1908–88) was prime minister from March 1971 until December 1972 when he became the first Liberal to lose an election in 26 years. The other distinguishing features of his tenure were his kowtowing to the United States and his beautiful wife Sonia, who once startled the nation by wearing a dress with a daring thigh-length side-split at an official event.

MacPherson, Elle
'The Body' had a beaut business head, but also once remarked that the only books she read were ones she wrote.

Macquarie, Lachlan
Macquarie (1762–1824) was Governor of New South Wales from 1809 to 1821. Appointed after the turmoil of

Mad Max starring Mad Mel

The cover of a modern *Magic Pudding*

Farming the Mallee

the Rum Rebellion, he became one of the colony's most successful administrators, through a program of public works and the encouragement of exploration and expansion. He had a humane policy towards Aborigines and emancipated convicts.

Mad Max

Archetypal 'lone warrior' character created by writer-director George Miller and convincingly portrayed by Mel Gibson in a series of iconic movies – *Mad Max* (1979), *Mad Max 2* (1981) and *Mad Max Beyond Thunderdome* (1985). *Mad Max* was one of the few Australian movies to have influence overseas.

Magpies

(1) Black and white native bird with an engaging warble and the disconcerting habit of dive-bombing intruders during the nesting season, sometimes drawing blood with a peck on the top of the skull.
(2) Any of a number of Australian Rules football teams sporting black and white jumpers, most notably Collingwood, an inner Melbourne suburb, and Port Adelaide in South Australia. Both teams have fierce reputations and once enviable records in their competitions.

Magic Pudding, The

The canonical Australian children's story (1918), written and illustrated by artist Norman Lindsay (1879–1969), it tells the story of Bunyip Bluegum as he sets off to see the world, meets up with Bill Barnacle and Sam Sawnoff and their inexhaustible 'magic pudding', Albert, and assists them through many adventures in protecting the valuable pudding from scurrilous and unprincipled 'puddin' thieves'. A celebration of mateship and the joys of a peripatetic life in the bush, it uses colloquial Australian idiom with great verve.

Mallee Root

The bulbous root of small scrubby eucalypts that grow in the arid regions of central Australia. They are excellent for heating as they take a long time to burn out, and they were synonymous with a good fire in many Australian homes until the exhaustion of supply and greater environmental awareness led to replacement by the gas wall heater. The obstacle to cultivation by mallee roots still in the ground led to the invention of the stump-jump plough.

Ern Malley edition of *Angry Penguins*

A close-up of the Mambo logo

Man magazine saves Australia from the flood

M

Malley, Ern

Ern Malley was a previously unknown mechanic whose 'modernist' poems were sent posthumously by his sister Ethel to the avant garde literary magazine, *Angry Penguins*, where they were enthusiastically welcomed and published by editor Max Harris. Unfortunately for Max, both the poems and their progenitor were concocted with satirical intent by two bored army reserve officers in their barracks in Melbourne, James McAuley and Harold Stewart, with the intention of discrediting modern art. The subsequent scandal had a dampening effect not just on the careers of Max Harris and his associates (who included Sidney Nolan) but on the modernist literary movement as a whole in Australia. The hoax and the ensuing

controversy drew international interest. To add injury to insult, Harris was then prosecuted for obscenity over the allegedly indecent contents of one of the phoney poems by the moral crusaders of the South Australian police force. After a lengthy trial he was fined five quid.

Malouf, David

Prize-winning Australian author of Lebanese descent, Malouf (b. 1934) has published a number of volumes of poetry and the novels *Johnno*, *An Imaginary Life*, *Fly Away Peter* and *Remembering Babylon*.

Mambo

A surf and streetwear company founded by Dare Jennings in 1984 with a few T-shirts smothered in incomprehensible but somehow lewd

images, Mambo has since grown into an international design and fashion empire. More than just a fashion label, Mambo has become one of the true underground art institutions in the country, offering its gloriously perverse scratchings and unique visions to the world. Its stable of artists includes Jeff Raglus, ex-Mental As Anything singer/songwriter Reg Mombassa, Bruce Goold, Bob Tillery, Marcelle Lunam, Mark Falls and Jim Mitchell. Now creating board shorts, Mambo 'loud' shirts, a Goddess range for women and all kinds of accessories, Mambo also mounts regular exhibitions for its artists.

Man

From 1936 to 1974 *Man* magazine was every adolescent Australian male's introduction to the mysteries of the

A postcard of Manly Beach

A scene from *The Man from Snowy River*

A stern Christina Stead

A.B. 'Banjo' Paterson (right) at Narrambla

female body. However, unlike *Playboy*, it was implausible to claim you were only reading it for the articles, and it was surreptitiously smuggled from desk to desk, locker to locker, until parental or educational authorities intervened. Hopefully, by then you had had a chance to remove some of the 'better' pictures for inclusion in your secret collection.

Man from Ironbark, The
Subject of one of A.B. 'Banjo' Paterson's humorous poems, the archetypal country innocent from Ironbark is the victim of a practical-joking city barber, who pretends to cut his throat. The joke backfires when the Man from Ironbark wrecks the shop in what he mistakenly believes are his death-throes, leading to a fashion in bushy beards.

Man from Snowy River, The
Even more famous than the *Man from Ironbark*, the *Man from Snowy River* by A.B. 'Banjo' Paterson has become perhaps Australia's most famous poem and its eponymous hero has become the paradigm of an Australian bush horseman, skilful and courageous, daredevil and unrelenting. To the nostalgic, he has come to symbolise the old self-reliant individualistic bush Australia, now lost in the miasma of contemporary corporatisation and urbanisation. The poem has spawned two feature films and a 26-part TV series. Various bushmen have been suggested as the original inspiration for Paterson's poem, including Jim Troy, Jack Riley, Owen Cummins, Jim Spencer, Jack Clarke and Lachie Cochrane, but the jury is still out.

Man Who Loved Children, The
Novel by expatriate Australian author, Christina Stead (1902–83), published in 1940 and set in the USA.

Manly Beach
Along with Bondi, Manly is the quintessential Sydney beach. Legend has it that the locality got its name from Governor Phillip's remark that the 'natives' there looked very 'manly'. Successive generations of Australians have used the beach to show off their 'manly' and 'womanly' qualities.

Manly Ferry
Like the legendary Bondi Tram, the Manly Ferry has achieved iconic status in Australian culture, being, along with the bridge and later the opera house, a standard visual image symbolising life in the harbour city.

Archbishop Daniel Mannix

M

QUADROOPED

Neil Curtis' take on the effects of atomic testing at Maralinga

Mannix, Archbishop Daniel

The most influential ecclesiastic in Australia's history, Daniel Mannix (1864–1963) arrived in the country from Ireland on Easter Saturday, 1913, to take up the post of Roman Catholic co-adjutor Bishop of Melbourne. In 1917 he became Archbishop, a position which he held until his death 46 years later. A charismatic leader and speaker, his support for Irish independence led him to oppose Australia's participation in the First World War, which he was not alone in regarding as merely an irrelevant struggle between rival European imperialists. The debate began to focus around the issue of conscription for overseas service and when the 'little digger', PM 'Billy' Hughes, introduced a series of referenda to bring about conscription,

Mannix became his principal opponent. Both of Hughes' referenda were lost, and after the war Mannix renewed his involvement in the movement for Irish independence. He travelled overseas in 1920–21 and spoke in New York but was prevented by the British Government from returning to Ireland. Back in Australia he continued to take an active role in political and social issues and formed a close relationship with the many Catholics in the Australian Labor Party and the Australian union movement. He encouraged Catholics led by B.A. Santamaria to oppose Communists in the union movement and the struggle between the two groups escalated until it caused the Australian Labor Party to split in 1954. The resulting Democratic Labor Party, set up with Mannix's support, did

little except keep the conservative coalition in power in Australia for the next 17 years. Mannix was memorably portrayed by Bruce Spence in Barry Oakley's 1971 play at the Pram Factory, *The Feet of Daniel Mannix*, which also starred Max Gillies as Santamaria.

Maralinga Test Site

When the British Government wished to test highly lethal atomic weapons at a site far removed from sentient life forms they naturally chose Maralinga in South Australia, whose only inhabitants were already endangered native animals (so what's the difference?) and nomadic tribes of Aborigines, who just needed to be persuaded to be a bit more nomadic than usual and move out of the detonation area until things settled back to normal. The information that

Ray Martin thinking hard for the camera

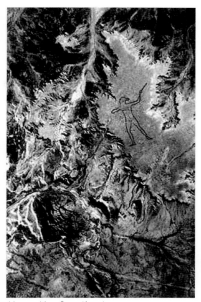
Marree Man from the air

A scene from *I Can Jump Puddles*

in the case of atomic radiation this might entail a wait of 250 000 years seems to have lost something in the translation. The first of four atomic bombs was exploded at Maralinga on 27 September, 1956, and Australian soldiers a few miles from the site respectfully turned their backs on the explosion to protect their eyes. On 17 December 1984, the 76 000 square kilometre reserve was handed back to the remaining Aborigines, and the site was supposedly rehabilitated over the next 15 years.

Marathon Swimmers
A strange sport that seems to have originated in the deeds of the Channel swimmers – including Australian Des Renford. Recently swimming in the ocean has become part of the World Championships, giving the sport some respectability. Susie Maroney (b. 1971) is the best of the women competitors, having swum the Channel, Cuba–Florida and around Manhattan Island. Tammy van Wisse, another champion, swam down the length of the Murray River in 2001, a bizarre Federation event.

Marree Man
In 1998 a four-kilometre tall man was mysteriously gouged into the desert on a remote plateau 60 km outside the town of Marree on the Oodnadatta track. No one claimed authorship of the giant spear-throwing man, said to be authentically Pitjantjatjara, and no one knows why it was done. Best seen from the air, it began to fade back into the desert after a few months. Marree Man remains a mystery.

Marshall, Alan
Crippled from the age of six by infantile paralysis, Alan Marshall (1902–84) began writing at an early age, and by the age of fifty he had carved out a career involving writing newspaper columns, a 'lonely hearts' column, a cartoon strip and numerous short stories. He did not gain significant recognition however until the publication in 1955 of the autobiographical *I Can Jump Puddles*, which gave him international renown, especially in Eastern Bloc countries. An award-winning film of the book was made in Czechoslovakia and Marshall began to be treated as a national treasure at home.

Martin, Ray
Like so many commercial radio and TV 'personalities', Ray Martin

Christina MacPherson wrote Matilda's tune

Marvellous Melbourne 'the play'

M

(b. 1944) served his apprenticeship with the ABC, before moving across to *Sixty Minutes* in 1985. His TV persona was so genial that in 1993 he replaced Mike Walsh as host of Nine's *Midday* show, which earned him the adoration of the largely female daytime audience and a number of Gold Logies. He later hosted *A Current Affair* until the late 1990s.

Mathers, Peter
Author of darkly comic novels *Trap* (1966) and *The Wort Papers* (1972), Peter Mathers (b. 1931) is the reclusive genius of Australian fiction.

Matilda
No one knows why the bushman's 'swag', his stash of food and possessions rolled up in his sleeping blanket and tied around with a belt or rope, came to be called 'matilda', but this led to the phrase 'to waltz matilda' or carry one's swag on the road, which in turn led to A.B. 'Banjo' Paterson's poem, which in turn led to the famous song, which in turn led to the folkloric bunfight about whether Paterson wrote the words from scratch or adapted them from pre-existing folk poetry or folk songs; about which of the competing tunes by Christina MacPherson, Marie Cowan and others is the most 'authentic'; and upon which Scottish, English or Irish folksong the music was based.

Marvellous Melbourne
In 1885 the visiting English journalist George Augustus Sala used this phrase to describe the thriving southern metropolis, high on its gold-generated wealth. The phrase stuck in the public imagination and in 1889 actor-manager Alfred Dampier used it as the title for a new melodrama set in the city. The play starts at Spencer Street Station and ends happily when the heroine's horse wins the Melbourne Cup. The less successful Sydney version was called *Slaves of Sydney*. The title was revived in 1970 at the Pram Factory when the Australian Performing Group presented a satirical extravaganza largely written by Jack Hibberd and John Romeril.

Mavis Bramston Show, The
The first Australian TV revue comedy show to be a ratings winner, *The Mavis Bramston Show* ran on Seven

Mavis Bramston steps out in style

Douglas Mawson, Antarctic hero

from 1964–68 with witty and irreverent comment on news, current affairs and middle-class Australian culture. Regulars included Gordon Chater, Carol Raye, Noeline Brown, Barry Creyton, June Salter and Ron Frazer, and others who appeared included Miriam Karlin, John Bluthal, Dawn Lake and Reg Livermore.

Mawson, Sir Douglas

Australia's greatest Antarctic explorer, Mawson (1882–1958) emigrated here from England when he was four and studied at Fort Street High School and Sydney University. In 1905 he was appointed to teach mineralogy at Adelaide University, where he taught with distinction until his death. In 1907 he was invited to join Sir Ernest Shackleton's expedition to the Antarctic and this was the beginning

of a life-long fascination with the icy continent. The expedition reached Antarctica in 1908 and Mawson and two companions climbed the nearby Mt Erebus, nearly twice as high as Kosciuszko, in five days. Mawson, Edgeworth and Mackay were then assigned to travel to the South Magnetic Pole, calculated to be 1800 kilometres away. It turned out to be even further away than at first thought, but despite blizzards and declining food supplies they achieved their objective. However on the return journey, when they were in sight of their ship, Mawson fell down a crevasse and the others were too weak to pull him out. He was eventually rescued but this misadventure did not dampen his enthusiasm and he jumped at the opportunity to lead an Australian

expedition in 1911. Base camps were built by January 1912 but the weather did not allow major expeditions until the following November. Mawson, Ninnis and Mertz set out across the treacherous terrain. Before long one of their sleds disappeared down a crevasse. A fortnight later, Ninnis and the second sled disappeared into a crevasse, along with most of the group's food supplies. Mawson and Mertz struggled on, gradually eating the remaining dogs. On January 7 Mertz died leaving Mawson alone and 160 kilometres from the camp without food. He struggled on through blizzards, himself fell down a crevasse and managed to climb out then, 8 kilometres from his goal, had to shelter for a week in a cave because of intense storms. He finally managed to make a dash for the

The Mean Machine celebrates another win

Phil May Picture Book

M

camp and safety, only to find the ship back to Australia had left that morning and he had to wait till the next summer to get back to civilisation. Largely due to Mawson's work, Australia established itself as a major force in Antarctica and consolidated its claims on a substantial portion of the continent.

May, Phil
English cartoonist Phil May (1864–1903) came to Australia to work on the *Bulletin* in 1885 and helped to establish its reputation as a publisher of superior cartoons and sketches. After three years he returned to England and worked on *Punch*.

Mean Machine
The original Mean Machine was the men's 4 x 100 swimming relay team at Moscow in 1980, but the term was coined by Ian Hanson at Brisbane Commonwealth Games in 1982 when the team of Neil Brooks, Greg Fasala, Graeme Brewer and Michael Delany won gold with shaven heads. The Australian success in men's relays continues through Sydney 2000.

Meanjin
Arguably Australia's premier literary journal, *Meanjin* started publication in Brisbane as *Meanjin Papers* in 1940 under the editorship of Clem Christesen, who brought the publication to Melbourne in 1945, despite the fact that the name 'meanjin' comes from the Aboriginal word for the original site of Brisbane. Under Christesen's editorship the magazine flourished and became a major vehicle for the publication of new Australian poetry and fiction, as well as significant critical writing on Australian literature. Christesen remained at the helm until 1974. Under a succession of subsequent editors including Jim Davidson, Judith Brett and Jenny Lee, the magazine began to cover socio-political areas without losing its literary focus.

Melba, Dame Nellie
Born Helen Porter Mitchell in Melbourne, from which city she took her stage name, Dame Nellie Melba (1861–1931) had many setbacks in her early career, not least being European prejudice against a colonial upstart, but after studying in Paris with the highly regarded teacher Madame Marchesi in 1886–87 she launched an opera-singing career during which she eventually conquered all the

Phar Lap wins the 1930 Melbourne Cup

Melbourne *Punch*; right, a Melbourne House game

great operatic centres of the world, developed into the leading diva of her day and became a national icon in her homeland. She demanded the highest fees, dressed and entertained lavishly and lived like royalty when on tour. Melba toast and peach Melba were named after her, the latter created in her honour by the great French chef, Escoffier. Her numerous 'final' performances became legendary. In 1927 she sang the National Anthem at the opening of the new (now old) Parliament House in Canberra.

Melbourne Cricket Ground

In the greatest sporting city of the greatest sporting state of the greatest sporting nation in the world, the Melbourne Cricket Ground, or the 'G', holds pride of place as the sporting arena non pareil. It is the only place (in the world) where a national football code and Test cricket were born, and where an Olympic Games has been held.

Melbourne Cup

The race that stops the nation was first won in 1861 by Archer, who according to legend walked from NSW to perform the feat. A great Australian boast is that we are the only country that has a public holiday, albeit only in the Melbourne metropolitan area, for a horse race.

Melbourne House

Australia's finest videogame development studio, Melbourne House began life in 1980 as Beam Software. Since then they have produced over 75 games for many different platforms, including the memorable 'Shadowrun' and 'Smash TV' for the Super Nintendo and more recently, 'KKND' for the Playstation and 'Test Drive Le Mans' for the Sega Dreamcast. Purchased in 1999 by French super publisher Infogrames, they are positioned at the forefront of world software development.

Melbourne *Punch*

A long-running and more or less successful attempt to imitate its famous London namesake, Melbourne *Punch* was published from 1855 until it merged with *Table Talk* in 1929 and inter alia played a major role in the development of the Australian tradition of political caricature, especially through the cartoons of Thomas Carrington and Nicholas Chevalier.

Max Meldrum with paintbrush

Ian 'Molly' Meldrum on the *Countdown* set

Men At Work pose for publicity stills

Dr MacKenzie and his Menthoids

Meldrum, Max

For Max Meldrum (1875–1955) painting was a scientific enterprise based on nineteenth-century rationalist principles, which left him poised between the conservatives who thought him too modern and the modernists who thought him too conservative. He was, however, a dominating figure in the Melbourne art scene for many years, mainly though his strongly held views and the influence of his art school. He was a pacifist during the Great War.

Meldrum, 'Molly'

The name of Ian 'Molly' Meldrum (b. 1945) has become synonymous with the promotion of rock music in Australia. His career started with *Kommotion* in the late 1960s but his major vehicle was *Countdown* which he hosted for 12 years (1975–87) and which he made a showcase for local popular music performers. He subsequently became a regular on *Hey Hey It's Saturday*. He received a special achievement award from ARIA in 1993. He drives a Rolls-Royce and barracks for St Kilda.

Men At Work

Formed in early 1979 from the acoustic duo of Colin Hay and Ron Strykert, with drummer Jerry Speiser, sax/flute player Greg Ham and bass player John Rees. Their first single *Who Can It Be Now* was an immediate smash. But it was 1983 that saw them truly hit the global stage, and their single *Down Under* would become a staple of radio stations for decades to come. Both the album and single spent 15 weeks at number one in the U.S. It was the anthem of the 1980s, and the 1983 America's Cup win. 'We come from a land down under, where beer flows and men chunder.'

Menthoids, Dr MacKenzie's

Cough lollies. The word 'menthoid' is a marketer's invention but Dr MacKenzie's became a household name during the postwar years owing to a highly successful TV promotional campaign in which he said in a Scots burr 'Em-eee-en? Tee Aitch Ohhl. Dee-ess!'

Menzies, Sir Robert

Robert Gordon Menzies (1894–1978) overcame many adversities, some of his own making, to become Australia's longest serving prime minister, from 1949 to 1966. A

Sir Robert Menzies appears on the first ABC news broadcast, 1956

Indoctrination Mickey Mouse style

scholarship student at Wesley College, Melbourne, and the University of Melbourne, after a brief but meteoric legal career which saw him become the country's youngest KC, he entered Victorian state politics in 1928 and by 1932 he was Attorney-General and Deputy Premier. In 1934 he transferred to federal politics and was elected to the seat of Kooyong which he retained for the next 32 years. He became federal Attorney-General in the UAP government and in 1939 after the death of Joseph Lyons he became prime minister for the first time. His handling of the war, and especially incidents such as his selling of iron to the Japanese before the war which was then used in the Japanese war effort and earned him the epithet 'Pig-Iron Bob', and the notorious 'Brisbane Line' which

conceded the northern half of the nation to the putative invaders, led to his replacement by the ALP Government led by John Curtin for the duration of the war. Many believed Menzies' political career was over, but he used his time out of office to unite the conservative forces in Australian politics, launched the Liberal Party of Australia in 1944 and won a landslide victory in 1949. His long term in office was assisted by the Petrov affair, which helped him win the 1954 election and by the split in the ALP which kept him in power in 1955 and for the rest of his term of office. One of his major achievements was the support for education and especially universities and the place of the humanities in higher education. Nostalgia for old-fashioned Menzian suburban white

picket fence conservatism remains the heart of Liberalism in Australia.

Mickey Mouse Club

If there were two words that all 1950s Australian children knew how to spell they were 'Mickey' and 'Mouse', as even those whose televisions did not blare out the program every evening would have heard other children sing the song as this awful piece of Walt Disney kitsch dominated our screens during peak kiddies' viewing time for many years. Many lads' first screen romance was with Annette Funicello.

Mietta

Known to everyone simply by the affectionate diminutive 'Mietta', Maria Fernanda O'Donnell (1950–2001) was a key figure in Melbourne's eating and cultural scene from 1974

Vlado, Jean Jacques and Mietta at Pellegrini's

Peter Mathers, Miles Franklin winner

George Miller scaring a cameraman

when she founded her eponymous restaurant in Brunswick Street, Fitzroy. In 1985 she and her partner Tony Knox moved the restaurant to the luxuriously appointed former Naval and Military Club building in Alfred Place in the CBD and as well as overseeing one of Australia's most elegant eating venues, they were able to indulge in their other passion, as patrons of the arts. Mietta encouraged intellectuals, actors and musicians to both perform and relax in her establishment. In 1995 Mietta and Tony sold the restaurant and began writing and publishing food guides and recipe books. Mietta died in a car accident in January 2001.

Miles Franklin Award
Australia's Booker Prize, the Miles Franklin Award was established under the terms of Miles Franklin's will and has been bestowed annually since 1957. Winners include Patrick White, Randolph Stow, Thea Astley, Peter Mathers, Thomas Keneally, David Ireland, Xavier Herbert, Ruth Park, Peter Carey, Elizabeth Jolley and Tim Winton, many of them more than once. The most notorious recipient was the 1995 winner, Helen Demidenko.

Miller, George (x 2)
There are two leading Australian film directors of the 1980s and 90s called George Miller, who both steadfastly resist suggestions they should add a middle initial or some other identifying device to distinguish them from the other, presumably because they each believe that they are the George Miller and if any

changes are to be made it should be by the other (less prominent) George Miller. This confusing state of affairs could not be tolerated however by writers on film, and since one of the Georges happens to be a medical graduate from Sydney University he is conventionally and conveniently referred to by others, though not by himself, as Doctor George Miller. So, in a sense, the other George Miller has won simply by virtue of deficiencies in his formal education. However Doctor George Miller (b. 1945) has achieved greater critical acclaim as the director of the trendsetting and cult-generating *Mad Max* movies and of the Hollywood movies *The Witches of Eastwick* and *Lorenzo's Oil*, and as producer of numerous films and TV series including *Bodyline*, *Bangkok Hilton*, *Dead Calm*, *Babe* and John

Kylie Minogue opening Fox Studios in Sydney

Sir John Monash in uniform

Our Glad, Gladys Moncrieff

Duigan's *The Year My Voice Broke* and *Flirting*. The other George Miller (b. Scotland 1943) has directed inter alia the films *The Man from Snowy River*, *Bushfire Moon* and *Gross Misconduct*, and the TV series *Cash and Company*, *All the Rivers Run* and *Anzacs*.

Minogue, Kylie

Supported by their ambitious mother, the Minogue girls, Kylie and Dannii, both tried to carve out careers for themselves in the world of showbiz. Kylie (b. 1968) was the one who made it to iconic status, principally through her starring role in the high-rating soapie *Neighbours*, for which she won a Gold Logie in 1988. The huge momentum from this show, which by this time had achieved cult status in Britain, enabled her to use

her talents to launch a more or less successful recording career in the 1990s. Her sister Dannii has also issued a number of CDs but has been less successful as a singer and in women's mag romance.

Moccasins

Another Australian favourite, the moccasin is a fleecy foot covering designed to be worn about the house but which has been seen adorning the feet of the tasteless in shopping centres, at the beach and about town. Simple in design, a thin, gripless foam sole supports a soft envelope of lambskin, with the fluffy bits turned toward the skin. Recently the lambskin has been replaced by all manner of synthetic fibres, but the true aesthete will gravitate toward the original.

Monash, Sir John

John Monash (1865–1931) graduated in Law and Civil Engineering from the University of Melbourne and at the same time made his way up through the ranks in the army reserve. In 1914 he became commander of the 4th Infantry Brigade and saw action first in Gallipoli and then in France where he was promoted to Major-General and led his troops with great success at Ypres and Passchendaele. He was the first Australian to command the Australian troops and his contribution to halting the last great German offensive in 1918 was decisive. After the war he was invited the lead the State Electicity Commission in his home state of Victoria and he was instrumental in developing the State's power grid, in tapping the State's hydroelectric

M

Lola Montez and her lewd dancing

Alan Moorehead, war correspondent

The cover of Frank Moorhouse's *Conference-Ville*

potential and in utilising the huge brown coal resources of the Latrobe Valley. His career was a demonstration of how democratic and open Australia was.

Moncrieff, Gladys

'Our Glad' (1892–1976) was Australia's major light opera star between the wars. Her performance in *Maid of the Mountains* ran for three years in Australia, and later in London. She added up that she had sung in 58 musicals.

Moneghetti, Steve

Ballarat marathon man Steve Moneghetti (b. 1962) took over the mantle from Rob de Castella, competing at the Olympics since Seoul 1988, best place fifth. He trained on junk food and Mars Bars.

Montez, Lola

Lola Montez (1818–61) brought her lewd Spider Dance to Australia in 1855, and was horsewhipped in Ballarat, a great publicity stunt. Mistress of Franz Liszt, Alexandre Dumas and Mad King Ludwig of Bavaria, among others, she died in poverty in New York.

Moomba

Sad Melbourne festival whose name is supposed to mean 'let's get together and have fun', it really is a local Aboriginal scatological joke.

Moorehead, Alan

An outstanding journalist and war correspondent, Alan Moorehead (1910–83) later made an international reputation as an author of mainly historical narratives, including

Gallipoli (1956), *The White Nile* (1960), *Cooper's Creek* (1963) and *The Fatal Impact* (1966). *Gallipoli* did much to recreate interest in Gallipoli and the role of the Anzacs.

Moorhouse, Frank

Frank Moorhouse (b. 1938) is a politically radical, short story writer and novelist informed by the Libertarianism of the Sydney Push and the contingencies of life in the inner Sydney suburb of Balmain, which are described in *Days of Wine and Rage*. Notable publications include *The Americans*, *Baby* and *The Electrical Experience*, which won the National Book Council Award in 1975, and his big pair of novels set in between-wars Europe, *Grand Days* (1993) and *Dark Palace* (2000).

Baron Ferdinand von Mueller

Warwick Capper's 100 Goal Mullet

Cricket writer 'Johnny' Moyes, right

Cricketer Mullagh after touring England

Morant, Harry 'Breaker'
Breaker Morant (1865–1902) was a *Bulletin* poet under the name 'The Breaker', who joined up to fight in the Boer War. After a mate was killed and mutilated by the Boers, Breaker and P.J. Handcock returned the favour, summarily executing a prisoner, and undertaking other reprisals. Breaker and Handcock were court-martialled and executed by the British in 1902, to the still continuing protests of Australians. Their deaths were the main reason that Australian soldiers could not be executed in World War I.

Moyes, A.G. 'Johnny'
Alban George Moyes (1893–1963) was always known as Johnny. He was a fine first-class cricketer, once chosen for Australia on a tour cancelled because of World War I. But he was,

with Ray Robinson, the best cricket writer of his day. Moyes wrote more than 20 cricket books, including the first full-scale history of the game in Australia, published in 1962.

Mudrooroo
Christened Colin Wilson and raised in a Catholic orphanage, Mudrooroo (b. 1939) has been active in Aboriginal affairs and a prolific writer for many years, including novels such as *Wildcat Falling*, much poetry and some plays.

Mueller, Baron Ferdinand von
In 1853 von Mueller (1825–96) became Victoria's first government botanist, and foundation director of the Melbourne Botanic Gardens until 1873. He wrote the splendidly titled *Eucalyptographia*, 1879–84.

Mullagh, Johnny
Johnny Mullagh Unaarrimin (1841–91) was a champion Aboriginal cricketer, outstanding on the 1868 tour of England, averaging 23.7 from 71 innings. He played for Victoria against Lord Harris' touring English team in 1879 making 36 and creating such an impression that spectators raised fifty pounds for him. This was the only game he could be persuaded to play for Victoria. A monument was erected in Harrow, Western Victoria.

Mullet, The
The mullet is by no means an Australian invention and the familiar short-cropped top and long 'mullet' tail out back have been in vogue for hundreds of years. However Australians seem to have a particular affinity for the haircut, and especially

The arid climes of Lake Mungo

Keith Murdoch during World War I

Rupert Murdoch will buy it all

during the 1980s helped popularise it worldwide with celebrities such as Jason Donovan and Guy Pearce sporting it on *Neighbours*.

Mungo Man

Mungo Man was discovered by geologist Professor Jim Bowler on 27 February 1974 in the sand dunes of the Walls of China at Lake Mungo, part of the Willandra Lakes National Park and World Heritage area, in south-west NSW. Initial dating of the overlying layers made the burial, a skeleton sprinkled with red ochre, at least 25 000 years old. Since then the dates have been pushed back to at least 43 000 years, making Mungo Man nearly the earliest evidence of human occupation in Australia. A team of scientists led by Dr Alan Thorne in 2001 announced,

controversially, that new DNA dating techniques meant that Mungo Man was 63 000 years old. Further, Thorne argued that this was evidence that human evolution was not simply 'out of Africa' but that humans evolved on many parts of the world, and that not all genes were passed on. Mungo Man might not be an ancient modern Aborigine, but of a line that died out before Aboriginal occupation. This is a view rejected by Aboriginal leaders.

Murdoch, Keith

Journalist Keith Murdoch (1885–1952) was influential in having the British commander Sir Ian Hamilton withdrawn from Gallipoli and later used his contacts with powerful people such as Billy Hughes, the British (1914–18) War Cabinet and

newspaper baron Lord Northcliffe, and his own organisational skills, to rise to power as managing director of the Melbourne Herald group, masterminding its expansion into other states. He was also a patron of the arts and served as Chairman of the National Gallery of Victoria. His wife Elisabeth was also a prominent arts patron and philanthropist.

Murdoch, Rupert

The 'dirty digger', Rupert Murdoch (b. 1931), son of Sir Keith, returned to Australia from Oxford in 1952 to find that the family fortune more or less consisted solely of the impecunious Adelaide *News*. He used this as a base to take over the rest of world, largely by pandering to the lowest common denominator reader, but also partly by producing quality newspapers

Stephen Murray-Smith lights up

Myer's opening sale in Sydney

such as the *Australian*. By the 1980s he had large newspaper interests in England and the US, and had moved into TV, book publishing and even air transport. He later acquired 20th Century Fox and has vast pay TV interests in Britain, China, USA and in Australia through News Ltd's partnership, Foxtel.

Murnane, Gerald
Gerald Murnane's fiction has moved from the slightly surreal mock naturalism of *Tamarisk Row* (1974) to the austere modernism of *The Plains* (1982), *Landscape with Landscape* (1985) and *Emerald Blue* (1995).

Murray, Les
Les Murray (b. 1938) is perhaps the leading Australian poet of his generation, often tipped to win a Booker, or even a Nobel Prize, but he only became known to the public at large when in 1999 he was brought in to help PM John Howard write his disastrous and ill-fated preamble to the Australian Constitution. The poet laureate of the Country Party.

Murray-Smith, Stephen
Stephen Murray-Smith (1922–88) founded the influential left-wing literary magazine, *Overland*, in 1954, edited many anthologies and was a leading figure in Melbourne intellectual life for many years.

Myer, Sidney
The original Myer was Sidney Baevski Myer (1878–1934) who migrated to Australia from Poland in 1897, and opened a store in Bendigo with his older brother, Elcon (1875–1938). He soon bought his brother out, and by dint of persuasive advertising and astute marketing became Bendigo's Busiest Drapers. After a visit to Europe Myer expanded, buying a Bourke Street drapers, Wright and Neil, in 1911, opening with a grand sale. Further expansion followed when the reunited brothers opened the Myer Emporium in 1914, with naturally enough a giant sale. Sidney converted to Christianity, got divorced and married his second wife, Marjorie Merlyn Baillieu, in 1920, thus uniting two of Melbourne's trading dynasties. The eleven-storey Lonsdale Street store opened in 1926. Sidney Myer rebuilt Bourke Street during the Depression to create jobs. He was a benefactor of worthy causes, a tradition continued by the Foundation established at his death.

N

Sidney Nolan, man behind the iron mask, by Michel Lawrence

Albert Namatjira and wife

Percy Leason on narks and nature strips

Namatjira, Albert

A member of the Arrernte Aboriginal people, Albert Namatjira (1902–59) became an almost overnight sensation with his European-influenced landscape watercolours. In 1957 he gained the dubious honour of being made an Australian citizen – ten years before the same right was bestowed on all Aboriginal people. His first exhibition in Melbourne in 1938 saw all 41 paintings on display sell.

Nation Review

Published weekly in Melbourne 1972–81, *Nation Review* was formed after a merger between the *Sydney Nation* and the *Melbourne Review*. It gave itself the nickname 'The Ferret' to match its controversial articles, animated reviews and literary debates. Among its frequent contributors was a young cartoonist named Michael Leunig, who used the national exposure to bolster his career.

Nature Strip

A feature of suburban Australia, the nature strip is a length of grass between footpath and road, traditionally and grudgingly maintained and mowed by the adjacent property owner. Nature strips are the prerogative of middle, perhaps middle-class suburbs, not the old macadamed inner bohemia.

Neighbours

Australia's premier soap opera, *Neighbours* was created by Reg Watson and made its debut on Channel 7 in 1985. The trials and tribulations of the residents of Ramsay St got off to a shaky start however, and the show was cancelled after 171 episodes – and was promptly picked up by Channel 10. *Neighbours* finally went global when it became a smash hit in England, and has been a ratings bonanza virtually ever since. Centring around the lives (especially early on) of two families, the Robinsons and the Ramsays, many dubious Australian stars have made their debut on the long-running soap. Witness the hit list: Kylie Minogue, Jason Donovan, Craig MacLachlan, Guy Pearce, Natalie Imbruglia and more!

New Idea

The first weekly Australian publication designed specifically for women, 1904.

N

Newk wins 1967 Wimbledon, with no mo

Sir Douglas Nicholls, first Aboriginal Governor

Olivia Newton-John, cute

Newcombe, John

John 'Newk' Newcombe (b. 1944) is one of the greatest tennis players Australia has ever produced, winning Wimbledon in 1967, the last year of amateur competition, and repeating the feat in 1970 and 1971. He is also one of our finest tennis coaches, leading the resurgence in Australian Davis Cup challenges with Tony Roche, his doubles partner for much of his career. Their many personal victories, including Wimbledon doubles victories in 1965, 68–70, were capped off when they coached Australia to win the 1999 Davis Cup.

Newton-John, Olivia

In 1965 Olivia Newton-John won a Johnny O'Keefe talent contest and scored a recording contract and a trip to England, and then in 1972 she became a regular on Cliff Richard's TV show. However it was *Grease* (1978) and co-star John Travolta which took her to the top. The film and album tie-in were hugely popular, and a string of hit albums followed, including five number one songs in the US, with *Physical* becoming her swan-song in the 1980s. Her business venture, the 'Koala Blue' chain of Australiana stores, filed for bankruptcy in 1991, but she has risen again in recent years.

Nicholls, Sir Douglas

Sir Doug Nicholls' (1906–88) life is a litany of great achievements. In 1972 he became Australia's first Aborigine to be knighted and became Australia's first Aboriginal Governor in 1976. A lifelong campaigner for land rights and racial equality, he had previously played 54 games of Australian football for Fitzroy, 1934–37, and competed in the Stawell Gift.

Nicholson, Peter

Peter Nicholson (b. 1948) sold his first cartoon to *Nation Review* for five dollars and never looked back. In 1976 the *Financial Review* offered him a job doing daily cartoons and six months later he was on staff at the *Age*, remaining there for 17 years. He also produced and directed the seminal *Rubbery Figures* show (1987–92) which used puppets to parody Australian politicians as cleverly as his cartoons. In 1994 a one-man show of his caricature sculptures, called *The Rubbery Years,* was toured around Australia by the National Museum. He joined the *Australian*'s sharp stable of black and white artists in 1994.

The cast of *Number 96*

Sid Nolan in his Parkville studio, 1940s

Greg Norman, driving

Nolan, Sidney

Largely self-taught, Sir Sidney Nolan (1917–92) made his name with his series of Ned Kelly paintings, begun in 1946. He moved to England in 1955 and continued to paint, as well as designing stage sets, such as the opera *The Rite of Spring* at Covent Garden in 1981. Nolan's reputation rests securely as the mythology and controversy around Ned Kelly grows. The black outlaw mask, with the eyes looking back at us, and the landscape behind, is surely the most potent image created in this country.

Norman, Greg

One of the world's greatest golfers, Greg 'The Great White Shark' Norman (b. 1955), and his Akubra have been wandering up and down golf courses as a professional since 1976. He was

ranked as the world's top player in 1986 and has won the Australian Open three times and the British Open twice. Also a powerful force in marketing, his face has appeared on everything from alcohol and cars to golfing equipment. He has been fated never to win a US major.

Nossal, Gustav

Gus Nossal (b. 1931) came to Australia with his family in 1939. Apart from two years as Assistant Professor of Genetics at Stanford University, a year at the Pasteur Institute in Paris, and a year as a Special Consultant to the World Health Organization, all Nossal's research career has been at the Walter and Eliza Hall Institute, of which he served as Director (1965–96). Nossal's research is in fundamental immunology, and he

has written five books and 510 scientific articles. He was Deputy Chairman of the Council for Aboriginal Reconciliation and Australian of the Year in 2000.

Number 96

Combining comedy, traditional soap opera elements, a dose of sauciness and then cramming the lot into a block of Sydney flats, *Number 96* titillated and amused Australian audiences for 1218 episodes on Channel 10 from 1972 to 1977. Its first screening was 'the night Australian TV lost its virginity'. The show not only saved Australian viewers from TV tedium, it saved Channel 10 from bankruptcy. The stars of the show became so popular that their early train journey to the Logies brought larger crowds than The Beatles tour.

O

Johnny O'Keefe's *Six O'Clock Rock* in full swing

Oarsome Foursome's golden moment

Lowitja O'Donoghue, stolen

Dinny O'Hearn, champion of Australian writing

Oakley, Barry

Playwright, columnist, novelist and literary editor, Barry Oakley (b. 1931) has been acerbically cataloguing Australian mores and manners in stories, novels and newspaper columns since his first novel *A Wild Ass of a Man* (1967). In 2000 friends and enemies discovered that Oakley had been keeping a diary all those years, published with the modest title *Minutudes*. His other major novels include the football tragicomedy *A Salute to the Great McCarthy* (1970) and *Let's Hear It for Prendergast* (1971) who was the tallest poet in the world. Plays include *The Feet of Daniel Mannix* (1970), *Beware of Imitations* (1973), *Bedfellows* (1975), *Scanlan* and *The Ship's Whistle*, about the forgotten poet Richard Hengist Horne (1979).

Oarsome Foursome

It all began in 1990, when a scarcely known team of four Australian coxless rowers won the European championships. This crew, James Tomkins, Sam Patten (later replaced by Andrew Cooper), Mike McKay and Nick Green, were tagged the Oarsome Foursome. However it was their gold medals in the 1992 and 1996 Olympic Games that cemented their place in Australian folklore.

O'Donoghue, Lowitja

Lowitja O'Donoghue (b. 1932) was born into the Yankunjatjara community in remote SA but was taken from her mother as a two-year-old and brought up in Quorn. Her first struggle was to be accepted as a trainee nurse in Adelaide, which she was in 1954. Joining the Department

of Aboriginal Affairs in 1967, she became the first Aboriginal person to be made a Regional Director in 1975. O'Donoghue was the inaugural chairperson of ATSIC, 1990–96, and was the subject of controversy in 2001 when she said she thought of herself as a 'removed' rather than 'stolen' child. This individual event was exaggerated by right-wing commentators as a denial of the label 'stolen generations', whereas it was an authentication of the complex fact that children were taken and hurt.

O'Hearn, D.J.

Dinny O'Hearn (1937–93) was a larrikin Irish Australian academic who managed to administer the Arts Faculty at Melbourne University at the same time as contributing mightily to the cultural life of

219

A postcard of the 1956 Olympic city, Melbourne

Melbourne – through talking, sponsoring, partying and reviewing, and helping establish such institutions as the Australian Centre, the Melbourne Writers Theatre and *Book Show* on SBS.

Old Melbourne Gaol

Ned Kelly was hanged there in 1880 and now it makes money as a museum to that moment, preserving his death mask, armour and the gallows on which he was hanged. Built in 1852–54 and closed in 1929, the current Old Melbourne Gaol was actually the third such structure to be built on the site. The surviving entrance buildings, central hall and chapel were begun in 1860. In 1862–64 a block for female prisoners was built, and the perimeter wall was finally completed in 1864.

Oliphant, Sir Marcus

Nuclear physicist Sir Marcus Oliphant (1901–2000) worked on the atomic bomb project at Los Alamos 1943–45. Oliphant was Director of the Research School of Physical Sciences, Australian National University 1950–63, and first President of the Australian Academy of Science 1954–56. Governor of South Australia 1971–76, he later argued strongly against America's policies regarding nuclear secrecy and further nuclear development.

Olympics

Australia is one of just three countries to have competed at every modern Olympic Games, and has been rewarded with two stagings of the Games, Melbourne 1956, the 'friendly Games', and Sydney 2000, the most successful Games 'ever'.

Australia's addiction to sport and spectacle, and seeing itself in the world through sports-tinted glasses, makes the Olympics a genuinely felt and experienced national ritual.

One Nation

The phrase 'One Nation' has had a currency since the time of Federation – 'One Nation, One People'. The predecessor of the AFL, the VFL, celebrated its jubilee in 1908 with the phrase, 'One People, One Nation, One Code of Football'. More recently Paul Keating used the phrase as the title of his anti-recession package of 1993, but he meant it inclusively. The xenophobic One Nation party would seek to exclude some Australians. Somewhere between 3–6 per cent of Australians support this idea.

A camouflaged version of Evelyn Owen's gun, the Digger's friend

Sir Marcus Oliphant, nuclear critic

'Tiger' Bill O'Reilly, champion of leggies

Oppy, the Bradman of bikes

Onus, Lin

Melbourne-based Aboriginal artist Lin Onus (1948–96) taught himself to paint after twenty years with the Country Fire Authority. Influenced by Western and Japanese art as well as traditional Aboriginal art practices, Onus' art illustrates his deep political concern over the plight of his people and the land they inhabit.

O'Keefe, Johnny

Legendary Australian rock singer, Johnny O'Keefe (1935–78) was king of rock'n'roll by the mid 1950s. *The Wild One* hit the charts in 1958, the first local platter to do so, and for the next six years he had a number of hits, including *Shout*, *She's My Baby* and *I'm Counting On You*. His ABC rock show, *Six O'Clock Rock* was also a first – first rock show on TV, in 1959–60,

and then on Seven as *The J O'K Show*, and *Sing Sing Sing* (1963). O'Keefe was never endowed with much of a voice, but that never stopped him.

Opperman, Hubert

Oppy (1904–96) was the Bradman of the bike in the 1920s, and later entered Federal politics as a Liberal in 1949, serving until 1966.

O'Reilly, Bill

'Tiger' Bill O'Reilly (1905–92) was a tremendous leg spinner for Australia, and a great cricket journalist for the *Sydney Morning Herald*. He played 27 Tests, and took 144 wickets, 1931–46, at 22.59, with a best of 7/54.

Overland

Overland began publication in 1954, edited by Steven Murray-Smith with

the motto 'Temper democratic, bias Australian'. It has had a renewed lease of life under editor Ian Syson in the 1990s.

Owen Gun

Designed by Evelyn Owen of Wollongong, the light and portable submachine gun was initially ignored by the Army, but after being taken up by Port Kembla manufacturer Lysaght's eventually 45 000 were produced.

Oz Magazine

Oz launched in 1963 in Sydney, edited by Richard Neville, Richard Walsh and Peter Griose, art directed by the graphically extraordinary Martin Sharp. Satire wasn't popular with the pooh-bahs and *Oz* was sued in 1964, editors jailed and freed on appeal. Circulation boomed. It closed in 1969 after Sharp and Neville left to start *London Oz*. More trials ensued in 1971.

P

The Pram Factory in 1973. Front Theatre on the first floor, market in the former panel beaters shop below.

Sir Frank Packer: he who must be obeyed

The *Bulletin*, bought by Sir Frank in 1960

Australia's most popular weekly in 1934

Packer – A Dynasty

The Packer dynasty begins with Sir Frank's father Clyde, known as R.C. Packer (1879–1934) journalist, editor, NSW Chief Scout in 1909, and co-founder of *Smith's Weekly* in 1919, the daily *Guardian* in 1923, *Sunday Guardian* in 1926 and founder of the Miss Australia Quest as a promotion for the newspaper, in 1926. He sold out for cash and shares to Sir Hugh Denison's Associated Newspapers in 1930, but returned in 1931 as managing editor after the Guardians ceased publication, to protect his investment. He died on his first overseas trip, off Marseilles. R.C. had problematic relationships with business associates and politicians, a trait passed on down the family line. Meanwhile Frank (Douglas Frank Hewson Packer, 1906–74) had begun

working life as a cadet on the *Guardian* in 1923, and had various tasks including accompanying the first Miss Australia, Beryl Squires, on a tour of the United States. In 1932, Frank became involved in a plan to publish a rival afternoon newspaper to the Associated Newspapers' *Sun* (R.C. was by now MD of AN). The deal was eventually struck that Frank and his partner E.G. 'Red Ted' Theodore were paid £86 500 if they did not publish an afternoon rival for three years. This was an extraordinary deal, and financed Frank and Theodore's gold mining venture in Fiji, and then the foundation of the *Australian Women's Weekly* in 1933.

In 1934 with the non-publication agreement about to lapse, Frank considered starting a new daily, which frightened Associated

Newspapers into folding its struggling morning paper, the *Telegraph*, into a new company, Consolidated Press, run by Packer and Theodore. The Packer company Television Corporation Ltd acquired a Sydney licence in 1955 and began broadcasting as TCN-9 in 1956, and in 1960 it bought GTV-9 in Melbourne, becoming the first TV network. Frank also acquired the *Bulletin* magazine in 1960, and his right-wing views and interference in both places became legendary. The Telegraph newspapers were losing money, and were sold to Rupert Murdoch's News Ltd in 1972. Frank Packer was a sportsman. He was NSW amateur heavyweight boxing champion in 1929, a polo player, yachtsman and financier of *Gretel* which challenged for the America's Cup in 1962 and 1970.

James Packer, a quick rise to the top

John Spooner's portrait of Australia's richest man

Packer, Clyde

Clyde Packer (1935–2001), son of Sir Frank, was a cadet on the *Canberra Times* in the early 1950s, and joined the family business in 1955. He was general manager of Consolidated Press 1960–66, and of TCN-9 1966–72, and deputy chairman of ConPress 1966–73. He resigned from Nine in 1972 because Sir Frank had ordered him not to run an interview with Bob Hawke, then President of the ACTU. He died in 2001.

Packer, James

Formerly Jamie, by 2000 James Packer (b. 1967) had been groomed by father Kerry to prosper the family business into the new century and the new media. James married Jodie, a semi-supermodel, and after a stint as assistant to Al 'Chainsaw' Dunlap in 1991 –92, James was General Manager of Consolidated Press Group 1992–96, CEO of Publishing and Broadcasting Ltd 1996–98 when he became Chairman, and CEO of Consolidated Press. The Packer heir apparent is on the board of NineMSN, Australia's most popular internet portal, Foxtel, and Ecorp and was on the board of OneTel.

Packer, Kerry Francis Bullmore

Australia's richest person, and the major local media mogul, given that Rupert Murdoch is an American. Kerry (b. 1937) took over the Packer empire on his father Frank's death in 1974, sold the Nine Network to Alan Bond for a billion dollars in 1987 ('You only get one Alan Bond in your lifetime') and then bought it back three years later in the Bond fire sale for $250 million. A leviathan punter whose rumoured losses and wins in London, Las Vegas and on Australian racetracks are legend, Packer is feared and disliked by politicians, journalists and the politically correct crowd. Australians, however, have a respect for someone who wins on the punt, and have made most of his media assets very successful. His battle for the TV rights to a modernised cricket competition, resulting in World Series Cricket in 1977, proved traumatic for many and changed the game – probably not for the better. One day cricket and the television coverage of it however, has proved the saviour of the game. Nine is by far Australia's most popular TV network. Consolidated Press magazines such as the *Women's Weekly* are popular also, the *Bulletin* less so.

Damien Parer with a couple of Diggers near Mubo, New Guinea, in 1943

Australia's much-loved writer Ruth Park

Pancake Parlour

Launched in Adelaide in 1965 by Helen and Allen Trachsel (who still manage the business), Pancake Parlour is one of the few native Australian fast food chains. Serving pancakes and related merchandise from an arcane menu decorated in a peculiar Alice in Wonderland style it has remained a success. In 1969, they brought the restaurant to Victoria and in 1978 to New South Wales.

Pandora, HMS

His Majesty's Ship *Pandora* was sent in search of the *Bounty* mutineers in 1791 at Tahiti, but failed to find Fletcher Christian who had sailed to Pitcairn Island. It picked up the men who had remained at Tahiti but ran into the Great Barrier Reef on August 28, 1791. The *Bounty* men were cruelly

chained in a cage known as Pandora's Box, and four drowned (31 of the *Pandora* crew had also perished) because they were not released, ten others joined the 89 *Pandora* crew, and rowed to Timor. Three of the *Pandora* men were eventually hanged for mutiny, the others were acquitted or pardoned.

Parer, Damien

One of Australia's greatest war photographers, Damien Parer (1912–44) worked with Charles Chauvel on the camera crew for the films *Heritage* (1935) and *Forty Thousand Horsemen* (1940). He joined a Commonwealth Film Unit in 1939 and followed the AIF to the Middle East in 1940 and New Guinea in 1942, where he worked producing documentaries of Australia's involvement in the war.

His documentary *Jungle Warfare on the Kokoda Front* won an Oscar in 1943. A legend because of his courage and determination in appalling circumstances, he had nearly as much trouble with Australian bureaucrats as the enemy. Parer was killed in the Philippines after joining the Americans in 1944. His images, especially of the 1942 Kokoda campaign, are the defining images of Australians at war.

Park, Ruth

Born and educated in New Zealand, Ruth Park (b. 1922) came to Australia in 1942 where she married the writer D'Arcy Niland. The pair proved themselves a successful writing duo, working on everything from short stories to radio jingles to make a living. Park also wrote several novels,

The Father of Federation, Sir Henry Parkes

The sinking of HMAS *Perth*, Parkin's first book

The Banjo, a prominent racing identity

including *The Harp in the South* (1948) which won the 1946 *Sydney Morning Herald* novel competition, and *Swords and Crowns and Rings* (1977) which won the Miles Franklin Award. She is also the author of children's fiction and is the creator of the 'Muddle-Headed Wombat' series.

Parkes, Sir Henry

Sir Henry (1815–96) came to Australia in 1839 after several unsuccessful business ventures in England. Work in many areas followed before a career in politics was launched when he was elected in 1854 to the NSW Legislative Council and the first Legislative Assembly in 1856. His position was never certain, but Parkes managed to become premier of NSW in 1872, and was later dubbed the 'Father of Federation'.

Parkin, Ray

One of the best writers and illustrators of any nationality to survive World War II, Ray Parkin (b. 1910) served with the Royal Australian Navy from 1928 to 1942 when HMAS *Perth* was sunk under him. He became a POW in Java, then on the Burma–Thailand Railway, and in Japan. Parkin wrote three classic accounts of this time in his life. *Out of the Smoke* (1960), tells the story of the sinking of the HMAS *Perth*, while *Into the Smother* (1963) follows the Burma–Thailand Railway in an extraordinarily humane manner, and *The Sword and the Blossom* (1968) deals vividly with Parkin's experiences in Japan. His massive illustrated work *HM Bark Endeavour* (1997) is a seaman craftsman's tribute to another great sailor's ship.

Paterson, Andrew Barton

'Banjo' Paterson (1864–1941) could lay claim to being Australia's national poet, if only for penning the words to *Waltzing Matilda*. But there is of course more, Banjo (the pseudonym he adopted for his first contributions to the *Bulletin*) became famous following the publication of *The Man From Snowy River and Other Verses* in 1895. It remains the highest selling book of poetry in Australian history. Clancy of the Overflow, Mulga Bill, the Man from Ironbark are other classical Australians. Paterson was a war correspondent during the Boer War, covered the Boxer Rebellion in China, and served with the Remount Service in the Middle East in World War I. He was a great racegoer, raconteur and writer about horses and an unchauvinistic nationalist.

Sir Les tips us a wink

Anna Pavlova is delighted with the shoes

Lovely shirts, still Australian owned

Paterson's Curse

A purple weed valued by apiarists, hated by all others, poisonous to stock. The name comes from a Paterson of Albury from whose garden the curse spread.

Patterson, Les

'Sir' Les was created by Barry Humphries in 1974. Overweight, red-nosed, vulgar and hilarious, this ex-politican has survived the fall of the Whitlam government to poke fun at the elitism, cronyism and government support for the arts.

Pavlova

Although some claim this dessert originates in New Zealand, it was perfected by Perth chef Bert Sachse at the now demolished Esplanade Hotel and named for the visiting Russian ballerina Anna Pavlova in 1935. The 'Pav', as it is affectionately known, is a meringue made from egg whites, sugar, cornflour, lemon juice and topped with whipped cream and passionfruit. Anna was a superstar, and much sought after by local advertisers.

Pelaco Shirts

Famed Australian-owned clothing company, Pelaco commenced business as a shirt-making partnership between Messrs J. Pearson and J. Law in 1906. In 1917 they established Pelaco Ltd from the first two letters of Pearson, Law, Company. Their first great advertising success was using a Geelong character called Mulga Fred, who became known as Pelaco Bill in the late 1930s. His slogan was 'Mine Tinkit They Fit'. While not exactly racist, the pidgin slogan is certainly patronising. In the 1950s the ads changed to a picture of then supermodel Bambi Shmith saying (in print) 'It is indeed a lovely shirt sir!' By 2001 the company was still Australian owned, with the slogan 'Pelaco – Australian Made', but its future looked doubtful.

Penguins, Angry

Angry Penguins was originally a quarterly magazine edited by Max Harris and John Reed between 1940 and 1946 devoted to modern writing, painting and the arts. James McAuley and Harold Stewart set up an elaborate hoax, inventing the late motor mechanic poet Ern Malley and writing his poems, and submitting them to *Angry Penguins*. They were enthusiastically published in 1944, to

The first edition of the magazine *Angry Penguins*

Young John Perceval

Legendary *Age* editor Graham Perkin

the ridicule of conservative Australian poets who joyfully exposed the scam. Modernists thought the poems were better than Stewart and McAuley realised or understood.

'Angry Penguins' has also become a shorthand title for the great florescence of painters in Melbourne in the 1940s around John and Sunday Reed's salon at Heide – Sid Nolan, Arthur Boyd, John Perceval, Albert Tucker, Joy Hester and others.

Penguins, Fairy

Australia's only resident penguins are the fairy penguins (*Eudyptula minor*) and their most famous mainland rookery is at Phillip Island in Victoria. Here the cute little birds have created a large tourist industry as people from all round the world go to see the penguins parade in the evening.

Perceval, John

An Angry Penguin, John Perceval (1923–2000) was born Linwood Robert Steven South at Bruce Rock Base Hospital, 220km east of Perth. He contracted polio during the summer of 1937–38 and, while recuperating, spent most of his time painting. He regained the ability to walk, albeit with some difficulty, and after a period in the army continued painting in earnest. Garish colours and potent subject matter combined to create a powerful visual style. The image of the child, a symbol of isolation and anxiety, would become central to his work which included sculpture as well as painting. His painting 'Scudding Swans' sold for $552 500 in June 2000, the highest amount ever paid for a painting by a living Australian artist.

Perkin, Graham

Graham Perkin (1929–75) became one of the most influential editors of the age when he became editor of the *Age* in 1966. He was 36, and turned what was a stodgy and conservative newspaper into a modern, independent, and influential one. He raised the standards of the paper by encouraging investigative and analytical journalism, occasionally campaigning, insisting on accuracy and responsibility. His time is looked back on as the golden age of the *Age*.

Perkins, Charles

Charles Perkins (1936–2000) was a fierce controversialist on behalf of the Aboriginal people. Born in Alice Springs, he was separated from his mother at the age of nine, and lived in Adelaide till he was in his mid 20s,

Charles Perkins' 1975 autobiography

Kieren Perkins wins another gold

Peter Pan, Andy Knox up

where he first became involved in campaigning, and took up soccer. He was a very good soccer player, and moved to Sydney in 1961 where he played for the Pan Hellenic team. In Sydney Pastor Ted Noffs encouraged him to go back to school, and then university where he became the first Aboriginal male to graduate in 1965. He led the legendary Freedom Rides through NSW in 1965. He joined the Aboriginal Affairs Department in the late 1960s and despite controversy was eventually made the first Aboriginal secretary of the department, 1984–88. He continued in public and business life, outspoken to the end. His biographer, Peter Read, wrote that in Perkins' lifetime a great and continuing change had been achieved in what Aboriginal people believed themselves capable.

Now 'Aboriginal individuals could achieve anything they chose and that negotiations must be as between equal partners. For this shift in public perceptions, Perkins was to a remarkable degree responsible, as much for the possibilities he demonstrated to younger Aborigines as what he achieved.'

Perkins, Kieren

The epitome of the modern Australian Olympic sportsman, Kieren Perkins stopped the nation when he won his second gold medal in the 1500 metres freestyle in Atlanta. He barely made the final, but turned in an extraordinarily courageous performance to win from lane eight. This made him into something larger than just a world-record breaking swimmer with a nice smile. He now

had a heart as big as Phar Lap, and was elevated from the common level of champion to that of a legend, up there with Dawn Fraser. We watched him struggle into the Sydney 2000 team, and hoped the dream would come true. It didn't, but not for want of grace – he was beaten by another Australian, Grant Hackett, and had to be content with silver. At the time he still held the world record for the 1500 metres; nobody else has swum very close.

Peter Pan

The spiritual successor to Phar Lap, Peter Pan was a tall, chestnut horse with a remarkable silver mane. Bred by Rodney Dangar, Peter Pan was a star of Australian racing in the 1930s with highlights being victories in the Melbourne Cups of 1932 and 1934.

229

Bruce Petty has a look at a spy scandal of the 1970s, when the American use of the Pine Gap base was controversial. What did they do there?

Petrov Affair

In 1954, Vladimir Petrov, third secretary of the Soviet Embassy in Canberra, defected and was granted political asylum by the Menzies government. The Soviets tried to fly Mrs Petrov out of the country but the aircraft was intercepted at Darwin, and dramatic pictures taken of Mrs Petrov and the plane. She too was granted asylum, and let it be known that they had been spying, handing over documents to ASIO. A Royal Commission was held into Soviet espionage, 1954–55. It revealed, among other things, an allegedly genuine document which named the Leader of the Opposition, Dr H.V. Evatt. He claimed it was a fabrication, used to stir the Red menace and help the Menzies government win the Cold War election of 1954.

Vladimir Mikhailovich Petrov made the headlines in 1954. With wife Evdokia, he was naturalised an Australian in 1956, and vanished.

Petty, Bruce

The elder statesman of Australian cartoonists, Bruce Petty (b. 1929) is much more – he is an Academy Award winning animation film maker, for *Leisure* (1977). Petty's intelligence, wit and scribbled line marked him as something more complex than a one cell joke maker. His work in the *Australian* from 1964–73, especially on the question of Southeast Asia and the Vietnam War, were powerful aids in understanding what was going on. He cartoons for the Melbourne *Age*, and makes films. They include *Australian History* (1971), *Marx* (1981), *Money* (1998) and *The Mad Century* (2000). Petty's view that the world works like a mad Heath Robinson-ish machine operated by Franz Kafka has influenced a generation of newspaper readers.

Phar Lap in his prime, with strapper Tommy Woodcock; a booklet published in 1931 extolling his greatness; Eric Thake's take on the great horse as a work of art

Phar Lap

One of the more likeable aspects of Australia is the sorts of things that have insinuated themselves into the national consciousness and become heroic emblems, images of the place. Military failures, strange sports, unique backyard apparatus, for example. There are not too many generals or kings, but plenty of privates, and a few cross-dressing comics. And there is a horse, typically not even born here, ugly, purchased for not much, and that won a single Melbourne Cup before being 'murdered' by the Yanks. Phar Lap. Carbine, winner of the 1890 Melbourne Cup, was probably a better horse, just as brave, and his bloodline runs in 40 more Cup winners, but his hide is not preserved in pride of place in a museum. He has not inspired song, theatre, movie, a postcard industry. We don't hear of a heart as big as Carbine's. Carbine raced, in a way, before publicity, and Phar Lap was recognised as the best advertised horse in Australia in his meteoric rise and fall – which occupied less than three years. Phar Lap became the symbol of hope in the Great Depression, and even when he lost he won because he was crippled by the weight. A country that had lost a generation in World War I, that was being pounded by the Depression and unemployment, that could see a worse war on the horizon, loved the certainty and the uplifting of the spirits that backing a winner like Phar Lap (or Bradman) brought. And only the good die young. Gangsters in the employ, so they say, of bookmakers standing to lose a fortune on Phar Lap, shot at him before the 1930 Melbourne Cup. He won anyway. Then with Australia conquered, and huge weights handicapping him at home, Phar Lap voyaged to the United States in 1932 to show the world what we were capable of. There he had his apotheosis. Phar Lap's 36th win on the dirt track at Agua Caliente took his total winnings to $332 250. The Americans could see a champion when they saw one. But 16 days after his win, Phar Lap was dead. Naturally conspiracy theories sprang to life, it being an Aussie in America. His death was certainly mysterious, and while modern explanations of strange bacteria are no doubt true, they do not satisfy. An accidental death by disease does not really befit the only horse who has become a national legend. He surely was got at.

Arthur Phillip ashore at Port Jackson

Anne Louise Lambert at the Picnic

William Edwin Pidgeon – the great WEP

Phillip, Arthur

Commander of the First Fleet to NSW, Captain Arthur Phillip (1738–1814) was Governor of NSW 1788–92. Well organised, humane under the circumstances, Phillip laid the foundation for the success of the colony. He was an advocate of conciliation with the Aboriginal people, despite being speared, and returned to London in 1792 with Bennelong who later returned to Sydney. Phillip's career is as varied as Captain Jack Aubrey's (without the fighting) in Patrick O'Brian's novel series about naturalists and the Royal Navy of Phillip's dotage.

Picnic at Hanging Rock

Peter Weir's 1975 mystery film about a party of sexually hysterical yet gauzy girls who go for a picnic at an ancient rock formation on Valentine's Day 1900 and disappear is based on Joan Lindsay's 1967 novel. Lindsay published the novel originally without a final chapter, and without a resolution. What did happen? Was the disappearance based on a real incident? Or is the story and the film a mystery of the old Australia, the bush having a magical impact on the inappropriate European invader/settlers. Probably the latter. The film was important in restarting the Australian film industry in the 1970s, and in creating an image of Australia in the minds of cinema audiences around the world.

Pidgeon, W.E.

William Edwin Pidgeon (WEP) was a cartoonist, war artist and three-time Archibald Prize winner (1951, 1961, 1968). His portrait of Sir Robert Menzies (completed 1968) is well remembered. WEP was also a famous cartoonist and illustrator for the *Daily Telegraph* in Sydney and for the *Australian Women's Weekly*. He became renowned for his covers of the *Weekly* from its inception (and in fact, WEP helped create the original dummy back in 1933) through to the 1950s.

Pie Floater

A traditional dish from that home of fine Australian cuisine, Adelaide, the pie floater is a rare and subtle delicacy. A single pie embraced by a bowl of thick, green pea soup and often garnished with a crimson splatter of sauce. The floater can be eaten with a spoon, a fork or your hands, outside the Adelaide Station.

232

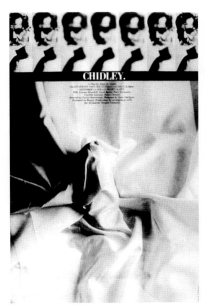

The first Playbox production, 1976

Three soulful 70s types – Playbox founders Hutchinson, Blundell and Gantner

Pieman, Flying

William Francis King (1807–74) arrived in NSW in 1829, and was known as the Flying Pieman. He was a famous athlete, fabulously be-ribboned itinerant pie seller and record breaker of his day. One advertising soubriquet was 'the Ladies' Walking Flying Pieman'. He could run faster than the coach, running 1634 miles in 39 days and twice beating it from Sydney to Windsor. He carried a 42 kilogram goat from Brickfield Hill to a pub in Parramatta in nine hours. He won a bet to run a thousand quarter miles in a thousand quarter hours, having himself horsewhipped towards the end to complete the feat.

Pig Iron Bob

In 1938 Robert Menzies, then Attorney General in the conservative Lyons government, opposed and overcame a waterside union ban on the export of pig iron to Japan, and earned the nickname Pig Iron Bob. The wharfie's view was that the iron was to be used in Japan's war in China, and just might end up used against Australia. The Menzian viewpoint was that the government made foreign policy not the unions, no matter who was right about the pig iron. He had the melancholy duty of declaring war, on Germany, as prime minister in 1939. Japan was to come later.

Playbox Theatre

The Playbox had its direct origin in Hoopla Productions, set up by Graeme Blundell and Garrie Hutchinson in 1976 to produce *Chidley* by Alma de Groen and *The Golden Oldies* by Dorothy Hewett.

Carrillo Gantner joined, and the trio took on the lease of the Playbox Theatre in Exhibition Street Melbourne for the tour of Gordon Chater in Steve J. Spears' *Elocution of Benjamin Franklin* in 1977. A determination to produce Australian work saw the theatre struggle through to 1984, by which time Gantner alone remained of the originals, and the theatre burned down. CUB donated its old Malthouse in South Melbourne in 1986, and a new two-theatre complex opened in 1990.

Play School

One of the longest running children's TV programs in Australian history, *Play School* and its cast of trapped-in-resin presenters have been singing along and reading out picture books

233

The scoreboard tells the tale, Ponsford 352

Lyndall Barbour at the microphone in the long-running radio soap, *Portia Faces Life*

since 1966. Remarkable for its long-serving presenters, who have included Benita Collings since 1969, John Hamblin since 1970 and Noni Hazlehurst since 1978.
See: Bananas in Pyjamas

Ponsford, Bill
Record-breaking Victorian and Australian opening batsman, Bill Ponsford (1900–91) is the only batsman to have made over 400 in two innings in first class cricket, and averaged 48 in 29 Tests. He made 352 in Victoria's awesome 1107 against NSW in 1926–27. The Ponsford Stand at the MCG is named for him.

Poppy (King)
Lipstick princess Poppy King was named Young Australian of the Year in 1995 after Poppy Industries (set up

when King was only nineteen) hit the big time with sales to most major Australian retailers. Despite a fall-out with her original investors, her business is now estimated to have an annual turnover around the four million dollar mark and her lipsticks are being sold internationally. Somehow lipstick also equals political nous and she was elected to the Constitutional Convention in 1998.

Portia Faces Life
Hitting the airwaves for the first time in 1952, *Portia Faces Life* would run an incredible 3544 episodes. Starring Lyndall Barbour as Portia Manning along with Leonard Teale, Owen Weingott and Aileen Britten, the show would become one of the most popular daytime radio serials in the country.

Powderfinger
Hailing from Brisbane and named after a Neil Young song, Powderfinger has been one of the true success stories of 1990s rock in Australia. Between the rhythmic, guitar-driven sound of Darren Middleton, John Collins, Ian Haug and Jon Coghill and singer Bernard Fanning's alternately rough and soulful voice, the band was always destined for success. Not that it came easy at first, however. Their debut album *Parables for Wooden Ears* (1994) didn't sell, but its follow-up *Double Allergic* (1996) and its break-out single *Pick You Up* both did, while their third album *Internationalist* went triple platinum and took four ARIA awards in 1999. Already gaining international exposure, watch them go global in the new millennium.

Max Gillies, Back Theatre, Pram Factory 1976

Margaret Preston at home, 1940s

Glowing Princess Panda and Happy Hammond

Pram Factory

A theatre built in a perambulator factory, in Drummond Street, Carlton around the corner from La Mama. It was the home of the Australian Performing Group (APG), and was set up in 1970 with its first production, the lively *Marvellous Melbourne*, based on an old melodrama, and scripts. The Pram Factory provided a venue not only for the APG but other parts of the new Australian theatre. There was a Front Theatre which seated about 150 uncomfortably, a Back Theatre for even smaller works, an Office, where strategies were devised, and a Tower where some members lived, and a ground floor known as the Panel Beaters, which housed a mess and a flea market. The Pram Factory was sold in 1980 and the site is now a mall and a carpark.

Preston, Margaret

Margaret Preston (1875–1963) was an early champion of Aboriginal art, and the influence of bark painting can be seen in her extraordinary still lives, wood cuts, and book and magazine designs in the 1920s to the 1940s. She was a 'natural enemy of the dull' according to Sydney Ure Smith, and a belligerent, some thought, advocate of an Australian art that had nothing to do with 'Grandpa G Britain' and the threat of internationalism. Despite her own misgivings about the term, Preston has become a decorative artist, some might even say 'kitsch'.

Prichard, Katharine Susannah

Katharine Susannah Prichard (1883–1969) was a journalist on the Melbourne *Herald* 1908–12, before winning Hodder & Stoughton's All Empire Novel Competition with *The Pioneers* in London. Further novels devoted to working class and bush life followed, including *Coonardoo* (1928) and *Haxby's Circus* (1929). A romantic Communist, she married Captain Hugo Throssell VC in 1919, and was deeply troubled by his suicide in 1933.

Prickly Pear

The prickly pear was introduced into New South Wales around 1839 and Queensland around 1843. Its spread was so rapid that as early as 1844, the Brisbane *Courier* was calling for some means to counter its growth. A tall cactus with large, pear-shaped pads covered with razor-sharp spines, it became one of the greatest pests ever to hit Australian soil. Farms, properties and homes were unable to

A tense moment in *Prisoner*

A 1930s anti-prohibition ad drawn by Percy Leason

Puff puff Puffing Billy

P

stand in its way and by 1925 the prickly menace had overwhelmed 26 million acres with another million acres disappearing each year. In 1926–27 a tiny caterpillar named the *Cactoblastis* was introduced and within two decades it had completely defeated the plant.

Princess Panda
Beautiful 'straight woman' to Happy Hammond, Vic 'Funnyface' Gordon and the gang in the early 1960s kids' rating success, *The Happy Show*. Real name Panda Lisner, she was Victoria's first Miss Television, the innocent object of desire of small boys.

Prisoner
Another cult Australian TV program, *Prisoner: Cell Block H* first aired in 1979 and ran for eight years and 692

episodes, much longer than the 16 episodes cast or crew had originally planned. Featuring memorable characters like the hard-nosed Bea Smith (Val Lehman) and the nasal whine of the slightly 'touched' Lizzie Birdsworth (Sheila Florance), it was an immediate cult hit. One of the earliest Australian soaps, it traced the trials and tribulations of the staff and inmates of Wentworth Detention Centre, a prison for women. A pseudo-spoof musical was also made many years later and toured internationally to much confusion.

Prohibition
Numerous attempts have been made by temperance groups and wowsers to limit and even ban Australia's drinking habit. Referenda were held in South Australia in 1915, in NSW in

1916 (after a drunken rampage by 15 000 Diggers) and in Victoria, which brought about six o'clock closing. The restriction was not ended until 1954 in NSW, 1965 in Victoria, and 1966 in SA. Further, unsuccessful referenda were held advocating the complete prohibition of alcohol in the 1920s, as the wowsers took heart from the US example. None succeeded in Australia.

Puffing Billy
Australia's century-old steam train is still running on its original track through the Dandenong Ranges near Melbourne every day of the year except Christmas Day. In 1954 however things looked grim, and a *Sun* journalist David Bourke organised a 'last trip' on Puffing Billy as part of his column. The event was such a

Clifton Pugh takes a break

A plea from *Punch*, 1925, drawing by Percy Leason

success that another was scheduled which in turn inspired the formation of the Puffing Billy Preservation Society. The Society proved a professional and accomplished unit and has ensured its success for future generations.

Pugh, Clifton

Clifton Pugh (1924–90) was a 'romantic impressionist' who won the Archibald Prize three times, in 1965, 1971 and in 1972 for his portrait of Gough Whitlam, a sign of his enthusiastic Labor politics. He was gobsmacked when he first saw Nolan's Kelly paintings, and is associated with a later generation of painters – Don Laycock, Charles Blackman, John Brack, Leonard French, John Olsen, Rick Amor, Fred Williams. John Olsen once remarked that

Pugh 'produced some of the best and worst paintings in Australian art history'.

Punch

Beginning as *Melbourne Punch* in 1855, dropping the 'Melbourne' in 1900, *Punch* was a satirical magazine along the lines of the London version. It was Australia's first illustrated popular magazine, having great fun lampooning politicians and local pretensions. It was especially strong on cartoonists, a tradition which Keith Murdoch tried to re-establish when the Melbourne Herald group took over *Punch* in 1924. Murdoch hired Kenneth Slessor as a contributor, pinched the great Percy Leason from the *Bulletin* and lured Will Dyson back from London. With Bancks, Hugh McCrae and Murdoch

money it should have succeeded, but it was closed in December 1925 and folded into the general interest magazine *Table Talk*.

Puppetry of the Penis

A unique, albeit shortlived, blip on the Australian cultural radar, *Puppetry of the Penis* hit the mainstream following a documentary by Mick Molloy titled *Tackle Happy*. Featuring the ancient art of genital origami and starring Simon Morley and David Friend, a sold-out national tour saw international dates and a stint on the West End. To finish with a quote from their ads: 'Be amazed at the hamburger, taken away by the windsurfer and cheer at the slow emerging mollusc, a camera and large screen enables shocking detail of these truly classic installations.'

237

Q

Sydney's Queen Victoria Building in its early twentieth-century heyday

Rod Quantock: Father of Bus, son of Tram

The QVB today

A Qantas ad (1946), and first flying kanga (1947)

Qantas

Registered in 1920 by two ex-World War I pilots, Wilmot Hudson Fysh and Paul Joseph McGinness, Qantas commenced operations in 1922. The flying kangaroo symbol was introduced after the government takeover of Qantas in 1947, from the name of the Indian Ocean hop of the kangaroo service.

Quantock, Rod

Comedian with a conscience, Rod Quantock (b. 1948) burst onto the international scene in the 1980s with a loudhailer and a rubber chicken in his show *Bus* which took an audience wearing Groucho Marx masks on gatecrashing escapades through casinos and men's clubs. Later TV shows like *Australia, You're Standing In It* and a bevy of live gigs saw him

become a fixture in Australian comedy. A vocal opponent of former Victorian Liberal premier Jeff Kennett, he has been a pioneer in a new generation of political Australian comics.

Queen Victoria Building

A market site from Governor Macquarie's time, the Queen Victoria Market Building was developed by the Council of Sydney Town in 1893 to replace earlier decrepit structures. Designed by the town architect in Romanesque style and built at a cost of £300 000. Opened on 21 July 1898, it proved uncommercial – despite Mei Quong Tart's popular café and an assortment of taxidermists, flower sellers, fortune tellers, corset fitters, herbalists and wine merchants. It was remodelled in 1916, the verandah

removed in 1918 and in 1927 a report recommended it be demolished to improve access to the new Sydney Harbour Bridge. Fortunately this didn't happen, and it became the headquarters of the council's Electricity Department in 1935. Further suggestions that it be demolished surfaced in the 1950s and 1960s. By this time it had been classified as a national treasure by the National Trust, and in the 1970s it was slated by the Council for preservation. In 1977 submissions were called for sympathetic development plans. None seemed to be commercially viable. Further submissions were called for in 1980, and just when it seemed that failure would again be the result, Yap Lim Sen of Malaysian company Ipoh Investments noticed the sign calling for expressions of interest on his way

The *Quetta* afloat

A couple of desert queens view the back of beyond

to the airport. Six years later the restored shopping complex opened, at a cost of $75 million.

Queen Victoria Market

The Queen Victoria Market is miraculously still thriving in inner city Melbourne, where it has been a cultural fixture since its official opening on 20 March 1878. It is still crammed with fresh produce, bargains and remains the source of fresh rabbits. Many of its old sheds are now heritage listed and with over 130 000 visitors per year is Melbourne's most popular attraction.

Queensland

A state of mind in northern Australia, where the beauty of reef and rainforest contrasts with the dark political corners. The weather seems to have induced a Deep North view of the world. Traditional bolthole of conservative southerners in retirement. Home state of the politically incorrect Pauline Hanson and Bill Hayden. Said to be beautiful one day, seamy the next night.
See: One Nation

Queens of the Desert

Australia's gay, transsexual, and cross-dressing culture reached a kind of apotheosis in Stephan Elliott's film *The Adventures of Priscilla, Queen of the Desert*. Credited with 'feminising' the 'harsh' Australian outback with its signature image of fabric streaming from the bus against the red landscape. Further heights were reached when the bus reappeared with cross-dressing accompaniment at the Sydney Olympics closing gala.

Quetta

At 9:30pm on 28 February 1890, the steamship *Quetta* on her way to London from Brisbane hit a submerged rock in Torres Strait and sank, taking 133 of the 290 on board down with her. Among the survivors were three girls, including 16-year-old Emily Lacy who was rescued after spending 36 hours in the water. Relics of the event are preserved in the so-called Quetta Cathedral on Thursday Island.

Quids

Quids were Australian pounds, indicated by the sign £. In 1966, when dollarisation of the Australian economy began, a quid was worth $2. The expression, 'wouldn't be dead for quids' meant something in those days, and even more today.

The Quiz Kids , with John Dease (centre) ponder another curly question

Mei Quong Tart; Adrian Quist by Noel Counihan

Quiros, Ferdinand de

Portuguese-born Spanish navigator, de Quiros (1565–1615) was a member of the expedition that attempted to colonise the Solomons in 1595. In 1605 he led an expedition to search for Terra Australis, the dreamed-of Great South Land, from Peru. De Quiros abandoned the near-mutinous co-expeditioners including Luis de Torres, who sailed on through the eponymous strait. De Quiros returned to Spain in 1607, and tried for seven years to get another ship. He died in Panama before he could sail again.

Quist, Adrian

A member of the early golden age of Australian tennis, Adrian Quist (1913–91) was most famous as a doubles player partnering John Bromwich. They won the Australian doubles title 1936–40, and 1946–50, US doubles in 1939 and Wimbledon in 1950. He was Australian singles champion in 1936, 1940 and 1948.

Quiz Kids

In the 1950s budding geniuses could test their knowledge against Australia's own *The Quiz Kids*. Compered by John Dease, the show was one of several popular radio quiz programs at the time, such as *Pick-a-Box* and *Give It a Go*.

Quokka

The Quokka is not a rat. Honestly. In 1616, when Dirk Hartog named Rottnest Island (shorthand for Rat's Nest) after witnessing firsthand the huge number of Quokkas found there, he was mistaken. In fact, the Quokka is a small scrub-wallaby which lives exclusively in the south-west of Western Australia and is the faunal emblem of that state.

Quong Tart, Mei

Quong Tart (1850–1903) arrived in Australia when he was nine and by the time he was 18 his success as a merchant and entrepreneur on the goldfields had brought him a small fortune. In Sydney he opened a number of successful tea rooms and cafés, most memorably in the Queen Victoria Building in 1898, and organised a series of Chinese-run horse racing meetings in the 1870s. He was also a campaigner for better conditions for Chinese miners and acted as an unofficial mediator between Chinese and Europeans in Australia until his death after a racist beating at age 53.

R

Lloyd Rees photographed by Michel Lawrence in 1988

The PPP Rabbit Annihilator

A rabbitoh shows his wares in the 1890s

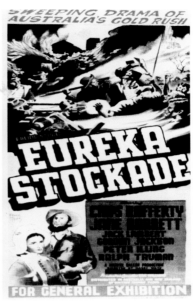

One of Chips Rafferty's epic Australian roles

Rabbit, The

Rabbits have been a problem in Australia since white settlement when they were introduced from England for sport by Thomas Austin near Geelong in 1858. By 1879 farmers were predicting their own ruin if the problem could not be stopped. In 1880 Victoria passed the Rabbit Suppression Act. Since then many eradication methods have been tried, including myxomatosis – the 'myxo'. This traumatised many Australian children who had to hand over their pets in the 1950s. The rabbit calicivirus was released in 1998, and has been relatively successful in drier areas. A by-product has been the eradication of the rabbit shooter, and the rabbit stew on Saturday nights.
See: Celia; Myxomatosis; Prickly Pear; Rolls, Eric

Rabbitoh

The itinerant rabbit seller was fondly regarded in Sydney during the Depression. Yabba, the legendary SCG Hill barracker, was a rabbitoh.

Rabbitohs, The

Nickname of the green and red working-class NSW Rugby League club South Sydney. Controversially eliminated in 1999 from the News Ltd backed national competition, its supporters fought on despite losing a series of court battles in 2000.

Rabbitproof Fence, The

Various methods of rabbit control were attempted, the most memorable being rabbitproof fencing. Between 1902 and 1907, 3276 kilometres of fence was constructed across Australia at a cost of £250 000.

Rafferty, Chips

Chips Rafferty (1909–71) was the archetypical old Australian in a series of films because he was one. Before he took up acting he was a pearl diver, shearer, drover and cane cutter, among other things. Born John Goffage, his first major role was in Charles Chauvel's *Forty Thousand Horsemen*, where he created his character as the self-reliant, determined but fun-loving man of action. Later films included *Mutiny on the Bounty*, *The Overlanders*, *Eureka Stockade*, *The Sundowners* and *The Rats of Tobruk*. His last film was *Wake in Fright* in 1971.

Rafter, Pat

Pat Rafter's rise to the number one ranked tennis player in 1998 marked a resurgence in Australian tennis. His

Chips Rafferty, left, in *40 000 Horsemen*

Some Rats of Tobruk defend the line in 1941

National Reconciliation Week 2000 postcard

R

brief reign featured back-to-back US Open victories in 1997 and 1998, the second after John McEnroe called him a 'one-slam guy'. Rafter's career has been punctuated by a shoulder injury, preventing a long stay at the peak. Everyone likes Pat – the way he plays (the Australian way) and the way he's big on family, helping kids and would genuinely rather play Davis Cup for Australia than make a million (more) dollars. Rafter reached the final of Wimbledon in 2000, and the 2001 Australian Open semi final, while retirement loomed.

rage

Video-clips successor to the ABC TV music shows of the legendary past – Johnny O'Keefe's *Six O'Clock Rock* and Molly Meldrum's *Countdown*. Not quite the same thing.

Rats of Tobruk

Lord Haw Haw, a Nazi propagandist, called the Australian (and other) troops defending Tobruk – a town now in Libya just across the border from Egypt – 'rats'. There were some 24 000 Australians from the 7th and 9th Divisions at Tobruk, which they held from April to December 1941. A German officer wrote in his diary of the Rats that they were not 'trained' but that they were 'men with nerve and toughness, tireless, taking punishment with obstinacy, wonderful in defence'. Australian football legend Ron Barassi's father was one of the thousands of fatalities at Tobruk. In an echo of the World War I diggers' appreciation of ancient Greek history's relationship to Gallipoli, the German went on to say 'Ah well, the Greeks also spent 10

years before Troy.' While 'rats' was ordinarily a term of abuse, especially in Labor Party circles where it means a deserter from a faction or the party, the Rats of Tobruk adopted the insult as a badge of honour.
See: Barassi, Ron; Blamey, Thomas

Reckless

Trained by Tommy Woodcock, Phar Lap's former strapper, Reckless almost pulled off the 'grand slam' of Australian racing by winning the Sydney, Adelaide and Brisbane Cups in 1977 before finishing second in the Melbourne Cup. His death in 1986 was mourned by all.

Reconciliation

Brought to the fore by the Keating government's Native Title Act, reconciliation has been contentious

The
Redgum Songbook
Stubborn Words, Flagrant Vices

Tombola Publishing Pty. Ltd.

Redgum announce their singing intentions

IT'S YOUR CHOICE: WHERE DO YOU DRAW THE LINE AGAINST COMMUNIST AGGRESSION?

Liberal Party Red Menace ad, 1963

Penfolds Grange Hermitage, the big red

ever since, with confusion over possible land claims on people's backyards (an impossibility) and arguments over the concept of retroactive guilt, and current Liberal Prime Minister Howard's steadfast refusal to apologise. The Australian government did not agree to the wording of the Council for Aboriginal Reconciliation's *Declaration Towards Reconciliation* in May 2000, thus missing an opportunity to mark a stage in the ongoing process. The Corroboree 2000 ceremonies at that time saw hundreds of thousands of people march together, before millions more saw Cathy Freeman light the Olympic flame at the Olympic Opening Ceremony, then win her race. Many Australians saw these events as 400 metres more along the track towards real reconciliation.

Redgum
A 1980s folkish band which had some biggish hits with *Virgin Ground*. John Schumann, its frontman, was prominent in office warfare in the SA branch of the Australian Democrats in the 1990s, accused (later retracted) by the Democrats Natasha Stott Despoja of being behind attempts to destabilise her position. He nearly won a House of Reps seat in 1996.

Redhead Matches
Redhead matches derive their name from the red striking head on the match and the flaming red hair of the face on its box. They were introduced in 1946 by Bryant & May of Richmond in Melbourne. The only changes to the design have been revisions to the hair-do, and the manufacture of the actual matches offshore.

Reds, Big
The biggest and most famous red of them all is the fabled Penfolds Grange Hermitage, made by Max Schubert from 1951 in a vineyard now located in a suburb of Adelaide. A bottle of the first vintage sold for $40 000 in 2000.

Reds, The
The threat from the north was luridly real in the 1950s and 1960s, depicted with relish in a 1963 Liberal Party handbill. It was geographical gravity, later dubbed the domino theory. If Korea, China, Vietnam, Malaya and Indonesia 'fell' to local Communists, whether aided or not by international comrades, this was a direct threat to Australian security. Reds are traditionally found under the bed.
See: Petrov Affair; Vietnam

Joseph Reed, Melbourne's great architect

Lloyd Rees by William Pidgeon

Strike him lucky, it's Roy Rene

R

Reed, Joseph

Architect of many of Melbourne's favourite buildings, Joseph Reed was born in Cornwall about 1823 and died of 'inanition' in 1890. He arrived in Melbourne in 1853 and won the competition to design the State Library in 1854. Among his other buildings are the Wesley Church, Lonsdale Street (1858), Baptist Church, Collins Street (1862), Independent Church, Collins Street (1866), Rippon Lea (1868), Melbourne Town Hall (1860s), Trades Hall, Lygon Street (1873), Exhibition Building (Carlton) 1879–80, Ormond College, University of Melbourne (1879). He counted among his friends the builder David Mitchell, Nellie Melba's father. Reed sang with them at the Collins Street Independent Church, and owned several Stradivarius violins. Reed's wife remarried after his death and gave her son the wonderful name Joseph Reed Stradivarius Boase. His firm survives as Bates, Smart.

Rees, Lloyd

Born in 1895, Lloyd Rees became the grand old man of Australian painting, much honoured before his death in 1988. He began his career at Sydney Ure Smith's commercial art school in 1917, using dramatic pen and ink to show off Sydney, and did not take up oil painting until 1935, when he began his celebrated landscape paintings. At first these were thickly layered oils, but later became lighter, freer and more abstract.

Rene, Roy 'Mo'

Comedian, clown and actor, Roy Rene (1891–1954) was born Henry van der Sluys and took his name after his debut as the Boy Roy in 1908 from a French clown, Rene. Roy Rene's most popular character was the bawdy and slobbery Mo, who was wildly popular across Australia from 1916 for decades. A film titled after Mo's famous catch-cry, *Strike Me Lucky*, was unsuccessful in 1934, although Mo continued to draw large audiences to his show with wife Sadie Gale until World War II. His radio career began in 1946 with *Calling the Stars* on 2GB and his spot 'McCackie Mansion'. He was plagued by ill health in the 1950s and died in 1954.
See: Stiffy & Mo

Renford, Des

Des Renford, marathon swimmer, crossed the English Channel the first of 19 times in August 1970.

Dick Reynolds, triple Brownlow medallist

Jack Dyer and Lou Richards

Ginger Riley, master painter

Republic, The

Ned Kelly is supposed to have yearned for a Republic of North East Victoria; a republic of Australia seems just as far away, after the hopes dashed at the 1999 Referendum, lost on the rocks of complicated waffle from the Sydney-based Australian Republican Movement, and contradictions from the absolutist direct election republicans. Symbolic Republicans like Ned and me who simply wanted the last colonial ties cut and the Queen of Australia deposed, just despaired.

Reynolds, Dick

'King' Richard played 320 games for the Bombers between 1933 and 1951, picking up seven best and fairest awards, four premierships and three Brownlow medals along the way.

Richards, Lou

Lou Richards (b. 1923), a unique character of Australian sport and media, played for Collingwood for 15 years, was captain from 1952 to 1955 and led the Magpies to a premiership in 1953. After his retirement he became a popular columnist in the Melbourne *Sun News Pictorial* and then the first multi-media sports star. In the 1950s and 1960s he was renowned for preposterous predictions such as, 'If Footscray win on Saturday, I'll cut Ted Whitten's lawn with nail scissors', and then having to do so. He had a long career on television, mostly sparring with Jack 'Captain Blood' Dyer on Seven's *World of Sport*, and *League Teams*, pioneer sports TV programs. He retired to the Nine network and was still going strong in the 1990s.

Riley, Ginger

Ginger Riley Munduwalawala, painter, was born in the saltwater country of the Mara people on the coast of the Gulf of Carpentaria around 1937. He was given a traditional Mara upbringing, and eventually went to work as a stockman until the late 1960s. At one time in the 1950s he met the watercolourist Albert Namatjira, which planted a seed that the colour of Ginger Riley's country could be captured in paint. After a series of other jobs, he came to experiment with paint at Ngukurr in 1986, and became a full-time artist in 1990. He is a painter of his Limmen Bight country, and the stories that exist there – and of other Australian stories. His Australian Football paintings were sensations at the National Gallery of Victoria in 1997.

Illustration, Rohan Rivett's *Behind Bamboo*

Eric Rolls, poetic historian

Lionel Rose defeats Fighting Harada

Rivett, Rohan

Rohan Rivett was interned by the Japanese in Singapore during World War II and despite a daring escape bid, joined thousands of other Australians on the Thai–Burma Railway. A journalist for the *Argus* newspaper, he brought the plight of POWs to life in his vivid and sometimes shocking book, *Behind Bamboo*. He later became editor of the *Adelaide News* and campaigned against the execution of alleged murderer Rupert Max Stuart.

Roberts, Victoria

Victoria Roberts, cartoonist and illustrator, was born in New York in 1957, grew up in Mexico and Australia and became famous with her whimsical series of drawings cutting into the biographical 'My Day' of such

luminaries as Rasputin. They first appeared in the 1980s *National Times*. Roberts returned to New York and her work appears in the *New Yorker*.

Robinson, Ray

Australia's greatest cricket writer (1905–82), Robinson's scrupulously researched and phrased books, including *On Top Down Under*, *Green Sprigs* and *Between Wickets*, are the sources for much that passes as Australian cricket folklore. He began writing as a cadet on the Melbourne *Herald* in 1922, and to the eternal shame of Australian newspapers was never given a full-time appointment as a cricket writer.

Rolls, Eric

Sensualist, farmer, poet, historian, autobiographer, Eric Rolls (b. 1923)

wrote a terrific book about the rabbit pestilence, *They All Ran Wild* (1969), and a similarly exuberant history of the Namoi River area, *A Million Wild Acres* (1981).

Romeo + Juliet

Aussie Baz Luhrmann's 1997 reinterpretation of Shakespeare's play starring teen idol Leonardo DiCaprio saw fast edits, snappy camera work and a perfect soundtrack modernise the story for easy digestion. Thankfully he didn't touch the dialogue.

Rose, Lionel

Lionel Rose (b. 1948) was the first Aboriginal Australian to win a world title, when in 1968 he beat Fighting Harada in Tokyo before an estimated television audience of 30 million. Rose was Australian flyweight champion in

Rosehill ad, 1896

Lance Hills, centre, outside his rotary clothesline factory in the 1940s

1963, represented Australia at the 1964 Olympic Games in Tokyo and was Australian bantamweight champion 1966–69. He lost his world title at his fourth defence in 1969.

Rose, Murray

A great freestyle swimmer in Australia's 1500 metre pantheon, he won the gold medal in Melbourne 1956, and won the 400 metres at both Melbourne and Rome 1960. He totalled four Olympic gold, one silver and one bronze. In 1964, in the great tradition of Australian amateur sports pedantry, he was denied selection because he couldn't make it to Australia for the trials, despite having just set a world record in the 1500. Rose was elected by his peers in 1983 as Australia's greatest Olympian.
See: Fraser, Dawn

Rosehill Racecourse

Rosehill was founded as private race track in 1885 in Sydney but became an Australian institution with the beginning of the Golden Slipper for two year olds by the Sydney Turf Club in 1957. This race is the Melbourne Cup's rival in stake money, if not in history and nation-stopping ability.

Rosella

The Rosella Preserving Company Ltd was formed in 1895. Its preserves, pickles and sauces have been favourites ever since, though the 'saucy bird' is most famous on the ubiquitous bottles of tomato sauce.

Rosewall, Ken

The greatest player never to win Wimbledon, Ken 'Muscles' Rosewall won almost everything else – French

and Australian Opens in 1953, US Open in 1956 – before turning professional in 1957. He was a Wimbledon finalist in 1954, 1956, 1970 and 1974, the last two after the 'pros' had returned to Grand Slam tennis. In all he won four Australian, two French and two US Opens. The nickname 'Muscles' derived from his small stature and lack of them, but he made up for it with a never-say-die attitude and a classical backhand.

Rotary Clothesline

Adelaide motor mechanic Lance Hill invented the backyard icon in 1945 in his backyard. He just wanted to solve a clothes drying problem caused by overhanging trees. The Hills Hoist, as it soon became known, took off like a motor mower after commercial manufacture began in 1946.

R

Roy & H.G.

Percy Leason's quick look at the 1937 Royal Tour

Rotary Hoe

The rotary hoe is a mechanical cultivator with a power-driven bladed rotor which tills the soil as the machine moves through the field. Invented by Cliff and Albert Howard in 1920, a petrol-driven version proved successful in 1925.

Rowe, Normie

An Australian 1960s pop star, Normie Rowe (b. 1947) had a few big hits including *Que Sera Sera*, *It Ain't Necessarily So* and *I (Who Have Nothing)* in 1965. He became a musician after the PMG (now Australia Post) objected to his long hair. His career suffered after he was conscripted and served in Vietnam, but made a career comeback in *Les Miserables* in 1987. Prominent in helping Vietnam vets.

Roy & H.G.

H.G. Nelson and 'Rampaging' Roy Slaven are a pair of likeable, knowledgeable and mock-ocker Australian sport-focused comedians. Their radio show *This Sporting Life* was a success for Triple J and has since spun off into TV shows for the ABC, and then onto Seven's Sydney Olympic coverage. *The Dream* was the gold medallist of the media circus, and their mascot, Fatso, the Fat Arsed Wombat, a hero.

Royal Visits

Alfred, Duke of Edinburgh was the first royal visitor in 1867–68 and suffered an assassination attempt. Others have been more popular, including the first reigning monarch Elizabeth II in 1954. Since then Royals have turned up more frequently, but

to less adulation and interest by most modern Australians.

Roycroft, Bill

Bill Roycroft (b. 1915) was a Victorian grazier who competed in five Olympics in three-day eventing, heroically climbing out of his hospital bed in 1960 after breaking his collarbone in a fall, to help Australia win gold in the Teams Equestrian event. He also won bronze in 1976 aged 61.

Rubinstein, Helena

The cosmetics queen before Poppy King, Rubinstein (1871–1965) came to Australia aged 18, and opened a beauty salon in Melbourne. After another shop in London she moved to the United States in 1915 and created a world-wide cosmetics empire.

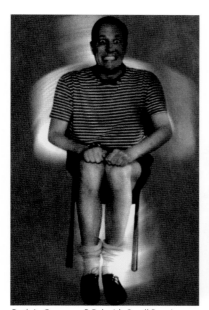

Rush in Company B Belvoir's *Small Poppies*

Peter Ryan's *Fear Drive My Feet* (1959)

Ronald Ryan handcuffed to Detective Charlton

Rush, Geoffrey

This Australian actor (b. 1951) began his career on the stage but gained his greatest acclaim in film. He won a Golden Globe and an Academy Award for his portrayal of eccentric pianist David Helfgott in *Shine*, and was nominated again in 2001 for *Quills*. He has appeared in many other movies, including *Shakespeare in Love*, but still calls the Australian theatre home, especially Company B Belvoir.

Rusty Bugles

Rusty Bugles by Sumner Locke Elliott was first performed in 1948 at the Independent Theatre in Sydney, and formed part of the slim canon of indigenous theatre until the 1960s. Banned for a time for its swearing, it is set in a remote army camp in the Northern Territory in 1944, and

describes the routines of a typical group of Australian soldiers waiting for the war before the last flings in New Guinea and Borneo in 1944–45.

Ryan, Peter

Born 1923, Peter Ryan was a patrol officer at the outbreak of war in New Guinea and served, beginning as an eighteen-year-old, alongside the Australian commandos, the 2/5th Independent Company, as part of Kanga Force around Wau, Lae and Salamaua in 1942–43. His plainly told but compelling book *Fear Drive My Feet* (1959) is based on his wartime experiences. He became director of Melbourne University Press in 1962, where he published Manning Clark's *History of Australia* – a publication which he later repudiated. After his retirement in 1990 he became a

curmudgeonly commentator and controversialist, especially on the subject of Manning Clark.
See: Kokoda Track

Ryan, Ronald

Ronald Ryan was the last man hanged in Australia. His execution, on 3 February 1967, has excited controversy and literature ever since. The trial and hanging created the campaign which made it the last. However culpable Ryan might have been, his fate has since served as an epitaph for the old-style Victoria of Henry Bolte, where judicial murder and flogging were acceptable. Barry Dickins' 1994 play *Remember Ronald Ryan* was a successful attempt to get inside the unlikeable character of the killer through his own voice and the people around him.

S

Click go the shears, boys: a shearer with hand blades at the ready

Ralph Sarich and his engine

Salvation Army

The first officers of the Salvation Army, Captain and Mrs Sutherland, arrived in Adelaide on 17 February 1881. The 'Salvos' have been at the forefront of innovation in their mission to save souls ever since. *Soldiers of the Cross* was their first multimedia show, almost a feature film. It boasted film, slides, and gramophone sound and was presented at the Melbourne Town Hall on 13 September 1900 to an audience of 4000.

Sarich Orbital Engine

Invented by Ralph Sarich and company in 1971, the Sarich Orbital Engine caught the attention of BHP after appearing (of all places) on the ABC TV show *The Inventors*. The resulting joint venture produced the patented 'orbital combustion process two-stroke technology'. Companies to license the technology include Ford,

The Salvation Army's Austral Guards, 1890s

General Motors and Fiat. The company holds an impressive 540 patents, and has stayed in business with engine developments, but not the original invention.

Sauvage, Louise

A truly remarkable athlete, Louise Sauvage's success is twofold. Not only

Louise Sauvage and her mum

has she been incredibly successful on the track, but she has helped lift the profile of Paralympians across the board. Born with myelodysplasia she has been in a wheelchair all her life and was introduced to wheelchair sports when she was eight. Training two hours a day for six days a week, she covers between 130 and 190 kilometres every week in addition to weight training. The hard work paid off however, and she became the highly successful face of the Paralympics. Sauvage won three gold medals at the 1992 Paralympics, four in 1996, and two at Sydney 2000.

Savage Garden

Queensland pop duo, guitarist Daniel Jones and singer/songwriter Darren Hayes, began their careers as a cover band but found massive commercial success with their self-titled debut album. It sold 11 million copies and clocked six times platinum before they followed it up with the album *Affirmation*. Savage Garden went separate ways in 2001.

SeaChange, something rich and strange

The Seekers at play

Harry Seidler's first modernist house

Scanlens Chewing Gum
Melbourne firm Scanlens is most famous for their football cards, but equally memorable is the rock-hard fluorescent pink stick of gum.

Schepisi, Fred
Australian film director Fred Schepisi began his career making television commercials with his company 'The Film House' in Fitzroy. He went on to help launch the Australian film industry with *Devil's Playground* (1976) and *The Chant of Jimmie Blacksmith* (1978) before making his mark in Hollywood on *Roxanne* (1987), *The Russia House* (1990) and *Six Degrees of Separation* (1993).

SeaChange
Brainchild of Deb Cox, the Artist Services/ABC production *SeaChange* first aired in May 1998, and was an immediate success. It touched a middle-class and middle-aged nerve, especially with women, many of whom dream of giving up the rat race, having an affair at the beach and still keeping the children. Three series later it survived the departure of Diver Dan (David Wenham) as the character of Laura Gibson (Sigrid Thornton) developed.

Seale, John
Australian cinematographer who began as camera operator at the beginning of the Australian film industry, with, among other films, *Alvin Purple* (1973), *Picnic at Hanging Rock* (1975), *Gallipoli* (1981). He was cinematographer on *The Perfect Storm* (2000), *The Talented Mr Ripley* (1999), *The English Patient* (1996), *Dead Poets Society* (1989), *Gorillas in the Mist* (1988) and *The Mosquito Coast* (1986).

Seekers, The
Featuring the talents of guitarist and singer/songwriter Bruce Woodley, lead singer Judith Durham, Athol Guy and Keith Potger, The Seekers formed in 1962. Among their many accolades, the whole group became Australian of the Year in 1967, and that same year played to an audience of 200 000 at the Melbourne Myer Music Bowl. Their single *The Carnival is Over* sold 93 000 copies in a day, and *Georgy Girl* became Australia's first number one song in America. Durham left the band in 1968 to pursue a solo career, but rejoined for their 'comeback' in the 1990s and played the 2000 Paralympics closing ceremony.

A trench at Gallipoli before the evacuation

Dean Semler, *Dances With Wolves*

Clem Semmler

The Songs of a Sentimental Bloke

Seidler, Harry

Architect, born in Austria in 1923, Seidler arrived in Australia in 1948 after studying under Walter Gropius at Harvard. He has won every major architectural award in Australia multiple times, and made his name with this modernist house, arguably Australia's first, designed for his parents in 1948 at Turramurra, NSW.

Self-Firing Rifle

The self-firing rifle was an Anzac invention used to create the illusion of manned trenches during the Gallipoli evacuation of December 1915. There were many variations, but the simplest involved two tins. The upper was filled with water that slowly dripped into the lower tin which, when it had filled, pulled a string attached to the rifle's trigger. Other versions involved candles which burned through string, releasing a weight attached to the trigger.

Semler, Dean

Cinematographer Dean Semler had his major break with *Mad Max 2* (1981) before going on to film a string of major American films, including *Young Guns* (1988), *Dead Calm* (1988), *Dances with Wolves* (1990) – for which he won an Academy Award – and the corny *The Power of One* (1991).

Semmler, Clem

Clement Semmler (1914–2000) was deputy general manager of the ABC 1965–77, but was also a distinguished biographer and editor of the work of Banjo Paterson, and collected Kenneth Slessor's World War II diaries and correspondence. Dubbed a 'highbrow lowbrow' by Ken Inglis in his history of the ABC.

Sennitt's Ice Cream

Sennitt's, along with Toppa and Peters, was a Melbourne ice cream icon of the 1950s and 1960s. The Sennitt's polar bear was a familiar sight at suburban milk bars. Peters, founded in 1929, licked the opposition and lasted the longest.

Sentimental Bloke

His name was Bill, and he wooed his ideal tart, Doreen, in C.J. Dennis' 1915 best-selling verse narrative. Probably no one had thought of the larrikin urban male as being such a softy, but Dennis latched onto something romantic in the Australian city, a theme that leads a furtive existence a century later in the work of Barry Dickins.

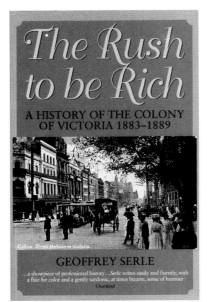

Geoff Serle's landmark history

Jimmy Sharman's boxing tent

S

Serle, Geoff

One of the leading postwar historians and writers, Geoff Serle (1922–98) served in the AIF and was wounded at Finchshafen in 1944. He wrote the pioneering histories of Victoria, *The Rush To Be Rich* (1971) and *The Golden Age* (1963), the great biography *Monash* (1982) and was joint editor of the bedrock work of Australian history, the *Australian Dictionary of Biography*, from 1975 for volumes 6–10, and sole editor of volume 11.

Shards

A controversial architectural feature of Melbourne's fin de siècle Federation Square promoted by then-Premier Jeff Kennett, built on a deck covering the railyards to the east of Princes Bridge, and formerly occupied by the city's ugliest towers,

the Gas & Fuel Building. The new erections designed by architectural consortium LAB+Bates Smart constituted a set of medium-rise jewel-shaped buildings, skinned in aluminium and other modern substances. One building, the 'western shard', was going to obscure St Paul's Cathedral when viewed from a certain angle, and was eliminated and then reduced by the incoming (1999) Labor Premier, Steve Bracks. *See: Sheds*

Sharks

Sharks are the marine section of the Australian bestiary, along with crocodiles, poisonous snakes and spiders. Australians tend to think of the place as fairly benign, compared to Africa or Asia – no lions or tigers – but visitors apparently have a

different view. They may no longer believe that there are kangaroos in Collins Street, but they are convinced there are sharks in the surf, crocs in the reservoirs and a redback under each dunny seat. The reason is perhaps the success of the Great White Shark, Greg Norman, in spreading the shark name around the traps and bunkers of the world.

Sharman, Jimmy

James (Jimmy) Sharman was born dirt poor in NSW in 1892, and took to fighting in boxing tents at the annual shows in the area. In 1906 he won £11.16 boxing at the Campbelltown Races, and began a career which saw 77 wins from 78 fights (according to him) to 1912. That year he fought one Jack Carter in a Wagga woolshed for the house plus a £20 side wager, after

256

Blade shearers in the 1840s

The book of sheds

A blade at Jeff's Shed

which he set up his career as a showman. By 1915 his troupe was well known, and 'Who'll take a glove?' became the catchcry to start proceedings which lasted for over 50 years. Sharman's Tent Show toured outback Australia and the main city agricultural shows, pitting good boxers against locals who fancied their chances of a 'pound or two for a round or two'. Sharman was the greatest 'ballyhoo merchant' of them all, and dominated the show ring until 1971. Jimmy's son Jim went into a different style of show business, and directed the Australian production of *Hair* in 1969.

Shearers

The human image of the European sheep business is the shepherd, even the shepherdess. In Australia it is the shearer: a rough, hard-drinking, often racist, probably sexist (if given the chance), boastful itinerant worker (often with a heart of gold) who has been at the centre of the labour movement for a hundred years – and at the cutting edge of technology as well, as hand shears have given way to mechanical blades and even to self-shearing sheep. Shearers are (or were) the quintessential Australian rural worker, the symbol perhaps of the older Australia of the *Bulletin* epitomised by Jack Thompson in the film *Sunday Too Far Away*. The noble failure of the 1891 Shearers' Strike in Queensland, broken by the government and biased judiciary, plays a major part in the foundation story of the Australian Labor Party. *Click Go the Shears* is the song of the blade shearer, and Tom Roberts'

painting *Shearing the Rams* is the classic image of the gun shearers hard at work.
See: Labour/Labor

Sheds

Every bloke is supposed to have a shed, a private space out in the backyard where a bloke can keep his tools, the bottle fridge, store things too good to throw away such as old bits of wireless, half-empty paint tins and useful lengths of wood. The romance of the shed has increased with its decline in the suburban Australian backyard, as pools, BBQs and dual occupancy have taken over. The apotheosis of the shed in urban imagery was the nicknaming of Melbourne's vast (the biggest shed in the southern hemisphere) Exhibition Centre as Jeff's Shed.

257

The Sherrin football, famous for 100 years

The *Cataraqui*, wrecked off King Island in 1845 with the loss of over 400 lives, just nine survived

S

Sheep's Back

Australia once 'rode on the sheep's back' because wool was then the major Australian export, rising to an extraordinary predominance in 1951 when wool amounted to two-thirds of exports. Arthur Phillip brought the first sheep to NSW in the First Fleet, acquiring them at the Cape of Good Hope in 1787. These were more for eating than shearing. The first fine-wool merinos were landed in 1797 by Henry Waterhouse and William Kent, also bought at the Cape. John Macarthur bought some, beginning the ride on the sheep's back.

Sherrin Footballs

Sherrin is synonymous with the actual Australian football, a ball developed by the Collingwood manufactory T. W. Sherrin (among

others) in the 1890s. The Sherrin was slightly smaller and had blunter ends than the imported English Rugby balls of the day, and thus had a deep influence on the kicking styles of the indigenous game. Ross Faulkner and Kookaburra are other brands.

Shilling, Last

Andrew Fisher said in 1914 'we'll defend Australia until the last man and the last shilling'. The last shilling was in fact issued in 1963 before Australia changed to decimal currency in 1966.
See: Dollar Bill

Shipwrecks

Shipwrecks were the transport disasters of Australia from the 17th to 19th centuries. We depended so much on people being brought by sea that

the ships and the stories of culpability, tragedy and heroism still live in the collective memory of Australia: Tom Pearce and Eva Carmichael surviving the *Loch Ard*; the awful loss of life from the *Admella*, and brave Grace Bussell.
See: Admella, Pandora, Quetta

Show, The

In the lead-up to each State's Royal Show the newspapers will be littered with endless listings of showbags and their prices. Filled with lollies, licensed memorabilia and overpriced plastic items of indeterminate origin, they are indescribably popular with children of all ages. Remember: kids do not want to see the animals, they do not want to look at the plant show, they want to go on a ride and get the showbags.

Jean Shrimpton, Derby Day, 1965

A Sidchrome bolt

Bob Simpson

Shrimp

Somewhere between Australia and America the translation had to be made for the benefit of Americans, turning our huge prawns into a tiny shrimp. Paul Hogan's BBQ advertisement (for the Australian Tourist Commission) invited Americans to come on down under and 'throw another shrimp on the barbie'. Another skinny thing was Jean Shrimpton, a.k.a. The Shrimp, who was a 1960s supermodel. She turned heads at the 1965 Melbourne Cup carnival when she wore a miniskirt, ten centimetres above the knee, on Derby Day.
See: Hogan, Paul

Sidchrome

American firm which began to make tools in Melbourne in the 1920s.

Became part of the folklore with the slogan 'You canna handa man a grander spanner', thought to be of local manufacture.

silverchair

Australian grunge phenomenon silverchair recorded their first single *tomorrow* with the winnings from a local demo competition in 1994. At the time, two of them were 14, the other 15. Soon after, singer/songwriter Daniel Johns, bassist Chris Joannou and drummer Ben Gillies recorded their first album, *Frogstomp*, in nine days. After watching it reach triple platinum status, they toured Australia and overseas to inevitable Nirvana/Pearl Jam comparisons, but also great success. Their follow-up albums, *Freak Show* and *Neon Ballroom*, have reached similar levels of popularity.

Simpson, Bob

Attacking middle-order batsman, brilliant slips fielder and Australian captain, Bob Simpson was a fine cricketer. However, it was his coaching which brought him most acclaim as he helped revive Australian cricket from his appointment in 1986 and create one of the most successful teams ever in world cricket, before poor health and the forces of change in Australian cricket forced his retirement in 1996.

Sixty Minutes

Based on a successful American formula, the Australian version of *Sixty Minutes* was tabloid current affairs and an early ratings topper from 1979. It usually made stars of its presenters, including Ray Martin, George Negus and Jana Wendt.

259

Triple Brownlow medallist Bob Skilton

Skyhooks still living in the 70s

Skippy and Sonny Hammond

The skipping boy Christopher Skase

Skilton, Bob

One of the greatest footballers ever to walk onto the field, Skilton played 237 games with South Melbourne as a rover and racked up virtually every achievement in the game – multiple times. Captain of South from 1961 to 1971 (and captain–coach in 1965–66) he won the best and fairest there nine times. He also won three Brownlow medals and represented Victoria on numerous occasions.

Skipping Boy – Skase, Chris

Former high-flying entrepreneur and owner of Channel 7 through his Qintex group, Christopher Skase fell from grace when he lost millions and skipped to a luxurious home on the island of Majorca. Attempts at extradition in 1994 failed in the fog of Spanish medicine and law.

Skipping Girl

The first neon sign erected in Melbourne during the early 1930s, the Skipping Girl was an advertisement for The Vinegar Company of Australia. When the company moved to Altona in 1968, the sign was deemed a traffic hazard and sold. However a public outcry and the efforts of John Benjamin saw her re-erected two years later and two doors down from her original location, on the roof of Benjamin's Crusading Plate Company, where she continues to skip today.

Skippy the Bush Kangaroo

One of Australian TV's most popular early exports, Skippy (the bush kangaroo) was Australia's answer to Lassie. Sold to 100 TV stations in the US, Skippy's adventures were a hit from its launch in 1968 through the early 1970s as she and her best mate Sonny Hammond (Garry Pankhurst) solved kid-friendly crimes.

Skyhooks

Seventies Australian rock group which attracted large audiences and had a string of hits in Australia, although they did not translate so well overseas. Several of its members went on to dubious roles on TV.

Smart, Jeffrey

Adelaide born (1921) and after 1963 resident traveller in Italy, Jeffrey Smart paints austere images of people trapped in dream-like urban environments, sometimes vast, sometimes overwhelmingly intimate – parking lots, freeways, container terminals, grandstands. He wrote in the 1960s that 'I find myself moved

Jeffrey Smart by Michel Lawrence

T.J. Smith as a young jockey

Sydney Ure Smith, R.H. Croll, Bob Menzies, 1938

by man in his new violent environment, I want to paint this explicitly and beautifully.'

Smith, Bernard
Bernard Smith's ideas have been important in placing Australia and Australian culture, particularly art, in its geographical and historical context. *Place, Taste & Tradition* (1945), *European Vision and the South Pacific* (1960), *Australian Painting 1788–1960* (1962) and his autobiography *The Boy Adeodatus* (1984) are as vital as any four books written in Australia. Born in 1916, he was spotted painting in a studio in the Victorian Trades Hall in the 1990s.

Smith, Dick
Australian entrepreneur and electronics whiz, he was Australian of the Year in 1987. 'Appalled' by the loss of Australian brands to overseas buyers, he launched his own versions of popular Australian staples in the 1990s, including Vegemite and peanut butter.

Smith, Sydney Ure
Pioneer art publisher Sydney Ure Smith (1887–1949) studied at the Julian Ashton school in Sydney where he ran into Norman Lindsay and Will Dyson, and began publishing *Art in Australia* in 1916. It continued until 1942, and was the most influential arts magazine of its day.

Smith's Weekly
Between 1919 and 1950, this Sydney-based newspaper gained an international reputation for its raciness and quality art. Named after Sir James Joynton Smith, it was aggressively nationalistic and sometimes racist, it supported the digger, promoted White Australia and was strongly anti-Communist. It also had a humorous bent, with a mix of cartoons and sporting news, and its cartoonists rivalled the *Bulletin*'s.

Smith, T.J.
Legendary horse trainer, T.J. (Tommy) Smith was born in NSW in 1918, apprenticed as a jockey at 13, took up training with the aptly named Bragger and had his first win with it in 1942. Smith won the first of his astonishing 33 consecutive NSW trainers' premierships in 1952–53. A 34th came in 1988–89. He won two Melbourne Cups with Toporoa and Just A Dash, and had two of the greatest horses in Australian turf

May Gibbs published by Angus & Robertson

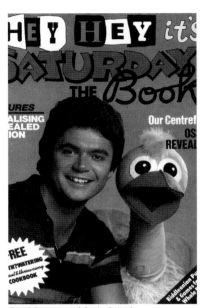

Daryl Somers and Ossie Ostrich

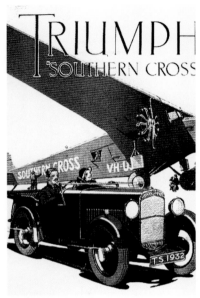

Southern Cross in advertising

S

history, Tulloch and Kingston Town. Tommy Smith died in 1998 but daughter Gai Waterhouse has continued the family's winning tradition.

Smithy

Charles Kingsford Smith (1897–1935) was a World War I flyer who became a record-breaking aviator in the heroic age of the 1920s. His US to Australia epic in 1928 in the *Southern Cross* was the stuff of boyhood legend.

Snugglepot and Cuddlepie

Created by May Gibbs, bush babies Snugglepot and Cuddlepie and their adventures (often involving the wicked Banksia Men) have been entertaining kids for almost a century. Featuring Australian characters in an Australian setting,

they, along with books like Norman Lindsay's *The Magic Pudding*, helped give Australian kids their own set of myths and stories. The characters' first appearance in the 1916 classic *The Gumnut Babies* was followed in 1918 by *Snugglepot and Cuddlepie*.

Somers, Daryl

Daryl Somers began a 28-year career as host of the variety/comedy show *Hey Hey It's Saturday* on Saturday mornings in 1971. It moved to an evening spot in 1986, and never looked back until it was axed in 1999 as a cost-cutting measure by the Nine network, despite winning two Logies that year. For many years Ossie Ostrich (Ernie Carroll) was a featured performer, and segments such as Red Faces (a mock talent quest) and the Wheel recalled a more innocent time

in Australian TV. Innocence was perhaps the secret of its success, something that by the end of the century was out of tune with commodified money-making media.

Southerly

Founded in 1939, this quarterly journal began by publishing American and British writers, but under Kenneth Slessor's editorship (1956–61) it added the subtitle 'A Review of Australian Literature' and switched its focus to domestic writers. Apart from 1960, when no issues appeared, it continues to the present day as a valuable source of criticism, fiction and poetry.

Southern Cross

The Southern Cross is the characteristic star sign of the

The southern cross, trademarked

Bookies off course in Bourke Street, 1887

Sovereign Hill ad, 1990s

southern hemisphere, adopted by Australians as far back as the Anti-Transportation League (1851), and most famously by the seamstresses of the Eureka Stockade (1854) who ran up the loveliest flag in the world. The Southern Cross appeared on the Australian national flag in 1901, after a competition run by the Melbourne *Herald* newspaper. Sir Charles Kingsford Smith's Fokker was named the *Southern Cross* for its heroic flight across the Pacific in 1928. The Southern Cross on the Eureka flag has been hijacked by both political left & right, as well as by advertisers.

Sovereign Hill

Tourist village just outside Ballarat, which recreates the sights, sounds and experience of gold rush Australia. Complete with costumed actors,

working stores and busloads of school children, it is an experience no young Victorian is allowed to miss.

SP (Bookies)

Off-course betting, or 'the SP' (starting price), has long been at the heart of Australian sporting culture and black economy because many people want to bet, but don't want to go to the races. Instead they seek to have a bet in a quiet corner of the pub, or on the phone. Or in the 1890s they would visit establishments such as John Wren's Tote in Johnston Street Collingwood. Racing clubs and governments don't like the SP because they don't make any money out of it, and have made it illegal. Despite difficulties, such as obtaining information, occasional police raids and the domination of TAB which

now allows phone betting, the SP still flourishes in the colourful corners of the racing industry.

Speedo

Swimwear once synonymous with Australian feats in the pool. The basic pair of togs was the small men's brief, and the figure-hugging one-piece for women. Now an American company that markets a body suit based on the skin of the shark – which won 83% of swimming medals at Sydney.

Spiderbait

Hailing from the sleepy NSW town of Finley, Spiderbait members Kram, Whitt and Janet were signed by AuGoGo records in 1990 and released their debut album *ShaShaVa Glava* in 1992. They hit the big time with their single *Buy me a Pony*.

263

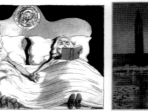

A Spooner in the works

The art of John Spooner
Introduced by Robert Manne

The 'Demon': Spofforth

John Spooner's collected works

STATE SCHOOL

WITH SPOFFORTH.

AN AUSTRALIAN ELEVEN THAT WILL BE SURE TO MEET WITH APPROVAL AT HOME.

Spofforth, Frederick Robert
One of NSW and Australia's finest early bowlers, Fred 'Demon' Spofforth (1853–1926) toured England in 1878, 1880, 1882, 1884 and 1886. His greatest moment was taking 14/90 in the Test than began the Ashes tradition at the Oval in 1882, Australia's first Test win in England. He took the first Test hat trick in 1878–79 at the MCG. In only 18 Test matches he took an amazing 94 wickets at an average of 18.41, and his overall first-class career averaged an even better 13.55. He settled in England in 1888.

Spooner, John
Black and white artist (b. 1946) whose illustrations, caricatures, cartoons and etchings have provided visual enlightenment for readers, mostly of the Melbourne *Age*, since 1977.

Sport
Sport is one, perhaps the only, field of endeavour that draws all Australians together, that puts the 'us' in AUS. Is this unique in the world? It probably is. Other countries have different creation stories, we have Gallipoli, and sport. In sport all Australians can find a place, and a story – Aboriginal Australians, children, women, the disabled and the non-participant. Before Federation the first Australian teams were the 1868 Aboriginal cricket team which successfully toured England, and the 1877 Test team. An indigenous football game developed in Victoria, instinctively based on aspects of English and Irish folk football, an Aboriginal game and some new ideas. Aboriginal footballers have provided a new dimension in the AFL since the 1970s.

Well before Sydney 2000, Olympics sport has long been a way of expressing a national solidarity and the Australian way of life to the world. Women have been an equal force for Australia in the Olympics since World War II. The Sydney Olympics provided further evidence that it is through sport that we can join together and show who we are. Cathy Freeman, Louise Sauvage, Tatiana Grigorieva and Ian Thorpe were representative of the different Australias we are now.

Sporting Globe
The last surviving example of the weekly or bi-weekly sporting papers that flourished in Australia from the 1890s to the *Globe*'s demise in the 1980s. The *Globe* was published twice a week on pink newsprint, hence its

S

Sporting Globe masthead, 1937

Ian Stewart receives his Brownlow Medal

Mel B. Spurr

Stiffy & Mo

nickname the 'pink paper'. The midweek edition was useful for racing form and footy previews, but the Saturday evening edition was most prized for its telegraph-style football match reports. It was the prime excuse for a bloke to stay in the pub after the footy until six (in the days of early closing) to 'get the *Globe*'.

Sportsgirl

The first major Australian fashion label for young girls. Eventually taken over following the over-ambitious launch of the Sportsgirl Centre in Melbourne at Australia on Collins.

Spurr, Mel B.

An English comedian and monologist, Spurr toured Australia to great acclaim in 1903–04, but died here on 19 September 1904. After his death, Hutton's adapted his 'don't argue' ad poster into the phrase 'don't argue – Hutton's is best' which has remained their trademark.

Stead, Christina

Christina Stead (1902–83) worked as a teacher, office worker and psychologist's assistant before leaving Australia in 1928 to pursue a literary career in London. Her first novel, *Seven Poor Men of Sydney*, and a book of short stories were both published in 1934. She returned to Australia in 1968 and published 15 books before her death.

Stephanie

Chef, former owner of Melbourne's fine dining restaurant 'Stephanie's' and author of the massive best-seller *The Cook's Companion*, she is now a culinary institution and co-owner of the Richmond Hill Café and Larder.

Stewart, Ian

Stewart is a triple Brownlow medallist, winning in 1965 and 1966 with St Kilda (129 games) and 1971 with Richmond (78 games). A brilliant centreman and glorious drop kick on the run, he was less successful as a coach at South Melbourne 1976–77, 1979–81 and Carlton for a few games in 1978.

Stiffy & Mo

Nat 'Stiffy' Phillips and Roy 'Mo' Rene were a pair of slapstick comedians who did their best to entertain audiences at the Tivoli Theatre in Melbourne during the early part of the 20th century.

LET STALK STRINE

Seven shillings and suspence — 75 cents

S

COMPILED BY AFFERBECK LAUDER

Stewnce, Vistas, New Strines! Learn the lingo!

Six steeds pull a five-furrow stump-jump plough

Stolen Generation
One of the central issues in the reconciliation debate, the 'Stolen Generation' refers to young Aborigines who were taken away from their families to be raised by whites. The situation was not helped by a Liberal government statement in early 2000 which claimed there 'was no stolen generation'.

Streeton, Sir Arthur Ernest
Australian Impressionist (1867–1943) and member of the Heidelberg School which included artists such as McCubbin, Roberts and Conder. He contributed 40 paintings to the *9 X 5 Impression Exhibition* held in Melbourne in 1889 – the first of its kind in the country. He was an official war artist during World War I and later a critic for the *Argus*.

Strictly Ballroom
Popular 1992 film credited with once again reinvigorating the Australian film industry. Starring Paul Mercurio and directed by Baz Lurhmann, its humorous (and vaguely camp) portrayal of the ballroom dancing scene won popular audiences in Australia and overseas.

Strine
Our language, the way we speak, was expounded by Professor Afferbeck Lauder in a book entitled *Let Stalk Strine* in 1965 (and later *Nose Tone Unturned)*, though the lingo might be thought to go as far back as the glossary in the back of C. J. Dennis' *The Songs of a Sentimental Bloke* (1916), and further. Examples of Strine are Straya (our country) and Emma Chisit (question in a shop).

Stump-jump Plough
Folklore holds that the stump-jump plough was designed by accident after Robert Bowyer Smith, a farmer from South Australia, broke one of the bolts holding the arm carrying the mouldboard of his plough as he worked uneven ground. Whether this is truth or fable, the stump-jump plough has its ploughshare loosely suspended from the frame by a single bolt, allowing it to ride over roots and stumps instead of being caught and damaged by them. Its invention made it possible to cultivate parts of Victoria and NSW which were previously thought untillable.

Sturt, Charles
Dreamer and explorer of the 'inland sea' which in the early 19th century was hoped lay at the centre of the

The set for the 1976 Melbourne Theatre Company revival of *Summer of the Seventeenth Doll*

The Sullivans – Lorraine Bayly and Paul Cronin centre back

Sunnyside Up, Bill Collins leading from front

continent. Sturt (1795–1869) set out to look in 1827, discovering the Darling River flowing west. In 1829 he explored the Murrumbidgee downstream to the Murray River and its conjunction with the Darling, then to the mouth of the Murray at Lake Alexandrina. He then rowed 1200 kilometres upstream, reaching Sydney in May 1830. In 1844–46 he set out again, this time proving there was no inland sea. Sturt is commemorated with a highway, a desert, a desert pea and a university.

Summer of the Seventeenth Doll

A defining moment in Australian theatre, Ray Lawler's play *Summer of the Seventeenth Doll* opened on 28 November 1955 at the Union Theatre. Featuring a contemporary setting in suburban Melbourne and centring

around the trials of two cane cutters, it has become an Australian naturalistic classic.

Sullivans, The

First screened in November 1976, period serial *The Sullivans* was a Crawford production following the trials and tribulations of a Melbourne family before, during and after World War II. Starring Paul Cronin and Lorraine Bayly, it was sold to more than 70 countries in Crawford's first big export success.

Sun, The

The Melbourne *Sun News-Pictorial* brought the tabloid morning paper format of pictures on the front page to Australia in 1922. It was acquired by the evening broadsheet *Herald* in 1925 and was an immediate success –

Melbourne's most popular paper. Changing habits of readers saw the afternoon paper decline in the 1980s, until it was folded into the *Sun* in 1992, becoming the *Herald Sun*, a seven-day-a-week morning tabloid.

Sunnyside Up

A Friday evening variety program on HSV-7 in Melbourne, *Sunnyside Up* was immensely popular for most of its run 1958–64, rating in the 40s after it moved to 7.30 in 1961. It evolved from radio 3DB's *The Happy Gang*. The gang comprised Dick Cranbourne, John Stuart, Lou Toppano and his Orchestra and versatile race caller Bill Collins, perennially in a dinner jacket. Collins became host, and comic Honest John Gilbert joined, and with another comic, Sid Heylen, they became big stars.

Midget lifesavers at Bronte beach, 1934

La Stupenda, Joan Sutherland

Sunshine Harvester
A harvesting machine which could strip, thresh, winnow and bag grain in a single continuous operation. Grain stalks were separated by the comb at the front of the machine, then the heads were stripped from the stalks by a five-bladed beater and threshed in a drum. Next the mix of chaff and grain was dropped onto vibrating riddles for winnowing. A fan blew any unthreshed heads back into the drum while chaff and straw were blown out under the machine, and separated grain dropped into a bag.

Super Sopper
One of Australia's finest contributions to the world of sport spends its time behind the scenes and if everything goes to plan, you never see it. The Super Sopper, invented in 1974 by Sydney inventor Gordon Withnall, only comes out in the rain. Designed to quickly and easily remove excess water from the field, it is relatively simple: a metal drum, coated in super-absorbent polyurethane foam, absorbs the excess water, while a roller above it squeezes it into a trough for easy disposal off-field.

Surf Lifesavers, Surfing
The surf lifesaver has been touted as becoming, after World War I, the apotheosis of Australian manhood, combining bodily perfection and civic duty, a kind of scout on a surf ski saving lives from sharks and rips. The image of the 'clubbie' was challenged by the freedom-loving surfer (originally known as a 'surfie') of the 1960s, getting stoked on the new aesthetic of finding and riding the perfect wave. Surfers have prospered, but surf lifesaving also has progressed into the commercial world, along with the new icons – iron men.

Sutherland, Dame Joan
Known throughout the operatic world as 'La Stupenda', Dame Joan Sutherland (b. 1926) has been one of the world's foremost sopranos since her debut in 1951 at the Conservatorium in Sydney where she sang the lead in *Judith*. She travelled to London to train at the Royal College of Music after winning several competitions, and after three auditions was accepted into the employment of the Royal Opera House, Covent Garden, making her debut there as the First Lady in Mozart's *The Magic Flute* in 1952.

268

A swaggie of the 1890s

'Fifteen minutes to last drinks, gentlemen' – the six o'clock swill in full flow

SWALLOW & ARIELL'S

BISCUITS · · CAKES
PLUM PUDDINGS
AND
COMPRESSED VEGETABLES

However it was the role of Lucia in *Lucia di Lammermoor* in 1959 which cemented her place as an internationally acclaimed singer and diva.

Sutton, Henry

Henry Sutton (1856–1912) was a self-effacing Australian inventor, who, among other things, was an early and independent inventor of the electric dynamo, the telephone, the electric light bulb, an electric storage battery, colour photography, photo-engraving and in the 1880s also designed but did not construct a system of television, devised to transmit the Melbourne Cup from Flemington to his home in Ballarat. His father, Richard Sutton, founded the long-lasting music firm Suttons in 1854 on the Ballarat goldfields.

Swagman

The pedlar of the 19th century, the swagman moved from place to place, peddling his wares, with no particular area or base. A common sight, especially during the 1930s, the swagman has been mythologised as the typical Australian, even though he is now long since extinct.

Swallow & Ariell Biscuits

When Thomas Swallow and Thomas Harris Ariell became partners in 1854, they established a reputation as ship's biscuit manufacturers, flour-millers and sugar refiners. Their original 1858 Port Melbourne factory was added to the Historic Buildings List in 1983. Along with other pioneer biscuitmakers, Swallow's was swallowed by Arnott's, in 1965. Teddy Bears were a Swallow's bikkie.

Swill, Six O'Clock

Temperance societies were a feature of Australia life in the early 1900s. A powerful lobby, they helped close 1300 licensed premises in Victoria and NSW alone between 1907 and 1914, but it was the outbreak of war in 1914 which saw them claim even greater ground. They then began to link temperance with patriotism and claimed that closing hotels earlier would force men to devote more time to the war effort, and that liberal drinking poisoned potential army recruits. So effective was the campaign that by 1918 all states had imposed early drinking laws. But men simply tried to cram an entire after-work evening's drinking into a single hour: the six o'clock swill. NSW was the first to extend hours to 10pm in 1955, Victoria followed in 1966.

269

The Bridge opening souvenir programme

Eric Thake's kitchen sink Opera House

Sydney Harbour Bridge

The meeting of the two gigantic spans of the Sydney Harbour Bridge took place on 22 August 1930, providing that city with one of its most recognisable landmarks. Costing about £10 million, it was the greatest single arch bridge in the world. Thousands turned out to watch the occasion and thousands more walked across it when it finally opened on 19 March 1932. Legend has it that by the time the bridge has been painted once, the workmen must turn around and begin painting the other end again, making it a circular task worthy of a Greek tragedy.

Sydney/Melbourne

After the depression of the 1890s put paid to the Melbourne ascendency, the Sydney century in Australian history began, reaching an apotheosis in the 2000 Olympic Games. Seen from the south, Sydney has represented a different kind of urban Australia from Melbourne. Perhaps it was the convict stain, the heat, the hills or the harbour – but Sydney was more relaxed and hedonistic, less sport and culture obsessed. In Sydney the drift is outdoors to the beach and the water, not inside to kitchens and dark night conversation. Sydney is clubs not pubs, ferries not trams. In the 1950s Australians left Australia for England to make it; from the 1970s Australians left the rest of the country and went to Sydney. The remorseless magnetism of the Australian metropolis attracted media moguls and their empire HQs and banks and businesses followed, undermining the old money down

south. Arts businesses and film studios, telcos and dotcoms, banks and corporations – that's Sydney. While the Olympic Games showed that the people of Sydney will turn out en masse for a party, it remains to be seen whether they will find anything to do with the vast arenas they constructed.

Sydney Morning Herald

On 18 April 1831, the first copy of the *Sydney Herald* (later to become the *Sydney Morning Herald*) hit the stands. Started by Sydney bookseller William McGarview (although it was soon bought out by F.M. Stokes and Ward Stephens and later by John Fairfax), it was originally intended to be a weekly publication. Its incredibly cheap cover price of fivepence and its bipartisan politics (as indicated by its

Happy days at Sylvania Waters

Sydney Morning Herald building, 1856

Sydney Mail celebrates the joining of the arch

Magda Szubanski as Pixie Anne Wheatley

original motto: 'In moderation placing all my glory, while Tories call me a Whig and Whigs a Tory') made it an instant success – a position it has maintained to this day.

Sydney Opera House
Taking 19 years and $100 million to build, the Opera House was designed by Danish architect Joern Utzon. The winner of a worldwide design contest held in 1956, Utzon offered a 'shell' design in a series of sketches whose appearance gave rise to much debate and controversy on how to build it and how to pay for it. It was opened on 22 October 1973 by the Queen. A notable absentee was Joern Utzon, who had resigned from the project in 1966 after a terminal dispute with the State government.
See: Bennelong

Sydney to Hobart Yacht Race
First raced on Boxing Day 1945, the Sydney to Hobart has an international reputation for yacht racing, and in 1999, tragedy.

Sylvania Waters
Bizarre hybrid of 'real-life' TV and *Neighbours*, this 1992 TV program showcased the banal lives of a family of (supposedly) 'real' Australians. Alternately depressing and riveting, their strange activities became increasingly self-aware until it actually seemed they were scripting their own lives to fit the formulas of an average soap opera.

Syme, David
Before buying a half share in Melbourne's enduring newspaper institution the *Age* from his brother

Ebenezer in 1856, Scots-born David Syme (1827–1908) was a gold digger and road contractor. He took over after Ebenezer's death in 1860, and soon had circulation up. He campaigned on land for the people, protection of local industries and for full rights of self-government. The *Age* was selling about 120 000 copies a day in 1890 in a city of less than a million, a daily circulation not changed much from that achieved in a city of nearly four million in 2000.

Szubanski, Magda
Popular comedian who has worked with the D-Generation and *Fast Forward* (and picked up a few Logies along the way) before finding international fame in a movie about a talking pig: *Babe*.
See: Babe; *D-Generation*; Fast Forward

T

Truganini

First bet at the TAB, 1961

Ron Tandberg sees the joke

Table Talk in 1933, Maggie Tyte, English Diva

TAB

The legalisation of off-course betting transformed Australian racing, beginning with the opening of the Victorian TAB (Totalisator Agency Board) on 11 March 1961. While it has not eliminated the black-money SP network entirely, the TAB has changed racing for many punters from a sport to a pure form of gambling. Except for the biggest races such as the Melbourne Cup and the Golden Slipper in Sydney, attendances at racing and revenue shared between on-course bookmakers has been in steady decline.

Table Talk

Covering a wide selection of general topics, from politics to the arts to fashion and social events (along with a smattering of sport), *Table Talk*

magazine survived a remarkable 54 years from its debut in 1885. The last issue hit the stands on 14 September 1939, leaving room for the similarly formatted *Australian Women's Weekly* to attract an even larger national readership.

Tandanya

Tandanya is the traditional name for the Adelaide city area of the Kaurna (pronounced 'Garna') people – the original inhabitants of the Adelaide Plains. 'Tarnda' means 'red kangaroo' and 'angka' means 'the place of'. It is also the name given to Australia's National Aboriginal Cultural Institute in Adelaide, South Australia.

Tandberg, Ron

One of Australia's finest political cartoonists, Tandberg's (b. 1956) acid

wit has appeared predominantly in the *Age* newspaper from 1973, with a brief stint at the *Herald Sun* from 1993–94. He was the conscience of Victoria and the nemesis of politicians, and won a number of Walkley Awards (including seven between 1976 and 1986, and Gold Walkleys in 1979 and 1986).

Tankard, Meryl

Time spent with the famously modern Pina Bausch and the Wuppertal Tanztheater in Germany 1978–84 transformed former Australian Ballet dancer Meryl Tankard (b. 1955) into an influential and controversial choreographer and company director. She became director of the Australian Dance Theatre in 1993 and left acrimoniously in 1999.

Les Tanner: self-portrait of a cartoonist at work

Leonard Teale in *Homicide*

T

Tanner, Les

An early start as a junior wooden lavatory seat maker proved ample preparation for a career as a political cartoonist. Les Tanner (1927–2001) started in newspapers as a printer's devil at the Sydney *Daily Telegraph*, where his family had strong working connections. He studied at the Julian Ashton school and went to London in 1960, drawing for the *Daily Sketch*. In 1961 he was at Frank Packer's *Bulletin*, where he famously got into trouble for drawing Victorian Premier Henry Bolte as a hangman in 1965. He worked at the *Age* from 1967 until his retirement in 1997. Over these 30 years Tanner's daily cartoon, and Tanner With Words on Saturday, became Australian institutions, at a time when cartoonists became as influential as journalists.

Target Stores

Target was the brainchild of George Lindsay, who opened his first store in 1925. It ran under the slogan 'Half the profit – Twice the turnover' and by the time of its merger with Myer Emporium in 1968, it had grown to a chain of 14 small stores around Victoria. Pronounced 'Tarjay' by shoppers seeking retail reassurance.

Tarzan's Grip

A strong cement, ideal for glueing flapping soles to school shoes, from the 1930s.

Tatts

In 1878, English-born George Adams and friends bought the Tattersall's Hotel in Sydney and he began running horse sweepstakes. Avoiding anti-gambling legislation throughout the 1890s, he eventually settled in Tasmania and Tattersall's became the official Tasmanian lottery. Today, Tattersall's runs Tattslotto, the largest lottery in the Australia, and 'winning Tatts' is still the dream of millions.

Teale, Leonard

An acting institution on the Crawford's cop show which began Australian TV production, *Homicide*, Leonard Teale (1922–94) was the deep-voiced but slightly nasally Det. Sgt Mackay, longest serving of all the *Homicide* detectives, appearing from 1965 to 1973. To an earlier generation he was equally famous as the postwar (he was a RAAF officer 1942–46) voice of *Superman* the radio serial, on the *ABC Children's Hour*, and the voice on the best-selling vinyl rendition of *The Man from Snowy River*.

Peter Thompson driving elegantly

Beautiful thongs

Sigrid Thornton looking serious

Howzat Jeff Thomson

Thomas, Rover

Rover Thomas (1926–98), an individualistic but influential Turkey Creek painter who uses black and brown 'flat' colour. He began painting and exhibiting in the 1980s.

Thompson, Peter

When he was 12 years old, Peter Thompson's grandfather gave him a two iron. Seven years later Thompson (b. 1929) turned pro and immediately won the first of nine successive New Zealand Opens, a feat almost as impressive as his five British Opens (including three in succession 1954–56). Never focused on the US tour, he still won the Texas Open in 1956 and finished fourth in the US Open that same year. After retiring, he began an international golf course design company.

Thomson, Jeff

Along with fast bowler Dennis Lillee, Jeff 'Thommo' Thomson (b. 1950) was one half of Australia's most lethal opening bowling partnership. Devoid of subtlety, his bowling was all about speed and bounce, his loping sling-arm style destroying English sides in particular from the mid-1970s to the mid-1980s. In 1978 he was at the centre of one of the sport's most famous court cases when the ACB denied his request to play World Series Cricket. The court found in favour of the ACB and Thomson sat out for a year before joining the side in 1979 for the West Indies tour. He took 200 wickets in his 51 Tests.

Thongs

Known in some northern lands as flip flops, and in Syria as Zenobias, thongs are the favoured footwear of millions of the true blue, especially in summer. They reached their zenith when a giant thong was ridden by Kylie Minogue in the Sydney Olympics closing ceremony.

Thornton, Sigrid

Sigrid Thornton (b. 1959) made her stage debut aged 9, her first TV appearance four years later and her first movie at 18 in *The Getting of Wisdom*. She found international acclaim in *The Man from Snowy River* and its sequel, but saved her most memorable performances for the lead role in the whimsical and universally loved ABC TV series *SeaChange*.

Thorpie – some people he knew thought 'crazy'

Ian Thorpe – the Thorpedo

Albert Thurgood – Albert the Great

T

Thorpe, Billy

As frontman for Billy Thorpe and the Aztecs and later as a solo performer, Thorpe and band were at the forefront of Australian pop music in the 1960s. 63 000 came to see them in concert at Melbourne's Myer Music Bowl and 8000 met them at the airport in Western Australia.

Thorpe, Ian

At 14, Ian Thorpe (b. 1982) became the youngest person ever to qualify for an Australian swim team. Blessed with incredible size 17 feet, the 'Thorpedo's' key events are the 100m, 200m and 400m freestyle. Even early in his career he showed he was capable of dominating the sport, picking up four gold medals at the Commonwealth Games in 1998. He has three Olympic golds – two in relays & 400 metres.

Thurgood, Albert

'Albert the Great' was one of the early greats of Australian Rules Football, with a career which ran from 1892 to 1906, although it was effectively shortened by eight years after a serious injury and the VFL's refusal to grant him a permit to play. At ruck and half-forward, Thurgood (1874–1927) was a goal-scoring machine, and his leaping mark and long kick redefined the sport. He is credited with one of the longest kicks ever – 98.48 metres at East Melbourne in 1899, and helped Essendon to four straight premierships in the 1890s.

Tiddas

Originally members of Aboriginal band Djaambi, Amy Saunders, Lou Bennett and Sally Dastey formed a new outfit for a performance in 1990.

The name 'Tiddas', meaning sisters, was coined on the day by Ruby Hunter and stuck with them through an EP, three albums and a live CD, which marked their break-up in 1999.

Tingwell, Charles 'Bud'

Bud Tingwell is as highly respected an actor and director as there is in Australia, in theatre, film or television. Born in 1923 he has appeared in films such as *Eliza Fraser*, *'Breaker' Morant*, *My First Wife* and *Malcolm*. He became a star to a new generation in the films *The Castle* and *The Dish*.

Triple J

On 19 January 1975 Triple J was first heard in Sydney, kicking off its broadcasts with Skyhooks' *You Just Like Me 'Cause I'm Good In Bed*. Originally called 2JJ and broadcast on

Charles Tingwell

Ross Moss, Marius Webb, Double J's first day

Truganini

the AM band, it moved on 1 August 1980 to FM under the name 2JJJ, and then in 1989 adopted its present name, Triple J. At the same time the station embarked on a campaign to expand into all capital cities in the country plus Newcastle in NSW, making it Australia's only national youth broadcaster. This plan was expanded in 1995 to include 18 rural centres across the country. It is also 100 per cent commercial free and plays at least 35 per cent local music, making it one of the loudest and most strident supporters of Australian music in the country.

Troedel & Co.

German-born Charles Troedel (1836–1906) was the master lithographer/printer of the 19th century in Australia. He came to

Melbourne in 1860 aged 24 and worked for a printer named Schuhkrafft for three years before setting up on his own in Collins Street. He employed a number of distinguished etchers and artists over the years including Percy Leason, Blamire Young, Lionel Lindsay and Arthur Streeton.

Truganini

Truganini was thought to have been the last 'full blood' Aborigine to have lived in Tasmania. She was born about 1812, and married Woorraddy at Bruny Island in 1829. After most of their people had been killed or died, Truganini and Woorraddy helped Protector G.A. Robinson collect the small number of survivors to Flinders Island in 1835. Truganini accompanied Robinson to Port Phillip in 1838, and in

1856 went with the remaining 16 Aborigines to Oyster Bay on the east coast of Tasmania. By 1873 only Truganini survived, and she went to Hobart where she died in 1876. Despite her express wishes, her skeleton was displayed in the Tasmanian Museum from 1904 to 1947. On 8 May 1976 her bones were cremated and the ashes scattered in the D'Entrecasteaux Channel.

Trugo

Trugo is one of two games indigenous to Victoria (Australian football is the other one) and was developed at the Newport railyards in the 1920s, played by railway workers at lunchtime. It is a croquet-style game which involves knocking a rubber disc through goals at the end of a 30-metre lawn court.

Victor Trumper takes block for the camera in the pre-war Golden Age of cricket

Trumper, Victor

Before Don Bradman, Australians could claim no greater batsman than Victor Trumper (1877–1915). Fluid and graceful, attacking but reliable, Trumper was a revelation. Soon after his debut in 1899 he scored a career-high 300 not out against Sussex at Hove. In 1902 at Old Trafford he became the first cricketer to score a hundred before lunch on the first morning of a Test. When he died tragically of a heart attack in 1915, the papers let news of the war run side by side with 'The Death of a Great Cricketer'.

Truth

A muckraking, anti-establishment scandal sheet, the *Truth* was first published in 1890 in Sydney by William Willis and William Crick, and edited by Adolphus Taylor, a sometime Mudgee politician and syphilitic drunk. It prospered, and was joined shortly after its establishment by the dubious Sydney identity John Norton. Norton soon rose to the top of the heap, replacing Taylor as editor in 1891, and taking a share of the ownership at the same time. Machinations of ownership continued amid libel and other law suits until Norton became undisputed owner of the failing paper in 1896. Under Norton's alliterative editing, and creative campaigning, it soon prospered again. Brisbane and Melbourne editions commenced in 1902, and a Norton media empire was born. John Norton died in 1916, leaving a deeply unresolved estate. Much legislation, litigation and fraud took place over the next few years until John Norton's son Ezra gained control in 1922 at the age of 25. Ezra obtained a licence to produce a daily newspaper in 1941, and established the *Daily Mirror* in Sydney, folding the Sydney edition of *Truth* (as the *Sunday Mirror*) in 1958. The Mirror papers came into the hands of Rupert Murdoch's News Limited in 1960. *Melbourne Truth* had become independent of the Norton empire in the 1950s, and was taken over by Owen Thompson and Mark Day in 1980, and by Mark Day in 1993, with Norton's aim of 'bringing the secret sins and crimes of public men to light' as well as a hefty amount of football and racing. Jack 'Captain Blood' Dyer was the mainstay of the

Albert Tucker by Michel Lawrence

Tulloch, the champ

Ian Turner, the 'Footy Professor'

football coverage in the 1960s and 1970s, and racing, boobs and celebrity scandals through the 1990s until its final demise in 1998.

Truscott, John

Designer John Truscott was an Academy Award winner for set and costume design on *Camelot* (1967), and later designed the interiors of the Victorian Arts Centre (1984).

Tucker, Albert

A self-taught painter, Tucker (1914–2000) was a central figure in the Angry Penguin painters which flowered around Heide during World War II. His interpretations of Australian morality during World War II and his photographs of Heide are central to our understanding of Australian art. In 1957, his paintings

became the first work of an Australian artist to be purchased by New York's Museum of Modern Art. He died of heart disease.

Tulloch

Perhaps the greatest horse of all time, Tulloch won or was placed in every race he ever entered – except one. Bought in 1965 by T.J. Smith, he won 15 of his first 21 starts including the Caulfield Guineas and Stakes, and finished second in the other six. Only the Melbourne Cup would elude him, first in 1958 when owner Haley declared his opposition to running three year olds and withdrew him from a race he would surely have won, and in 1960 when jockey Sellwood restrained him so long he could not make up the distance in the straight.

Turf

When smoking was as Australian as going to the races, Turf Virginia fags in the red packet, with flavoursome cork tips, were dead certs.

Turner, Ian

Known as the 'Footy Professor', Ian Turner (1922–78) was a critical thinker and writer about diverse Australian social issues, from labour history to children's rhymes, and was naturally passionate about Australian football. His series of mock-academic Barassi Memorial Lectures were heard with delight and respect at Monash University from 1968 to 1975. His social history of footy *Up Where, Cazaly?* (1981) was unfinished when he died in 1978. The book was completed by Leonie Sandercock and remains one of the best studies of the game.

279

U

Holden ute

Uluru, centre of Australia

Trevor Chappell's underarm

David Unaipon on the inventive $50 note

A wrecked 1933 Ford ute

Uluru

The centre of Australia, physically and perhaps spiritually as well. Made of arkose, a coarse-grained sandstone rich in the mineral feldspar. The oxidisation of the mineral gives it its rich red colour. The first white person to reach and climb the Rock was William Gosse in 1873. He named it Ayers Rock after Sir Henry Ayers, later premier of South Australia. It was returned to its Aboriginal owners in 1991, who successfully manage it jointly with the Commonwealth.

Unaipon, David

The first published Aboriginal writer, David Unaipon (1872–1967) is commemorated with a portrait on the $50 note – appropriately, as he was also a distinguished inventor. Unaipon was a Ngarrindjeri man,

born at the Point McLeay Mission near Tailem Bend in South Australia. In 1909 he patented an improved handpiece for sheep shearing, and as 'Australia's Leonardo' put forward ideas for a helicopter (based on the boomerang), mechanical propulsion devices and a multi-radial wheel. His writing first appeared in the Sydney *Daily Telegraph* in 1924 and included *Native Legends*, a booklet published in 1929. He was an advocate of equal rights for black and white and for the Commonwealth to take responsibility for Aborigines from the states.

Underarm

Notorious cricket incident which caused a diplomatic and social rift between New Zealand and Australia. For the final ball of a one-day international at the MCG in 1981,

Greg Chappell ordered little brother Trevor to bowl underarm, preventing the NZ batter from hitting the six required to win the game. It has become synonymous with bad sportsmanship.
See: Bodyline

Ute, The

In 1933 a Gippsland farmer's wife wrote to Ford Managing Director Hubert French with the following request: 'Could you please make a car that we can go to church in on Sunday and take the pigs to market on Monday.' The result was a design from Lewis Bandt who attached the front half of a sedan to the back half of a light truck and created the Coupe Utility. It entered production in 1934 and was soon being imitated the world over.

281

85 MEN MISSING — Voyager cut in two by carrier

PM: SHOCKING DISASTER

Captain missing

The Herald
63-0211   MELBOURNE, TUESDAY, FEBRUARY 11, 1964   26 PAGES
HOME EDITION
daily sales

Herald Staff Reporters

JERVIS BAY, NSW, Today. — Eighty-five officers and men of the destroyer HMAS Voyager are missing after the collision with HMAS Melbourne at 9 o'clock last night.

They include the Voyager's captain, Captain D. R. Stevens, 43, who is reported to have been on his bridge when the collision occurred.

The Voyager carried 324.

The Prime Minister, Sir Robert Menzies, said in Canberra today: "It is a shocking disaster, unparalleled in the peace-time history of Australia."

Sir Robert said he had ordered a prompt, thorough public investigation conducted by a judge. This was because the normal machinery for Naval investigations was not adequate for the present purposes.

The Navy Department announced early today that most of the Voyager's officers and men were known to have survived. It had high hopes that some of the missing were on board rescue craft still searching the area.

But, as the hours passed, the hopes gave way to the certainty of a massive deathroll. A Navy helicopter brought in only three more survivors to Balmoral Naval Hospital in Sydney. And a mine sweeper was reported to be heading for Jervis Bay with two bodies.

The Voyager, a 3500-ton Daring class destroyer, sank in 60 fathoms (360 ft.) of oily water, 17 miles south of Jervis Bay, about midnight. Jervis Bay is 120 miles south of Sydney.

Many of her crew were below decks — some of them playing the traditional Navy game tombola (housey-housey) in the forward section. Suddenly, the call "Collision Stations" was sounded.

There was a crash. Survivors' stories of what part of the Voyager was hit by the Melbourne vary. Several said she was hit in the side near the bridge, and was almost cut in two.

The Melbourne — 19,930 ton aircraft carrier and flagship of the Australian fleet, stood by the Voyager until she sank, and helped to pick up survivors. Now she is steaming slowly to Sydney with damaged bows. She is not expected to reach there until noon tomorrow.

More than 12 hours after the sinking, the Navy had issued no list of survivors although it told relatives to ring a Canberra telephone number — 70424, extension 261

The Minister for the Navy, Dr Forbes, at a Press conference early this afternoon gave the first official statement of the background to the accident.

Survivors at Jervis Bay

BLANKET-WRAPPED SURVIVORS of the Voyager photographed in a mess hall at Jervis Bay today after they had been brought ashore. FROM LEFT: Leading Electrical Mechanic Bernard Verwayen, 23, of Albury, NSW; Petty Officer Colin O'Flynn, 28, of Lilyfield, Sydney; Ordinary Tactical Communications Officer Owen Sparks, 19, of Bunbury, WA; Ordinary Draftee Robert John Vomarx, 17, of Myrtleford, Victoria. — Picturegram

Trapped below deck

JERVIS BAY, Today. — Scores of men playing cards in the Voyager's canteen are believed to have been trapped when the ship's side was stove in.

In other pages . . .

ON PAGE 2
● Herald men flee over damaged carrier
● Crash boats pick up 70

ON PAGE 3
● Voyager survivors tell of escapes — "mates were heroes"
● More pictures of survivors

The Melbourne *Herald* reports the HMAS *Voyager* tragedy

V

We've always been happy little Vegemites, bright as bright could be

Vegemite

Made from processed, concentrated and refined brewers yeast, Vegemite spread was developed by Dr Cyril P. Callister at the Fred Walker Cheese Company in 1922 and named by an unknown competitor in a £50 prize that same year. It was not an immediate success. To reinvigorate sales in 1928, a name change was proposed. The name? Parwill! A play on the slogan used in Britain for the popular spread Marmite – 'If Marmite . . . then Parwill!'. It didn't help, and the name Vegemite was quickly reinstated. Sales received a boost in 1935 when savings-conscious Australians cashed in the free coupons included in packets of cheddar cheese. An early pioneer of modern advertising techniques, Vegemite was involved in huge

contest giveaways; its labels were adorned with Disney characters and it secured promotion within British medical journals as a rich source of vitamin B. In 1954, the 'Happy Little Vegemites' song jangled in the ears of Australians for the first time and Vegemite switched to a transparent glass jar. Such is Australia's fascination with the spread that in 1983 a plaque was unveiled at Kerford Road in Melbourne. Another historic feat: in April 1984 at a Woolworths in Chullora NSW, a 115g jar of Vegemite became the first item to have its barcode electronically scanned at a supermarket checkout in Australia. The cost? 66 cents. In 1991 Vegemite mania reached its zenith, with an exhibition at the Powerhouse Museum in Sydney. A national search had been conducted to find early

Vegemite jars and memorabilia, and the results were shown throughout July. And finally, in 1997, this Australian icon hit its 75th birthday with these impressive statistics: Australians use 22 million jars of the spread each year, and 90 per cent of Australian pantries are hiding a jar.

Verge, John

John Verge (1782–1861) was a retired London builder lured by the promise of profit in NSW in 1828. He set up as a farmer on large grants of land but wasn't overly successful. However, initially at the invitation of Governor Darling, he left his mark on Sydney. Most prominent between 1830 and 1837, his extant masterpieces are Camden Park designed for John Macarthur and Elizabeth Bay House for Alexander MacLeay.

A Walter Vernon building

For a hard earned thirst

Carlton & United
AUSTRALIA'S OWN
OFFICIAL BEER SUPPLIER TO THE AFL
For a hard earned thirst

SECOND BOOK. 57

Skip, skip, skipping on the ends of their toes ran the hobyahs.
And the hobyahs cried, "Pull down the hut, eat up the little old man, carry off the little old woman."

Then yellow dog Dingo ran out, barking loudly. The hobyahs were afraid.
They ran home as fast as they could go.

The Hobyahs in a Victorian Reader

Vernon, Walter & Sons

Vernon was born in England, and came to Sydney in 1883 to recuperate from asthma. He was commissioned to design a department store for David Jones, on the corner of George and Barrack streets (1895) and was appointed government architect in NSW in 1890, with perhaps his major achievement being the Art Gallery of NSW (1909). He was on the committee which chose the site of Canberra, and appointed Walter Burley Griffin to design it. He retired in 1911, and died in 1914. His son Hugh Venables Vernon (1877–1935) was also an architect and was a major in the 1st Light Horse and landed at Gallipoli. He was later awarded the DSO at Fromelles. A younger son, Geoffrey H. Vernon (1882–1946), was also an Australian hero. A doctor, he

was regimental medical officer for 11th Light Horse in Palestine, and won the Military Cross in 1917. He lowered his age by eight years to join the second AIF in 1942, and was the revered Doc Vernon of the 39th Battalion on the Kokoda Track.

Victa

Mervyn Victor Richardson developed the idea of a lightweight rotary-action motor mower in 1952, and lodged a patent application in 1955. Despite the extraordinary success of the Victa in becoming an Australian icon and sales success (100 mowers in the first year of business, 1953, 60 000 in 1957) the basic idea was covered by an unexploited British patent of 1932. The Australian Victa was an idea whose time had come in suburban Australia.

Victoria Bitter

VB was first brewed in the 1890s and became part of the Carlton & United stable (now Foster's Brewing) – it is the choice of locals opposed to the Fosterisation of the world.

Victorian Readers

A series of reading books issued by the Victorian Education Department between 1928 and 1930 for each of the eight grades of primary school. Second editions appeared 10 years later, and the first six were phased out in the 1950s. The Fifth and Sixth Books survived into the 1960s, continuing to teach Grade Two students about Anzac but leaving many haunted by the Hobyahs and their fearful impact on the Little Old Man and the Little Old Woman, saved by yellow dog Dingo.

The first Vietnam headline

Steve Vizard and Michael Veitch in *Fast Forward*

Eugène von Guérard

Vietnam

The Vietnam War and the re-introduction of military conscription for 20-year-old males (1964) divided the Australian community as no war had done before. From the day (19 April 1965) Prime Minister Robert Menzies announced a commitment of 1000 Australian troops to join the United States forces in South Vietnam, a vocal and vigorous minority was opposed to the war and conscription for it. The Vietnam War and conscription added a political dimension to the rapid social changes taking place in Australia, as the phenomenon of the 'Sixties' took hold. From the visit of The Beatles in 1964, the times they were a'changin', especially for young Australians. Sex, drugs and rock'n'roll were part of it, as was a reflection of the momentous events of 1968 in Paris, Prague and Chicago. The heady mix added to a new nationalism expressed in theatre, the nascent film industry, poetry and publishing.

Vizard, Steve

Former *Tonight Live* show host and comic actor, Steve Vizard (b. 1956) has become a mid-range mogul in the Australian media as founder and director of Artist Services, producers of *SeaChange*, *Full Frontal* and *Fast Forward*. His business interests include a computer for the masses scheme with the ACTU, and internet services.

Von Guérard, Eugène

Von Guérard (1811–1901) was a heroically naturalistic landscape painter who had a good deal to do with the imagining of the Australian bush as weird and mysterious. He arrived in Geelong in 1852, and spent time prospecting on the Ballarat goldfields. In the 1860s he travelled and painted extensively and was appointed first Director of the Victorian National Gallery and School of Art in 1870. He left for England in 1881.

Voyager, HMAS

In the long list of Australian maritime disasters, the sinking of the destroyer *Voyager*, after a collision with aircraft carrier HMAS *Melbourne* on 10 February 1964, ranks with the worst. Two Royal Commissions attributed sole blame to the *Voyager*, on whom 82 men were killed. Decades later the survivors are still fighting for compensation in the courts.

W

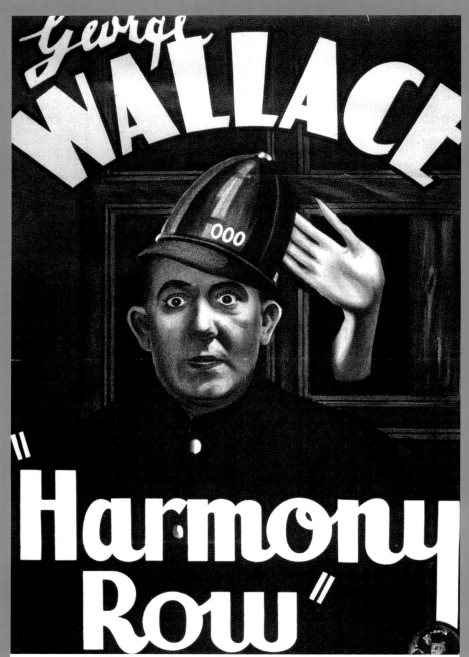

George Wallace starred in the Frank Thring Snr film production, *Harmony Row*

Mike Walsh, TV host, with Frank Thring whose father's company Efftee Films produced Wallace

The 1996 Wallabies head for the try line

Garnet Walch's Christmas Annual 1874

Walch, Garnet

Originally a Tasmanian, Garnet Walch (1843–1913) was educated in England before returning to live in Australia in 1860. In 1873 he moved to Melbourne and became a distinguished journalist and publisher. He wrote 30 burlesques and pantomimes.

Walker, Lennox

Over 42 years as a long-range weather forecaster, Lennox Walker (1925–2000) established himself as an Australian legend. After a stint as a jackaroo and a period serving in New Guinea during World War II, he began work at the Crohamhurst Observatory in Beerwah, north of Brisbane. Lacking modern forecasting techniques, he used sunspot activity, the revolution of the planets and weather records to help farmers around Australia pick

drought-breaking rains. He was also remarkably accurate in many predictions of major events including the weather for the 1956 Melbourne Olympics and Cyclone Tracy in 1974. However, he was not always accurate and the Queensland government criticised him for damaging tourism with his cyclone predictions. The Australian public, especially some young brides, stuck with him, right up to his retirement in 1994.

Wallabies

Nickname of the Australian rugby union side. First used in 1908–09.

Wallace, George

Comedian, film actor and composer of the World War II hit *A Brown Slouch Hat (with the Side Turned Up)*, George Wallace (1895–1960) was for over 30

years as popular an entertainer as there has ever been in Australia. First on stage at the age of three as a pirate with his father's song-and-dance act, he was on the vaudeville circuit from age 16. His breakthrough was in 1919 as half of a double act called Dinkus and Onkus. By 1925 he was solo on the Fuller circuit at £20 a week and predicted by *Theatre* magazine to become Australia's greatest comedian. He was a notable prat fall artist, patter merchant and song and revue writer. Through the Depression he appeared in films, musical comedy and pantomime. He made seven features, reworking an old revue script for *Harmony Row* in 1933. He joined the Tivoli circuit in the 1940s, and was on radio in the 1950s. Health problems forced him into retirement in 1957.

287

Fred Ward, Captain Thunderbolt

WALTZING MATILDA

Waltzing Matilda score

W

Waltzing Matilda

Defeated by *Advance Australia Fair* in a referendum to choose Australia's national anthem, *Waltzing Matilda* was penned by Andrew Barton 'Banjo' Paterson in January 1895. The term 'waltzing Matilda' is old slang for looking for work with your swag.
See: Swagman

Wannan, Bill

William 'Bill' Fielding Fearn-Wannan (b. 1915) has become a widely known collector and authority on Australian humour and folklore. He has compiled several books on the subject and is perhaps best known for his 'Come In Spinner' column in the *Australasian Post* (1955–78). Books include *Bill Wannan's Folk Medicine* (no warranties expressed), *Come In Spinner* and *My Kind of Country*.

War Memorial, Parkville

War Memorials

Thousands of war memorials commemorate lives lost in wars fought by Australians. They exist in nearly every city and town in the land. Ken Inglis in his great book *Sacred Places* guesses some 4000 of them, not counting the cemeteries overseas, where Australia remembers its dead in more than 50 places. The lone Digger on his plinth, Lest We Forget, the poppies on Anzac Day, the World War II names added to World War I names, the secular temples in Canberra and Melbourne.
See: Anzac, Australian War Memorial, Little Boy of Manly

Ward, Fred

Frederick Ward (1835–70), perhaps better known as 'Captain Thunderbolt', worked as a station

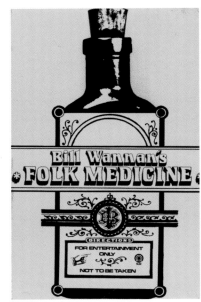

Bill Wannan's folkloric medicine

hand and horse breaker before being sentenced to 10 years imprisonment on Cockatoo Island for horse theft. He received a ticket of leave four years later but was again found guilty of horse theft. In 1863 he escaped the island and carried out a series of robberies in the New England District between 1865 and 1870. Gaining an unfounded reputation as an altruistic thief, he was finally killed in a shoot-out in Uralla, NSW. A folk hero after his death, his exploits have been celebrated in verse, literature and two films, *Thunderbolt* (1910) and *Captain Thunderbolt* (1953).

Warne, Shane

Shane Warne (b. 1969) is one of the greatest leg-spinners of all time. In a delicious twist, he began his sporting life trying to play football for St Kilda,

Shane Warne on his first tour of England

Steve and Mark Waugh – brothers in arms (above); Gai Waterhouse (right)

but issues about his weight saw him turn to cricket instead. He made his Australian debut against Zimbabwe in 1991 after only one match for Victoria. But it was England who saw Warne reach his peak. In 1993 he bowled Mike Gatting with his first Test ball in England, a delivery which spun from outside leg to take Gatting's off stump. Warne has performed similar feats virtually every time the two sides have met. Run-ins with bookmakers and the media prompted him to call his life off the field 'a soap opera', but on the field he is often unbeatable.

Waterhouse, Gai

After a long battle to secure a licence, Gai Waterhouse quickly proved herself one of Australia's finest horse trainers. The daughter of racing legend T.J. Smith, she was a dominant figure in Australian racing throughout the 1990s, working with champion horses such as Pharoah and Nothin' Leica Dane.

Waugh, Mark

One half of the Waugh twins, Mark Edward Waugh (b. 1965) has a reputation in the world cricket community for elegant strokeplay. He made his debut in the fourth Test against England in the 1990–91 series (at the expense of his brother) and has gone on to become a fixture in both one-day and Test teams for Australia. The low point in his career came in 1995 when he was fined by the ACB for giving pitch and team information to an Indian bookmaker, a controversy which dogged him through the 2000–01 season.

Waugh, Steve

The other half of Australian cricket's Waugh twins, Stephen Rodger Waugh made his debut against India in the Boxing Day Test 1985. Since then he has played in over a hundred Test matches and over three hundred one-day matches. Originally a fine all-rounder with a devastating slower ball, shoulder troubles have seen him focus on his batting in recent years. In 1999 he was appointed Australia's 40th Test captain, in the same year as PricewaterhouseCoopers had him rated the world's number one batsman. A half-dozen books (all without the aid of a ghost writer) has seen him become one of Australia's top-selling sports writers. Waugh has grown in the captaincy of his country, and untainted by scandal, epitomises what is good about Australian cricket.

289

WEG cartoon, 1984

W

Webb, Karrie
A revelation in women's golf, Queenslander Karrie Webb (b. 1974) began playing golf when she was eight years old and turned pro in October 1994. In 1996 she became the first woman to earn a million dollars in a season. In 1997 she fell just short of repeating the feat and had 21 top-10 finishes in 25 events contested.

Weddings, Parties, Anything
Through 14 members, eight albums, two managers, three record companies and 10 years, Weddings, Parties, Anything defined themselves as an archetypal Australian band. Their rough edges, their disinterest in the peripheral elements of the musical trade and their obvious love for music put them at the top of the pile from their debut *Scorn of the Women* in 1987 to their final best-of, *Trophy Night*, in 1998.

Karrie Webb

Weeties
Launched in 1913, Weeties is one of the oldest packaged breakfast cereals on the market today and contains nothing but wheat grain flakes.

WEG (William Ellis Green)
William Ellis Green, cartoonist and illustrator in the Melbourne *Herald* from the 1940s to 1980s. Perhaps most famous for his AFL/VFL Grand Final posters, available at the ground after the game from the 1960s.

Weir, Peter
Director Peter Weir made his name

The King of Weeties

with early features *Homesdale* (1971) and *The Cars that Ate Paris* (1974), breaking through with the eerie *Picnic at Hanging Rock* (1975), *The Last Wave* (1977), and the more conventional storytelling of *Gallipoli* (1981). American successes include *Witness* (1985), *The Mosquito Coast* (1986), *Dead Poets Society* (1989), *Green Card* (1990) and triumphantly in *The Truman Show* (1998).

Welcome Stranger
The largest gold nugget ever discovered, the 'Welcome Stranger' was unearthed in Bulldog Gully near Dunolly on 5 February 1869. It weighed more than 210 lbs (95 kg) and was

White Australia, a play in 1906

West Gate Bridge collapse

Jana Wendt and David Johnston, news on Ten

found by two diggers, John Deason and Richard Oates, who were so 'hard up' they had been refused a bag of flour on credit the week before.

Wendt, Jana

The 'Perfumed Steamroller' of Australian telejournalism, Jana Wendt has been the highest paid woman in Australian television. She has also performed a rare 'grand slam' of Australian TV, appearing on every free-to-air network: *Eyewitness News* on Network Ten, *60 Minutes*, *A Current Affair* and a series of interview specials for Nine, *Witness* for Seven, *Uncensored* for the ABC and *Dateline* on SBS.

West Gate Bridge

A 15 October 1970 disaster which killed 35 workers when a span of a new bridge spanning Melbourne's Yarra River fell. As distinct from natural disasters such as bushfires, this man-made disaster was especially deeply felt in Melbourne, coming after another bridge, King Street, had sunk and become something of a joke. The West Gate workers killed are recognised by a memorial under the bridge.

West, Morris

Born in St Kilda, Morris West (1916–99) was a member of the Christian Brothers for 12 years but left in 1939 before taking his final vows. The experience inspired his first novel, *Moon in My Pocket* (1945), which was published under the pseudonym Julian Morris. He left Australia in 1955 to pursue a writing career and found widespread acclaim

with his novel *Children of the Sun* (1957). However, it was *The Devil's Advocate* (1959) which won the Heinemann Award, the Black Memorial Prize and the Conference of Christians and Jews Brotherhood Award. It also raised him to the ranks of the international best-seller, where he has remained ever since.

White Australia

The White Australia Policy, restricting immigration to Australia by non-Europeans, was legislated by the new Commonwealth parliament in 1901, but was based on anti-Asian sentiment in the colonies dating back to the arrival of Chinese gold diggers in the 1850s in Victoria and to Queensland in the 1870s. The motto of the *Bulletin* magazine was 'Australia for the white man'.

Patrick White, Nobel Laureate

Gough Whitlam when it was time

Ted Whitten, Mr Football

White, Osmar
Osmar White wrote one of the best and most evocatively truthful books to come out of World War II, *Green Armour*, which was about Kokoda Track and the even worse Bulldog Track battles in New Guinea in 1942. White (1909–91) was badly wounded while reporting the Americans in the Solomons in 1943, but returned to work in 1944, writing for the Melbourne *Herald* in Britain, and in 1944–45 in France and Germany. His powerful book about the defeat of Germany, *Conquerors' Road*, was not published until 1996. After the war, he returned to write about New Guinea, Indonesia and South-East Asia, and wrote two important and influential books about New Guinea, *Parliament of a Thousand Tribes* (1965) and *Time Now, Time Before* (1967).

White, Patrick
Australia's greatest unread novelist, Patrick White's (1912–90) portraits of morality and the Australian social landscape were initally scorned in Australia even as they were being lauded in England and America. Eventually held up as one of Australia's greatest novelists, his plays were also revolutionary on the Australian stage. He won the Nobel Prize for Literature in 1973.

Whiteley, Brett
Brett Whiteley (1939–92) first made headlines when he won the international prize at the Paris Bienniale of art aged just 22. Whiteley's work was influenced by poets as well as by artists and his extensive travels. He worked in many styles, from landscapes and nudes to large 'assemblages' which reflected the political and social unrest of the 1960s and 1970s. He won all three of Australia's major art prizes: the Archibald, Wynne and Sulman.

Whitlam, Gough
Prime minister from 1972 to 1975, Gough Whitlam's (b. 1916) Labor government ended 23 years of coalition rule in Australia. A brilliant social reformer, his legacy is universal health care, the abolition of White Australia's last remnants, no-fault divorce and 'one vote, one value' electoral reform. His reign ended in the greatest confrontation between the House and the Senate in Australian history, a fracas which eventually saw him dismissed in 1975 by the Governor-General after he defied the Senate's deferral of Supply.

292

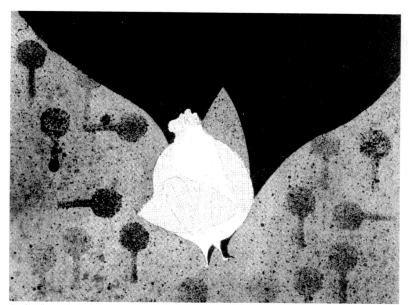

Fred Williams by Rick Amor, 1978

Robyn Williams, science radio star

R.M. Williams, the boot legend

Whitten, Ted

'Mr Football', E.J. 'Ted' Whitten (1933–95) was not only Footscray's favourite son, he was quite possibly football's favourite son. He played 321 games for Footscray between 1951 and 1970 and is regarded as the best all-round footballer of his era. Possessing a huge kick, a safe mark and peerless ball skills, he was appointed captain–coach of his team aged just 23. A vigorous supporter of state football, he revived the interstate clashes and was a Victorian selector from 1987 to his retirement in 1994.

Wiggles, The

A four-man kids' entertainment group, The Wiggles were the biggest thing a pre-schooler could imagine in the 1990s. Featuring the talents of Murray Cook, Greg Page, Anthony Field and Jeff Fatt, The Wiggles make fashion headlines with primary-coloured skivvies and sold-out performances across the country. Their workload at its peak was enormous, including around 500 performances a year, along with books, CDs and videos.

Williams, Fred

A revolutionary landscape painter, Fred Williams (1927–82) changed the way the Australian landscape is seen in art by choosing predominantly topographical and interior views. His work also included portraits and figure studies. Williams served on the board of the National Gallery of Victoria, and the annual Writers v Artists cricket match is played for the trophy of Fred's bat.

Williams, R.M.

Bootmaker and legend R.M. Williams (b. 1908) began making boots and other gear in the remote north of South Australia in the 1930s and was commissioned to make saddle packs for cattle king Sidney Kidman. He set up business as a bush outfitter in 1934, and, since leaving the firm that still bears his name in 1988, has been instrumental in setting up the Longreach Stockman's Hall of Fame.

Williams, Robyn

Robyn Williams (b. 1944) arrived in Australia from England in 1972, and has presented the influential and interesting *Science Show* on ABC radio since 1975. It is the longest-lived such organism in the world. He was Chairman of the Commission for the Future 1990–94.

David Williamson, world's tallest playwright

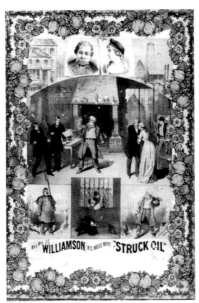
J.C. Williamson's *Struck Oil*

Tom Wills, founder of Australian football

W

Williamson, David

Considered one of Australia's premier playwrights, Williamson's (b. 1942) first full-length play was *The Coming of Stork* which had its premiere at the La Mama Theatre, Carlton, in 1970. His first commercial success as a playwright was *The Removalists* in 1972 which won an Australian Awgie Award and co-won the British theatre's George Devine Award. He is also the writer behind movies such as *Gallipoli*, *The Year of Living Dangerously* and *Phar Lap*. He was made AO in 1983 and was named one of Australia's 100 Living National Treasures in 1998 by the National Trust.

Williamson, J.C.

Australia's most successful theatrical entrepreneur, James Cassius Williamson (1845–1913) was born in America before coming to Australia in 1874 with the play *Struck Oil*, then returning in 1879 and leasing the Melbourne Theatre Royal. In 1882, he formed an association with his major competitors, George Musgrove and Arthur Garner. Coined 'The Triumvirate', they dominated Australian theatre, and their opposition to the avant-garde and commitment to long-running productions of star-studded shows did not help the development of local talent.

Wills, Tom

Thomas Wentworth Wills (1835–80) was the son of Sydney-born Horatio Wills (1811–61). Horatio was, before becoming a pastoralist, apprenticed to his mother's new husband George Howe, publisher of Australia's first newspaper, the *Sydney Gazette*. Horatio at age 18 set up a magazine of his own, the *Currency Lad*, a vigorous if short-lived publication whose motto was 'Rise Australia!' with the call 'See Australia floats with flag unfurl'd, a new Britannia in another world'. Tom grew up in western Victoria, where he apparently learned the local Aboriginal language and may have played some indigenous games. He was sent to Rugby School, England, in 1850, and became an excellent cricketer. He returned to Melbourne in December 1856 and was immediately selected to play for Victoria. In 1858 he wrote his famous letter to a Melbourne sporting magazine newspaper suggesting that cricketers take up football as a way of keeping fit, and umpired the first game between teams representing

Chester Wilmot on the BBC

Wirths' Circus poster

Wogs in work

two schools in August that year. He was an enthusiastic promoter of the new game, and played for Melbourne, Richmond and Geelong in its cause. He continued to play cricket and was for a time Secretary of the Melbourne Cricket Club. In 1861 he survived a massacre at Cullin La Ringo in Queensland which saw his father killed while overlanding sheep to a new property. Nevertheless, in 1867 Tom was the first coach of the Aboriginal cricket team which toured England in 1868. The team was raised from his boyhood district in western Victoria. He killed himself in 1880, suffering from depression.

Wilmot, Chester

Legendary war correspondent, Chester Wilmot (1911–54) was the son of R. W.E. Wilmot, who under the nom de plume 'Old Boy' was a prominent cricket and football writer in Melbourne in the 1920s and 1930s. Chester covered the Middle East and Tobruk, and went to New Guinea where he sealed his reputation among the Diggers by being banished by General Thomas Blamey. His book *Tobruk 1941* did for that place what C.E.W. Bean had done for Gallipoli. Unable to cover Australians, he worked for the BBC in Europe in 1944, the Nuremberg war crimes trials, and wrote the masterpiece *The Struggle for Europe*, published in 1952. He was killed in a plane crash.

Wirths' Circus

From its beginnings in the 1850s on the Bendigo goldfields, Wirths' Circus has been one of Australia's premier troupes. Run by the Wirth family, still resident in their 1916 Coogee home, the collection of midget horsemen, pinheaded Chinamen, ancient elephants and other oddities has been touring for over a century.

Wogs

Originally an insulting term applied especially to migrants from Italy and Greece, taken over by the comedy team led by Nick Giannopoulos and Simon Palomares in the hit show *Wogs Out of Work*. It reached its height in 2000 with the film *The Wog Boy*, a box office smash. Now a wog is almost a term of endearment, but only when used by one.

Tommy Woodcock, 1920

World of Sport handball competition

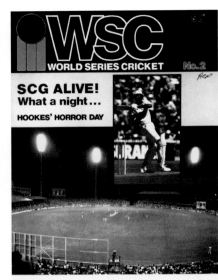

World Series Cricket program, 1978–79

W

Woodcock, Tommy

Tommy Woodcock (1905–85) was Phar Lap's strapper and trainer of Reckless, and a much-loved figure in the racing industry. The Tommy Woodcock Trophy is awarded to the strapper of the winner of the Melbourne Cup.

Woodhouse, Frederick

Fred Woodhouse (1820–1909) was a colonial sporting painter who arrived in Melbourne in 1858, and founded an equine painting dynasty.

Woodies, The

The most successful doubles tennis team in history, the Woodies have racked up an incredible 11 grand slam trophies, including a record-equalling five consecutive Wimbledon victories between 1993 and 1997, plus gold in Atlanta 1996, silver in Sydney 2000.

World of Sport

World of Sport was the original Sunday morning sports show, first screened by HSV-7 Melbourne in 1959, and created by Ron Casey, general manager of Seven, and later President of AFL club North Melbourne. *World of Sport* created a number of TV legends including 'Uncle' Doug Elliott who looked after the pies, Lou Richards, Jack 'Captain Blood' Dyer, and a number of folkloric segments including the handball competition, woodchopping, long kicking and roller cycling. It was last seen in 1987 after 1355 episodes.

World Series Cricket

A private cricket competition hatched by Nine's Kerry Packer in 1977 when denied the TV rights to official cricket. It split the game, ushered in professionalism and all that that has entailed since – including one-day international tournaments, coloured clothes and night games.

Working Dog

Working Dog is Rob Sitch, Santo Cilauro, Jane Kennedy, Tom Gleisner and Michael Hirsh, who have produced, directed and appeared in a number of Australia's most effective comedy shows on TV, and latterly on film with *The Castle* (1997) and *The Dish* (2000). It all began, like so much Melbourne comedy, with a Melbourne Uni revue called *Let's Talk Backwards* in the 1980s, which soon became the *D-Generation* on ABC TV, *The Late Show* in 1991–92, and progressed through the deadpan send-up of current affairs TV with three series of *Frontline* for the ABC, a

Jack Worrall, the great coach

John Wren, prominent racing identity

Judith Wright, environmental poet

fly-fishing romance *A River Somewhere* and a weekly panel show called *The Panel* on the Ten network.

Worrall, John

The first coach in VFL football, Worrall (1863–1937) was a renowned player for Fitzroy (1884–92) in the VFA, played cricket for Australia in 11 Test matches and was appointed secretary and coach of Carlton in 1902, winning premierships in 1906, 1907 and 1908. He coached Essendon to two flags in 1911 and 1912, and became a distinguished writer on football and cricket for the *Australasian* for 25 years, inventing much football lingo.

Wren, John

Prominent racing identity, alleged political fixer, businessman and friend of Archbishop Daniel Mannix, John

Wren (1871–1953) nearly played for Collingwood, and remained a patron and local hero throughout his life. He ran the illegal off-course betting operation, the Collingwood Tote, in the 1890s. He owned pony race tracks in opposition to the thoroughbred crowd, and raced some not-so-fast horses, including one named Pius. He was involved in the trots, the bikes, the ring, owning the House of Stoush, as the Melbourne Stadium was named. Not to mention cafés, theatres, grazing, mining – and the *Courier Mail* newspaper in Brisbane. He was a patriot, joining the first AIF at 44, organised the Sportsman's Thousand, gave Albert Jacka VC £500 and organised with Mannix the great St Patrick's Day march of 1920 with 14 VC winners on white horses. He was the fictional basis of Frank Hardy's

Power Without Glory. Wren died after a heart attack in the last quarter of Collingwood's 1953 premiership win. He remains a mystery at the heart of what Melbourne has become.

Wright, Judith

A remarkable poet, Judith Wright (1915–2000) was born and raised in Armidale, NSW, and her love for the Australian countryside runs through much of her early work. Acclaimed for the lyrical beauty, perfect craftsmanship and emotional honesty of her poetry, her best received work was *The Moving Image* (1946). This was followed by many others, including *Woman to Man* (1949), *Birds* (1962) and *Fourth Quarter and Other Poems* (1976). She was also the author of a book of short stories *The Nature of Love* (1966).

X

The Fourex man had some good advice

Another Aussie thing starting with 'X' – *Xanthorrhoea* grass trees in western NSW

Forgotten early 1980s band called Xero

Xenides, Adriana

Long-time spinner of the letters of the alphabet on a TV quiz show, Argentine-born Adriana Xenides was the world's longest-serving game show hostess. Her 18-year career with the likes of Tony Barber ended in 1996, and again in 1999, in tears. When asked what was her favourite vowel she said, 'Oh that's a big call. To separate the A, E, I, O and U is really a very hard thing to do. They are each as important, and each one we need to express our feelings, our thoughts and our deeds.'

XL Petroleum

Discount petrol company formed in the 1960s in Victoria and in 1970 in NSW to challenge the market power of the big companies. More recently, prices have skyrocketed anyway . . .

X-ray Crystallography

The 1915 Nobel Prize for Physics was won by the father and son team William (1862–1942) and Lawrence Bragg (1890–1971). William was born in England, Cambridge educated and appointed Professor of Mathematics and Physics at the University of Adelaide in 1885. Lawrence was born there, and later educated at Adelaide, and Cambridge, after his father had accepted an appointment at Leeds in 1909. William's interest in radium and radioactivity was sparked when President of the Physics section of the Australasian Association for the Advancement of Science in 1904. When Lawrence graduated in 1912, they worked together on X-rays and crystals. After their Nobel Prize only three years later, neither worked in Australia again.

XXXX

XXXX (or Fourex) is the Queensland beer, and was once marketed relentlessly by Queensland heroes such as King Wally Lewis, AB and Thommo as the only thing fit for a fair dinkum Queenslander to drink. Down south XXXX seemed like a swearword, but as one early 1990s commercial rhyme enthused:

Melbourne's got rain and Sydney's got yuppies,
Tassie got the chop and we got lucky.
Nobody does it like up here does it
We love it up here,
We don't just like it, we love it!
We don't just like it, we love it!
We love it up here,
The people, the places, the mates,
the faces
The XXXX, yep, the beer up here,
we love it up here.

Adriana Xenides and Tony Barber

Y

Yabby fishers in mythical Wiregrass by Percy Leason, 1926

Yabba was no bunny as a barracker

Young Talent Time team

Cliff Young trains but not in his gumboots

Yabba

Stephen Gascoigne, known as Yabba, was the archetypical Australian barracker in the 1930s from his spot on the hill at the Sydney Cricket Ground. A rabbitoh, well known for telling Bodyline captain Douglas Jardine, when waving away a sticky fly, 'Jardine, leave our flies alone.' And to a fieldsman who dropped a catch, 'Git a bag.'

Yothu Yindi

Yothu Yindi gained widespread recognition for their fusion of traditional Aboriginal music with modern Western sounds. Featuring both Yolngu (Aboriginal Australian) and Balanda (non-Aboriginal Australians) their debut album, *Homeland Movement*, earned them a contract with Mushroom Records and their follow-up, 1991's *Tribal Voice*, found immediate commercial and critical success. World tours and another four albums have followed.

You Am I

A rock'n'roll band born in the early 1990s, You Am I have since gained a large and devoted following in Australia and overseas. Its members, David Lane, Tim Rogers, Rusty Hopkinson and Andy Kent, have put together five albums so far, with *Hourly, Daily* being their biggest hit.

Young, Cliff

The remarkable marathon shuffler Cliff Young (b. 1921) made headlines when in 1983 he won the Westfield Sydney to Melbourne road race at age 61. Whilst the other runners slept at night, Cliff kept on running.

Young, Johnny

Born John De Jong (b. 1945), 'Johnny' Young began his career in the media by writing pop songs for other Australian artists and fronting a TV music show. He became an Australian icon after forming his own production company in 1970 and launching the children's music show *Young Talent Time*, which he hosted for almost 20 years.

Yunupingu, Galarrwuy

Chairman of the Northern Land Council 1977–79 and 1983–89, Galarrwuy Yunupingu came to prominence fighting the ultimately unsuccessful Yirrkala land rights case in 1970. With the Northern Land Council he negotiated mining rights for the Gagudju people, including the Ranger uranium agreement.

Z

Zig & Zag at the height of their fame

Z Class Tram of the 1980s

Craig McDermott's frightening zinc creamed nut does the trick against England's Alec Stewart

Z Class Trams

A more modern class of tram introduced to Melbourne in 1980, they have never achieved the status of the fresh-air conditioned W Class trams, which began service in the 1920s and rattled on into the 21st century. Z class trams were set to be replaced in the early 2000s.

Zable, Arnold

Arnold Zable is a Melbourne writer and storyteller, born in New Zealand, whose search for his family's past in Poland/Russia, *Jewels and Ashes* (1991) is an exquisite evocation of Jewish life before World War II. Zable explores what it means to be a survivor of the Holocaust. His new novel *Cafe Scheherazade* (2001) contains mezmerising accounts of suffering and survival, as told in a St Kilda cafe.

Zampatti, Carla

Fashion designer and business woman, Italian-born director Carla Zampatti (b. 1940) has had a successful label since 1965, opening her first boutique in Sydney's Surry Hills in 1972. Her style is cool and 'classical'. Married to John Spender, Australian Ambassador to France.

Zig & Zag

Jack Perry and Doug McKenzie were two ex-music hall clowns who fell into the earliest days of television – in fact the very first broadcast from the studios of HSV-7 Melbourne in 1956. They sold Peters ice cream, especially on *Happy Hammond's Happy Show*, an incredibly successful after-school show for children, were the faces of Moomba and raised lots of money for the Royal Children's Hospital Good Friday Appeal. (Perry was to face child sex charges in the 1990s.)

Zinc Cream

Primitive zinc oxide sun protection and antiseptic, used by cricketers and veterinarians before the ozone hole made total coverage prudent.

Zoot

Adelaide pop band founded in 1966 as Times Unlimited, by Beeb Birtles with Daryl Cotton as lead singer. Renamed Zoot in 1967, and infamous because they always wore pink gear. Backed the flip side of Farnham's hit *Sadie the Cleaning Lady* in that year. The band took off when Ricky Springfield, later a US TV soap star, joined in 1969. Broke up in 1971. 'We just couldn't escape our image – the pink thing haunted us,' said Cotton.

Acknowledgements

Making this book has been a long and arduous process, and many people need to be thanked for assistance and support: in particular Peter Ascot, Kimily Clark, Alex Hutchinson, Cate O'Dwyer, Ian Robinson for services above and beyond.

Production Design: David Lancashire Design

I thank the following copyright holders for permission to reproduce the images, as listed below. All other pictures are photographed by Garrie Hutchinson, or from the Ross, Hutchinson & Associates collection and other private collections. While every endeavour has been made to contact copyright holders, I welcome further information and advice to be published in a future edition: GH

T= TOP, L= LEFT, R= RIGHT, M= MIDDLE, B=BOTTOM

3	Bonds
5T	Associated Press AP/Rob Griffith
5BL	Ken Done
5BR	David Hughes
6	H.G. Nelson/Seven Network
7	H.G. Nelson/Seven Network
8T	Network Ten
8M	Melbourne Cricket Club
8BR	Melbourne University Press
9B	Michael Leunig
10TL	Mushroom Records
14TM	Melbourne Cricket Club
14TR	Akubra
15TR	Australian War Memorial 098700
15BM	Geoff Sharp/David Lancashire Design
16 TM	Carlton Football Club
17TM	Bryant & May, Swedish Match
17TR	Southcorp Wines/Penfolds
18BL	Bonds
18BM	Mambo Design
18BR	Qantas
19TL	Unilever Foods/Rosella
19 TM	Driza-Bone
19TR	Sportsgirl
19LM	Kraft
19M	Pelaco Pty Ltd
19BL	Just Jeans
19RM	Fosters Brewing Group
19BR	RM Williams
22	Harold Scruby/AusFlag
23	Harold Scruby/AusFlag
24TL	Reserve Bank of Australia
25BL	Museum of Australian Childhood
27BR	Associated Press AP
29T	Reuters/Mark Baker
31R	Associated Press AP/Elise Amenolola
34M	Thomas Nelson Australia
34R	Thomas Nelson Australia
39L	The *Age*/John Spooner
41M	Howard Arkley, *House With Native Tree*, 1996, The Estate of Howard Arkley, Alison Burton
49MR	Penguin Books Australia
53R	Sun Books/Pan Macmillan
56L	The *Age*/John Spooner
60L	Maggie Beer
61L	Maggie Millar
63M	*The Big Issue*
63R	3JJJ
65L	Penguin Books Australia/Nick Rains
68M	Angus & Robertson, HarperCollins Publishers
68R	Southern Star Entertainment
69R	Late, great Les Tanner
73L	Michel Lawrence
77M	Avon Books
79M	The *Bulletin*
79R	The *Bulletin*
82L	Margaret Gee
83R	Penguin Books Australia
85L	ABC
85M	Penguin Books Australia
89L	University of Queensland Press
90M	Working Dog Productions
91R	Ken Cato Design
96MB	Bonds
97TM	*Cinema Papers*
97BM	Sly Ink
101M	House & Moorhouse Films
103R	Patrick Cook
106R	Australia Post
119R	Ken Done
120TM	Driza-Bone
122R	Phillip Burgoyne
126	Barry Humphries
128R	HarperPrism
134	Roy & H.G./Seven Network
140L	*The Footy Show*/Nine Network
143L	Tony Feder
145L	*Cinema Papers*
151M	Melbourne Theatre Company/ Jeff Busby
166	Michael Leunig
170L	Penguin Books Australia
174L	The *Age*/John Spooner
175L	News Ltd/The *Australian*
184R	Michael Leunig
185L	Alex Stitt/Life Be In It
191L	Kimily Clark
194L	John Spooner/OUP
195L	ABC Books
197M	Angus & Robertson/ HarperCollins Publishers
198M	Mambo Design
200M	Neil Curtis
204L	*Meanjin*
205R	Melbourne House
208L	James Cant
210R	Angus & Robertson/Frank Moorhouse
214	Michel Lawrence
223M	The *Bulletin*
224R	The *Age*/John Spooner
227R	Pelaco
230	Bruce Petty
231R	National Gallery of Victoria
232R	Peter and Elizabeth Pidgeon
239M	Qantas
239R	Qantas
241L	Late, great Noel Counihan
242	Michel Lawrence
243TL	ABC
246M	Peter and Elizabeth Pidgeon
247R	Photograph of Ginger Riley Courtesy Alcaston Gallery, Photo B. Knight
249R	Unilever Foods
250L	Roy & H.G./Seven Network
253L	The *Bulletin*
253R	Columbia Records
254TL	Artist Services/ABC
255R	Angus & Robertson/ HarperCollins Publishers
256L	Melbourne University Press
257TR	HarperCollins Publishers
261L	Michel Lawrence
262L	Angus & Robertson/ HarperCollins Publishers
264M	John Spooner/Text Publishing
265R	Sportsgirl
270R	National Gallery of Victoria
274L	Late, great Les Tanner
281BL	Reserve Bank of Australia
283	Kraft
284M	Fosters Brewing Group
290L	WEG, William Ellis Green
293M	Rick Amor
298	XXXX Lion Nathan Australia/ Castlemaine Perkins/ photo Mimmo Cozzolino

The Ashes • *Aunty Jack* • Big Pineapple • Sir Donald Bradman • Brownlow Medal • Burke and Wills • Chesty Bond • *Cop Shop* • *Countdown* • Dad and Dave • Davis Cup • *Don's Party* • Driza-bone • Eight Hour Day • Esky • Eureka Flag • Federation • *Four Corners* • Gallipoli • Goanna Oil • Granny Smith Apple • Hill's Hoist • Harold Holt • *Home and Away* • Humphrey B. Bear • INXS • Jackeroo • Elizabeth Jolley • Barry Jones • Ned Kelly • Nicole Kidman • Kings Cross • Lamington • Lasseter's Reef • Henry Lawson • Leyland Brothers • Dennis Lillee • Jeannie Little • Eddie Mabo • Mad Max • Elle MacPherson • Manly Ferry • Ray Martin • Men at Work • Mietta • Kylie Minogue • Olivia Newton-John • Sidney Nolan • *Number 96* • Penfolds Grange • Phar Lap • *Picnic at Hanging Rock* • Pie Floater • *Play School* • Puffing Billy • *Punch* • Qantas • *rage* • Rats of Tobruk • Reconciliation • Fred Schepisi • The Seekers • Sentimental Bloke • silverchair • Skipping Girl • Dick Smith • Snugglepot and Cuddlepie • Speedo • *Strictly Ballroom* • *The Sullivans* • TAB • Tatts • Sigrid Thornton • Thongs • Truganini • Uluru • Vegemite • Victa • *Waltzing Matilda* • Steve Waugh • Weeties • Gough Whitlam • The Wiggles • R.M. Williams • Working Dog • Cliff Young • Carla Zampatti